Radio, Television and Modern Life

# Radio, Television and Modern Life

## A Phenomenological Approach

Paddy Scannell

BLACKWELL
Publishers

Copyright © Paddy Scannell 1996

The right of Paddy Scannell to be identified as author of this work has been asserted in accordance with the Copyright, Designs and Patents Act 1988.

First published 1996

2 4 6 8 10 9 7 5 3 1

Blackwell Publishers Ltd
108 Cowley Road
Oxford OX4 1JF
UK

Blackwell Publishers Inc
238 Main Street
Cambridge, Massachusetts 02142,
USA

*British Library Cataloguing in Publication Data*

A CIP catalogue record for this book is available from the British Library.

*Library of Congress Cataloging-in-Publication Data*

Scannell, Paddy.
    Radio, television, and modern life / Paddy Scannell.
        p.   cm.
    Includes bibliographical references and index.
    ISBN 0–631–19874–1. — ISBN 0–631–19875–X (pbk.)
    1. Mass media—Philosophy.   2. Broadcasting—History.   I. Title.
P91.S297   1996
302.23′01—dc20                                                96–13393
                                                                      CIP

Typeset in 10 on 12 pt Ehrhardt
by Graphicraft Typesetters Ltd, Hong Kong
Printed in Great Britain by Hartnolls Limited, Bodmin, Cornwall

This book is printed on acid-free paper

# Contents

| | | |
|---|---|---|
| Acknowledgements | | vi |
| Introduction | | 1 |
| 1 | Intentionality | 6 |
| 2 | Sociability | 22 |
| 3 | Sincerity | 58 |
| 4 | Eventfulness | 75 |
| 5 | Authenticity | 93 |
| 6 | Identity | 117 |
| 7 | Dailiness | 144 |
| | References | 179 |
| | Index | 185 |

# Acknowledgements

In writing this book I have, at certain points, made considerable use of under-graduate student work at what was the Polytechnic of Central London (now the University of Westminster) since the early 1980s. Dissertations by Margaret Foster, Jenny Williamson and especially Graham Brand have been invaluable sources of information and ideas. Nearly all the programmes considered in detail in the chapters that follow have been played and discussed in the class-room. It is from such discussion, as much as the authors mentioned in the Introduction, that I have come through to the particular understanding of broadcasting set out below. I thus have a deep sense of indebtedness to our students, over the years, and also to my friend and colleague, David Cardiff, with whom I have talked over much that has eventually ended up in this book.

I am, of course, especially grateful to my family – to my wife and daughter, Suzanne and Sonia – for putting up with my various moods and enthusiasms while writing. In spite of 'the boringness of Heidegger', for which they have shown a remarkably cheerful tolerance, I dedicate this book to them both, with love.

Grateful thanks are due to the following for their permission to reproduce copyright material:

British Broadcasting Corporation: for extracts from early BBC Radio pro-grammes, *Harry Hopeful, News Of 100 Years Ago, Have a Go, We Speak for Ourselves* and *Sincerely Yours*; and from BBC Television documentary series, *Police* (BBC1, 1982).

Blackwell Publishers: for extracts from Harvey Sacks: *Lectures on Conversation*, Volume 2 (Blackwell, 1992).

Campbell Connelly & Co. Limited: for extract from Vera Lynn's 'We'll Meet Again', written by Charles & Parker, Copyright © 1939 Dash Music Co. Ltd, 8/9 Frith Street, London W1V 5TZ. All Rights Reserved.

Curtis Brown Group Ltd: for extract from H. Jennings and D. Madge (eds) *May the Twelfth: Mass Observation Day Surveys* (Faber, 1937), Copyright The Trustees of the Mass-Observation Archive at the University of Sussex.

Faber & Faber Ltd: for extract from W. H. Auden: 'Musée des Beaux Arts' from *Collected Poems*, Copyright © 1940 renewed 1968 by W. H. Auden.

The *Guardian*: for extract from leader article in The *Guardian*, 4.1.82, Copyright © The *Guardian*, 1982.

David Higham Associates: for extracts from J. Dimbleby: *Richard Dimbleby* (Hodder & Stoughton, 1975).

*The Journal of Communication*: for permission to reproduce chapters one and six.

Random House, Inc.: for extract from W. H. Auden: 'Musée des Beaux Arts' from *Collected Poems*, Copyright © 1940 renewed 1968 by W. H. Auden.

Sage Publications: for article 'Talk, Identity and Performance: *The Tony Blackburn Show*' by G. Brand and P. Scannell from P. Scannell (ed.) *Broadcast Talk* (Sage, 1991).

Unfortunately it has not been possible to trace and contact all copyright holders prior to publication. If notified, the publisher will undertake to rectify any errors or omissions at the earliest opportunity.

# Introduction

This book picks up where the first volume of the *Social History of British Broadcasting* (Scannell and Cardiff 1991) left off. I do not mean it does so chronologically, for – although it is historical in temper – it does not follow straight on from the historical moment at which the first book ended: 1939, the outbreak of the Second World War. Rather, it picks up the fundamental thematic concerns of that book at the point where it breaks off. The preface to the *Social History* described it as the first volume in a series that would attempt to account historically for the impact and effect of broadcasting on modern life in Britain. There were two parts to this project, it was claimed: first, to describe 'the actual ways in which broadcasting developed and interacted with the society it was intended to serve; and second, to reflect on those accounts and their wider political, social and cultural implications' (p. x).

The key distinction I was trying to make was between different aspects of historical work. Now I would say, more simply, historical work begins with narrative, but does not end there. At the time of writing the *Social History* I often wanted to step out of its narratives to comment on them, reflect on them, think about their wider implications, what they showed about the impact of broadcasting in the moment of its decisive establishment in the form of the British Broadcasting Corporation. But it was impossible. The thing that had to be done in the first place was to give detailed largely chronological accounts of the formation of the work of broadcasting in the main areas of programme output. The task was to show – as fully as possible – how what we today recognize and take for granted as the utterly normal everyday output of broadcasting was, in the first place, actually discovered and set in place by broadcasters for listeners, in what ways, under what circumstances and for what reasons.

The most difficult aspect of the work was finding the right narrative structure for the book as a whole, which has a very deliberate architecture. It begins with the political formation of broadcasting. The key central section examines the formation of production practices in all the main areas of output in a sequence that begins with political broadcasting and moves through to music and entertainment. That leads into the final section of the book, which is about the broadcasters' relationship with their audiences. The last chapter of the book – 'The Listener' – takes a different stance to this theme. It shifts from institutional attitudes to audiences (as revealed in the three different systems of distribution for delivering the programme services on offer – namely local, regional and national forms of broadcasting) to the attitude of listeners to this new thing – a wireless set – and what you could hear on it if you bought one, and how it fitted into daily life and its concerns.

That is the point at which this book resumes a historical consideration of the impact of broadcasting. It is written throughout from the perspective of everyday life. The book is free-standing. It is not at all necessary to have read the detailed historical accounts in the earlier volume in order to understand what the present volume is about, or what it's trying to get at. But I feel it necessary to point to the links between it and its predecessor in order to indicate what is here taken for granted or – more exactly – taken as read. In the chapters that follow accounts are often given of the production history of particular programmes. Such accounts must be understood as situated within the overall context of production – the totality of output. For it is the meaningfulness of the whole that always structures in advance the meaningfulness of any particular part of the whole (i.e. any individual programme). It was the range and scope of production – across politics, information, culture and entertainment – that the earlier history tried to capture in detail. But although it provided a great deal of information about the genesis of programme policies and practices for mainstream output it was unable to focus in detail on any one programme in order to show how it worked. It is only when a preliminary account of the whole has already been put in place that one can return to the parts in order to reveal the inexhaustible vitality and meaningfulness of the whole, its duration in time and place, its world-disclosing function.

That is what this book tries to do. It presumes that making programmes is the *raison d'être* of broadcasting systems and that the analysis of programmes – showing how they work *for* audiences – is a central task in their study. If the first book was about the meaningful organization of the production process in its parts and as a whole, this book is about the meaningful organization of the programmes themselves. Its central concern might be stated as an attempt to show how understanding a radio or television programme is possible for me or anyone. That everyone *does* understand what they see and hear is – I take it – obvious. What is not obvious is how it is that radio and television are intelligible in just such a way that anyone and everyone can understand them. The chapters that follow explore the conditions of the intelligibility of any radio or television programme.

The first chapter sets out a preliminary 'theory' of communicative intentionality that connects the meaningfulness of programmes with *both* the organizing intentions of programme makers and the institutions in which they work, *and* the interpretations of any viewer or listener. A cardinal distinction is made between two levels of interpretation that are often conflated: the evaluations and assessments of programmes (the *opinions* we have about them) and the organization of those programmes in such ways as give rise to the possibilities of those opinions. It is to the latter, or first level of interpretative work, that this book attends. The bulk of the book consists of case studies of the meaningful organization of programmes in this way. I try to show, for instance, how it is that a performance that was widely regarded at the time of its broadcasting as being 'sincere' could indeed be found to be so by virtue of the way in which it was so organized as to appear as such. The case studies are arranged in a roughly chronological sequence (though that is not the organizing principle of the sequencing of the chapters) that goes from the mid-1930s to the end of the 1980s. The final chapter reinterprets all that precedes it (in this and the *Social History*). In particular, it reinterprets the first chapter and its initial attempt to account for the meaningfulness of output.

One real problem which the reader will encounter, when reading chapters two to six, is the unfamiliarity, for the most part, of the material being discussed. The literature and indeed the films of the thirties, forties and fifties are more accessible today than radio and television from those times. Doubtless older readers will be able to 'hear' the voices of say, Wilfred Pickles or Vera Lynn, as they read transcripts of their radio programmes. But even so, they will have to imagine the exact timbre of their voices, the timing and inflection of what they say, as well as the presence of the audience – whether in the studio or on location. Much of what I want to say hangs on what you hear in the sound of voices on air, on what you see in a look or gesture, and on how you interpret and assess what you hear and see. Ideally, this book needs a CD-ROM version so that readers may access the radio and television programmes that I discuss in order to compare their interpretations and assessments of the material with mine. I have done my best to provide accounts of the programmes I discuss – their production history, responses to and comments on them at the time, and so on. But even so, it will require some imaginative effort to 'hear' and 'see' the programmes I write about.

The last chapter will, no doubt, appear eccentric to many of its presumed readers since it introduces a quite new analytic frame with a different style and vocabulary from what has gone before. Any text deploys a rhetoric and what Richard Rorty calls a 'fundamental vocabulary' which is presumed as shared by both the author and his or her 'reading community'. To use words such as 'ideology', 'hegemony', 'texts', 'preferred reading', 'polysemy', etc. is to enter into an already established 'language game' which rests upon taken-for-granted normative assumptions about the object of discourse. That vocabulary (the normalized, normalizing language of 'media studies') and its operative assumptions is set aside in this book.

I set it aside because it gets in the way of the kinds of thing that I notice in radio and television and that I want to write about. Media studies is – in its own vocabulary – 'a discursive formation' that has captured a particular field of study and institutionalized it in the light of its own concerns. Fair enough. But the effect is to occlude the possibilities of other ways of seeing and other orders of reality. The only reality that media studies knows is a political reality, set in a field of discourse that – as it would say – mobilizes concepts of power, struggle, conflict, ideology. It has great difficulty with any idea of ordinary *unpolitical* daily life, and its everyday concerns and enjoyments. Since for the politically minded all things are political – and what is not is either marginal or incorrectly understood – it follows that the only *interesting* questions about the media are political. I of course do not think so. Politics is not denied in or by this book. But it is not a mobilizing concept for it.

What gets this book going is the thing that struck me increasingly as I worked on the early history of broadcasting: the unprecedented newness of radio as a medium of general social communication, and the problems that it posed for broadcasters in terms of discovering what 'doing broadcasting' meant. That meant most fundamentally, I came to think, making programmes in such a way that anyone turning on a radio or television set would (a) be able to figure out what was going on pretty quickly and (b) would find that what was going on might be worth listening to or watching. So that how to make programmes that were listenable to or watchable, within a coherently organized programme schedule, was the key problem in a broadcasting system whose *raison d'être* was to make programmes for audiences. That is the starting-point for this book and it is why I emphasize the *sociable* dimension of radio and television broadcasting as its basic communicative ethos. For it seems to me that if programmes are not, really and truly, sociable in the ways they address viewers and listeners, then no one would care to watch or listen.

I think that the books that you read choose you as much as you choose them. At any rate, when I reflect on the books and their authors that I have read and which have been absorbed into the bloodstream of this book I am struck by a common concern in all of them; namely, the conditions of the intelligibility of the social practices of everyday existence. At different times I read, in this way, the sociology of interaction (Goffman), ethnomethodology and conversation analysis (Garfinkel and Sacks), linguistic pragmatics (especially Brown and Levinson's brilliant analysis of politeness) and the recent social theory of Habermas and Giddens. Heidegger, whom I came to last, seemed somehow to gather in the concerns of all that I had previously read, and certainly to recast the question of the meaningfulness of the everyday world in a wholly new light.

I had thought, for a long time, that the temporality of broadcasting was a key to its understanding. Reading Heidegger's *Being and Time* clarified for me the specific character of broadcasting's temporality as *dailiness*. This I now argue is the particular ontological characteristic that most fully encompasses the specific nature and being of radio, television and (though not a focal concern here) the press. In the end I want to suggest that if we properly understand the dailiness of radio, television and newspapers we will have gone a long way to understanding how they (the media) matter for us in the ways that they do. Heidegger's incomparable analysis of everyday existence shows how and why it is, for each and all of us, the taken-for-granted, meaningful background that constitutes the horizon of all possibilities for all actual foregrounded social relationships and practices. In modern societies radio and television are part of both the background and foreground of our everyday dealings with each other in a common world. They are so by virtue of the ways in which they disclose the everyday historicality of the world every day. Or so, at any rate, I will try to show.

# 1

---

# *Intentionality*

## I

All day, every day and everywhere people listen to radio and watch television as part of the utterly familiar, normal things that anyone does on any normal day. 'Anything on telly?' 'No, nothing.' It is not, of course, that there is, in some literal way, *nothing* to watch. Rather, that what there is is nothing out of the ordinary; merely the usual programmes on the usual channels at the usual times. Nor does this necessarily imply a disincentive to viewing. We do watch a lot of 'nothing' on television, in fact we watch it nearly all the time. Broadcast output – like daily life – is, for the most part, largely uneventful, punctuated now and then, in predictable and unpredictable ways, by eventful occasions (Dayan and Katz 1992). Now suppose that it is not accidental or contingent that the output of radio and television is as we find it to be; that this ordinariness, this obviousness is *precisely* the intended, achieved and accomplished effect of broadcast output. The question remains – and it is a difficult one – as to how (and why) it is that it is as we find it to be.

Fully to answer the question would require the study of (a) the production process and (b) the output itself and (c) viewers and listeners as all combining to produce this 'ordinariness' as worked for (in production) and achieved (in output) and taken as such (in reception). We would then, indeed, have accounted for it as intended, achieved and accomplished. Now it has already been assumed, as our starting-point, that overwhelmingly it is the case that radio and television *are* taken as ordinary everyday things, and both common sense and receptions studies support this assumption.[1] If this is granted then we can

---

[1] See, for instance, Bausinger (1984), Morley (1986), Silverstone (1994).

here set aside the domain of audience studies and the kinds of assessments made by viewers and listeners of what they see and hear in order to focus on the first two elements (production and programmes). For it is an analytically distinct and prior question as to how people get to be able to make and express the views and opinions that they have about what they see and hear. Whether programmes are found to be biased, boring, interesting, entertaining, funny, informative, true, false, embarrassing (or not) and much more besides is a matter of empirical investigation, for these are personal matters that give rise to subjective moral, political and aesthetic judgements or opinions. But for programmes to be found to be any of these things they must have been understood (or even misunderstood) as those things. Our task here is to begin to show how such assessments *are there to be had* in the form and content of output as intentionally so organized as to enable (indeed, entitle) viewers and listeners to have the kinds of personal views and opinions to which they give expression. We will want to argue that personal opinions are created and entitled when – and only when – people are recognized and treated and addressed as persons (cf. Carrithers et al., 1987) and can recognize that they are so recognized, treated and addressed. We will want to show that such recognitions are there to be found (by anyone) in the output of radio and television.[2]

But what *is* it that people listen to and watch? Is it particular programmes – the news, favoured soaps, sit-coms, Saturday afternoon sport – or is it that people just watch television and listen to the radio irrespective of what is actually being transmitted? An adequate analysis must encompass both. It must be able to account both for how any particular programme is meaningfully organized and how the totality of output on any radio or television channel is meaningfully organized. That is, we must suppose that any particular meaningfully organized programme is embedded in a meaningfully organized programme schedule. We must attend to both, for they are inseparable. The meaningfulness of any particular element is dependent on the overall meaningfulness of the totality of output. And again this is obvious: programme output *has* an overall coherence. It is not a seemingly random jumble of things arbitrarily thrown together and transmitted any old how. It is not that there are islands of meaning in a sea of meaninglessness. To the contrary, programme output, as a whole and in all its parts, has a deeply settled, ordered, orderly,

---

[2]    Throughout this book radio and television are treated as naturally occurring phenomena which can be taken together, for the purposes of analysis, because (a) that is how they are meant to be and are, in fact, found and used for practical purposes in daily life, and (b) their technical development and historical formation are at all points interlinked. They are discussed here under the rubric of *broadcasting* as the classic, historic form in which both developed: i.e. as large-scale institutions offering nationally networked services of mixed programmes.

known and familiar character. Without it being so, how could we find our way about in it – as we quite clearly can and do – in a quite untroubled way. That we can do so – that the character of output is *essentially* unproblematic – is what needs accounting for.

Our task then is to account for the meaningfulness of programmes in this double sense: on the one hand as a particular kind of thing, on the other as part of a wider organized, ordered and orderly output. How to set about it? Let us ask once again, 'What is a programme?' and turn it round a little by asking 'How does a programme have its being?' This phenomenological twist enables us to make a distinction between *how* programmes come to occur and the *way* that they occur. In attending to how programmes come to occur we examine the conditions of their coming-into-being. In attending to the *way* that they occur we examine their *particularity* as that which we find them to be in the manner of their moment-by-moment coming-into-being. Or to put this slightly differently, we must attend to the conditions that give the *possibility* of being and the *actual* conditions of any coming-into-being for any programme.


## II


For a programme to happen it must happen sometime somewhere through someone's agency. The elementary components of an occasion are time, place and people. A realized occasion is always and everywhere context-specific: the *some*one *some*place *some*where is always in a particular here-and-now. What we are considering as an ontology of events (the horizon of their transition from a possibility into a reality) are the basic, mundane problems that broadcasters have to deal with in order to bring into being – and sustain as such – that continuous, unbroken and never-ending flow of output that we check out in television listings in the papers each day.

Any programme that gets transmitted has a complex prior history: a history of policy debates about whether it should be made (and for what reasons) and, if commissioned, of production debates about how it should be made. These two moments – of policy-making and of programme-making – are distinct. The moment of policy is the moment when institutional *motives* are considered: 'Will it make money?' 'Will it do us good?' 'Will we run into trouble if we do this?' Such may be the reasons that programmes do or don't get made, but they do not constitute the meaningfulness of programmes. Certain kinds of analysis think that if you find the motives for programmes you have explained them. But this is not so. Motives figure (on the whole) only indirectly in the meaningful organization of programmes and in the ways that they are understood by viewers and listeners. It would be more accurate to say that, for instance, the profit motive is a *by-product* of a 'successful' programme.[3] It may be the reason a programme gets made. It is not the reason it succeeds.

By now, ready-to-hand solutions to the basic problems of production have long-since been found so that programme-making appears, for those involved, at every level, essentially unproblematic. What is done is done according to accumulated institutional experience, well-tested rules-of-thumb, established precedents, etc. Everyone, more or less, knows what they're doing. But it is worth remembering that it once was not so, that there was a moment when 'how to do broadcasting' had, in all respects, to be discovered. The interest of a historical reconstruction of broadcasting is, in part, the recovery of that moment when practices had to be worked out, and methodical reproducible ways of doing broadcasting had to be found.

The medium in which radio and television exists is time. It is that which has to be filled with a content, it is that which is 'spent' in listening and viewing. At first, the task of broadcasters was a simple, overwhelming one of filling 'empty' time. Programmes were indeed produced any old way and transmitted any old how with little, if any, thought beyond the ever-present and pressing dilemma of how to get *something* on air and then something else to follow it.[4] The institutionalization of broadcasting (the formation of the networks in the USA; of the BBC in the UK) meant the stabilization of what it did and that, in effect, meant the routinization of production.[5] Routinization has a double aspect: it means the routinization of the making of programmes, and of their relationship to each other. The solution to the former was the serialization of production and to the latter, the development of fixed scheduling and continuity techniques. Both began (in the UK) at around the same time, in the mid-thirties.

Programme planning (scheduling) is crucial to the normalization of output as something that in its parts and as a whole is meant and is found to be 'user friendly'. Suppose that, from one day to the next, from one week to the next, you could never anticipate the times of programmes: if no programme was ever on the same day at the same time. You would never know when to listen to anything, because whenever you turned on the radio it would be purely a matter of chance whether or not you hit on something you wanted to listen to. In this sense listening to the radio would be *essentially* problematic. And to a considerable extent it was in Britain, at least until the late thirties. It went against BBC principles (in part influenced by fears of 'standardization' which,

[3]   On 'states that are essentially "by-products"', cf. Elster 1991: 41–108.
[4]   In the UK, for instance, cf. Scannell and Cardiff (1991): 307–14. In the USA, cf. Smulyan (1994). In Australia, cf. Johnson (1988).
[5]   Giddens (1984) emphasizes the importance of routines as the basis of ontological security for us in the conduct of daily life.

to the official mind, was almost synonymous with 'americanization') to make listening 'easy' (Camporesi 1994). The idea was that people shouldn't just have the radio on all the time: 'tap listening' was discouraged. Radio should be used as an occasional resource (like going to the theatre or a concert) and listeners should plan their weekly listening by consulting *Radio Times*, which contained the BBC's weekly programme schedules.

Programme *planning* began to develop in a systematic way in the BBC from the mid-thirties. It was linked to the establishment of a Listener Research unit (1936), one of whose primary tasks was to provide information about the availability or not of listeners for listening through the day and through the days of the week throughout the year. Thus, the notion of sequencing programmes through the day began to be worked on in a rational way, in an effort at matching different kinds of programme with different kinds of listener at different times of day, depending on their availability. This study of listening habits was a key factor in the normalization of the schedules (Pegg 1983). As this was understood so, too, was the value of 'locking' the schedules, of putting the same programme in the same time slot on the same day each week, so that listeners who were known to be there to listen, could know – in a taken-for-granted way – what was there for them to listen to. And the other key factor in relation to these two developments (sequencing the material, locking the sequence) was the discovery of 'continuity' techniques – of placing links and trailers for 'what comes next or later' between programmes. Thus, listeners would get a sense of the overall structure or flow of programmes as a regular, patterned kind of thing through the hours of each day and from one day to the next, and the next and the next.

Intimately linked to these developments was the discovery of serial production. In one sense this fundamental development (for *all* programmes on radio and television today are, with rare exceptions, serial in character) was a response to the severest problem of production – namely the supply of a ceaseless, uninterrupted never-ending flow of output. But at the same time it contributed to the creation of an easily recognizable *identity*, both for any programme and for the totality of output in the channel. A *single* programme has no identity: it is a transient thing that perishes in the moment of its transmission. For output to have the regular, familiar routine character that it has, seriality is crucial throughout the range of output. It creates that difference-in-sameness which is the hallmark of radio, television and newspaper production. The *content* varies from one occasion to the next, the format remains the same. The creation of a programme format as a template that allows for an indefinitely renewable number of broadcast occasions depends on a few basic methods which, again, are by now deeply familiar but which had all at first to be found and applied. They include the use of signature tunes, regular presenters, standardized openings and closings, set sequences for the programme

material and routines for moving through the sequences and maintaining continuity. The net effect of all these techniques is cumulative. In and through time
programme output, in all its parts and as a whole, takes on a settled, familiar,
known and taken-for-granted character as the recursive condition of its daily
occurrence. That it is so is by virtue of techniques discovered and applied to
make it so.

### III

Thus far we have considered the temporality of programmes: the basic ways in
which time is essentially implicated in their organization and production. The
spaciality of programmes comes more clearly into focus when we ask, not what
is a programme, but who is it for? Spaciality is implicated in the question
because it raises the issue of *direction*. It asks, towards whom do programmes
point? This was a question that broadcasters began to ask as part of the
normalization of output. A growing sense of talking into the void contributed,
in the BBC, to the creation of listener research to answer such basic questions
as who is out there listening, when can they listen and do they like what they
hear (cf. Silvey 1977)? It is not *necessarily* the case that programmes are for
audiences. They might be for profit. They might be for the powers that be.
They might be for those who make them. They might be for those who take
part in them.[6] And even if they are for audiences, it is still a particular thing
to make them for *anyone and everyone*. For a programme (indeed a whole
channel) may be conceived of and proclaim itself as for the chosen few, with a
clear intention of shutting out the rest. The BBC's Third Programme, which
began in 1946, was a highbrow channel that quite deliberately chose to avoid
widespread appeal. Its first controller, George Barnes, declared that the Third
would offer 'very few "hearing-aids" for listeners' (Whitehead 1989: 48) and,
not surprisingly, very few people indeed chose to listen. It requires a particular
thoughtfulness and care to make programmes that are listenable to or watchable
by anyone.

Commercial broadcasting is more quickly impelled in this direction than an
institution such as the BBC, whose public service ethos, particularly in the era
of its monopoly, was suffused with an assumption of knowing better than its
listeners what they wanted or needed. There was in the past (and still is) more

---

[6]    It is, for instance, a common feeling among participants in documentary programmes
that they have been 'used', and so they have. They think that because a programme is about
them it is for them. But it is not. It is for absent listeners or viewers. Likewise, as we shall
see in the next chapter, it can easily be shown that all game shows, chat shows, quizzes and
'people' programmes are not for the audience in the studio (which is, in fact, part of the
show) but, again, for listeners or viewers.

than a hint of the notion, among BBC producers (especially in the arts, drama and documentary departments) that they were making programmes for themselves as 'self' expression. All sorts of noble reasons are advanced to defend this principle of creative autonomy, but they bypass the question as to whom the broadcasters and their products are beholden. If they *are* beholden to audiences they must take those audiences into account. If it is a *service* it must serve, and this is something that must show itself to audiences *in* the form and content of programmes, so that audiences can *find* themselves in those programmes.

In discovering who they were broadcasting to, the broadcasters had to reflect on the circumstances of listening and viewing and the conditions in which these activities took place. They had to reflect on the implications and consequences of the evident fact that although they spoke from one place, they were seen and heard in another. They had to understand that while they could, and did, control what went on in their place (typically the studio), they did not, indeed could not, control what went on in the places of listening and viewing. And so they learnt that they must align their behaviour, their performance, to the nature of the places in which listening and viewing take place. It was they who must measure up to the expectations of their audiences, rather than requiring audiences to measure up to their expectations.

In most public events where the participants are co-present, it is the producer(s) of the event who control the behaviour of their audiences, with enforceable sanctions should they misbehave. But the relationship between broadcasters and audiences is *unforced* because it is unenforceable. There are no coercive edges to that relationship because there are no enforceable sanctions over the behaviour of viewers and listeners. To the contrary, power in this relationship (in the first and last instance) rests more with those on the receiving end rather than with those who produce what is on offer. And this is because no one can make anyone listen to or watch anything on radio and television. If listeners and viewers don't like what they find they can simply switch over or switch off. So that broadcasters *must* organize their affairs with the interests of listeners and viewers in mind by virtue, in the first instance, of the gap between the place of transmission and the place of reception and their consequent inability to control the behaviour of their audiences.

The 'discovery' of audiences, and of the need to give programmes listenable and watchable values has a complex history in the UK. It is intimately linked, in the early years, with the activities of the BBC's Talks Department (created in 1927) and their search for forms of talk that were appropriate to the situations in which listening took place (Scannell and Cardiff 1991: 153–79). Quite quickly, older public models of speaking (the lecture, the sermon, the political speech) were rejected and replaced by more direct, intimate, personal styles of speech (Matheson 1933). In short, broadcasting learnt that its expressive idiom must, in form and content, approximate to the norms of ordinary, everyday, mundane conversation, or talk. In talk-as-conversation participants treat each other as particular persons, not as a collective. So, too, with broadcasting. The hearable and seeable effect of radio and television is that 'I am addressed'. This means that *I* am addressed, and not someone else. In listening to radio I do not feel I am an eavesdropper, as if I had accidentally got a crossed line and was tapping in on a private conversation. The DJ in the studio does not appear to be talking to him- or herself (Montgomery 1986). When I watch television I do not normally feel like some peeping-tom or keyhole-kate (though there is currently, on British television, a show called *Through the Keyhole*). The interviewers and politicians that I see do not appear to be merely conversing with each other (Heritage and Greatbatch 1992). In these and countless other instances, *I am spoken to*.

The 'I' that is addressed by radio and television is me-or-anyone. In Heidegger's terms it is the *one*self, as when – for instance – one talks in such a way as to indicate that one's thoughts or actions are such as anyone might have or do. The oneself – a troubling term in Heidegger's thought, towards which he is decidedly ambivalent – is ontologically prior to *my*self.[7] This means that the possibility, for each and every one of us, of achieving a particularized self is necessarily derived from an always already prior ensemble of publicly available worldly possibilities of so self-becoming. Nevertheless, the oneself so addressed by radio and television is a *some*one, not just anyone; that is, a person, not a subject as in Althusser's notion of ideological interpellation (Althusser 1971). This shows up in the ordinary politeness norms of radio and television discussed below and, more particularly, in the ways that viewers and listeners are allowed (are entitled) to their opinions of what they see and hear. It is a structural feature of any programme that anyone can find that it is not 'for me'. That is, the possibilities of the myself are allowed for in the for-anyone-as-someone structure of any programme. The myself is the socially projected 'me'. me-in-my-particularity, me with my particular beliefs, tastes and opinions. There is a third structure of the self – what Heidegger calls

---

[7]    Heidegger's term is *das Man*, which his English translators render as 'the They'. Dreyfus (1994) argues for 'the One' as a better way of catching what is meant by the concept. He points out that it has the same force as French *on* (*On dit*, one says, they say). What is indicated by the concept is not so much public opinion at any time (though that certainly is how Heidegger uses it at times), as the essentially anonymous norms that regulate behaviours in any society at any time. It is what we invoke when we say such things as 'that's how one does it (in *our* society)', or that's 'not the done thing'. We each encounter these anonymous, unspoken public norms (the *non-dit*, we might say) as always already there (Heidegger 1962: 163–8). No matter what we might personally think of these regulatory norms no one can gainsay them: if we transgress them we find ourselves on the wrong side of that invisible line which is drawn between the morally acceptable and unacceptable.

the *own*most self – that is only obliquely addressed by public communicative forms such as radio and television. This incommunicable self – the cherishable, inexpressible aspects of a particular life with its ownmost experiences, memories, joys and sorrows – *can* appropriate public forms and make them its own (own them) in purely personal ways. Barthes explores the appropriations of the incommunicable self in his beautiful essay on photography (Barthes 1984). Such appropriations are, however, by-products rather than intended possibilities of programmes.

The construction of the listener or viewer addressed by radio and television is, thus, a complex phenomenological projection which is unobtrusively but pervasively embedded in programme output. What this overly condensed characterization attempts to account for is the for-the-sake-of-which of any programme: for whom, towards whom, on whose behalf is it made? The for-anyone-as-someone structure is a necessary precondition of any cultural product that can (a) be found as meaningfully available, without any difficulty, by anyone and (b) presents itself in such a way that it appears to be 'for me'. A clear example of this shows up in the, by now, utterly familiar look-to-camera of the television newscaster. This look has a hidden history as something sought for and worked at in order to achieve a particular performed communicative effect. Early television, which was of course live, found the presentation of news to be problematic in a number of ways. If news is a telling, how is it to be told? The BBC preferred, at first, not to have a newsreader in vision to read the news because it was felt that to do so would personalize a discourse that was supposed to be impersonal, impartial and objective. So an anonymous male voice read the bulletins over a visual sequence of charts, still photographs and captions. This was soon found to be not 'good television', and a newsreader was placed in front of the camera to read the news. But this, too, failed, as the newsreader's head flickered up and down from script to camera and back, leading one of the British tabloids (the *Daily Mirror*) to run a centre-page spread with photographs of the newsreaders with eyes downcast beneath a banner headline, THESE ARE THE GUILTY MEN.

To correct this distorted impression, and to secure an effect of honesty, directness and frankness, technical solutions were sought for and found in the invention of the variously called tele-prompter or auto-cue, a device first developed in the USA, whereby the text scrolled over or just below the lens of the camera into which the newsreader looked. Thus, the effect of a direct look from the screen was secured, a look which implicated a someone (who turns out to be 'me') to receive and return it. It was and is a consciously sought for, technically achieved and humanly accomplished device that contributes to the task of producing news-telling as a real-world interactive occasion between the institutions of broadcasting and each and every viewer, thereby securing the effect, for each and every one of them, of 'I am being told'. It is one tiny instance of how the meaningfulness of programmes is organized by those who make them as there-to-be-found by those for whom they are made.


IV

The argument thus far has been that the study of production (how programmes come to occur) shows that broadcasters had to learn what their business of 'doing broadcasting' consisted of. That fundamentally it consisted of producing programme services for audiences. That what had to be learnt was how to deliver a service that was, as a whole and in all its parts and down to the smallest particularities, ready-to-hand and usefully useable – in principle and in fact – by anyone and everyone who cared to watch or listen. That in so doing broadcasting produced and produces itself as part of and as for the ordinary everyday world, for that is the world in which listeners and viewers ordinarily live. That this 'ordinary effect' depends upon an achieved and accomplished and familiar coherence and intelligibility throughout the whole range of output. What has yet to be shown is how all these things are worked into that output as there to be found by any listener or viewer. So that our next task is to consider the general conditions of the intelligibility of output as worked into its form and content, and for this – it will be argued – a theory of communicative intentionality is needed.

It is after all obvious (in a deeply taken-for-granted way) that everything that we see and hear on radio and television is intended to (and does) make sense for us as viewers and listeners (the 'ordinary' effect). If you try to imagine, counterfactually, what broadcasting might be like that was not intended to make sense in this way (if its intelligibility was purely accidental) you can see what is the point of claiming an obvious intentionality in the arrangement of programmes as appropriate to the situations and circumstances for which they were designed.[8] So that, to take a very simple but key issue, for certain programmes to be recognized as *serious* (as dealing with serious matters – such as news – in a serious way) or as *entertaining* (as dealing with entertaining issues in an entertaining way) they must produce these effects as their very conditions for being accepted as that which they claim to be. If everything in social life is a performance in the sense that it has to be *done*, and has to be done in such a way that others will recognize what is being done (as being serious, or funny, or sincere, or real, or make-believe), then the doing of what goes out on radio

---

[8]  The notion of situational propriety is taken from Goffman, and I have in mind, throughout this book, the pervasive relevance and importance of his work on social interaction (1956; 1975), face-work (1972) and talk (1981) for understanding (for making sense of) the matters here under discussion.

and television can be studied in the same way as the rest of social life. With the key proviso that you look to see what difference – if any – there is in the fact of it being done on radio or television.

Thus, it is being claimed, the social organization of any broadcast programme partakes of the same 'logic' of everyday occasions. As in any ordinary circumstances, we monitor quite naturally what's going on, so too for radio and television.[9] We watch and listen with a background assumption that everything about the design of any programme is meant as meaningful. So that we can, in principle, say (analytically, now) in the first place: those making the programme did it this way (and no other way) because . . . (for reasons as yet to be discovered, but we assume they had a reason). Second, the intentions of the programme-makers are realized and expressed in every aspect of the programme (intentions are in the programme if they are anywhere, and nowhere else). Third, these intentions are retrievable by *any* competent listener or viewer (who knows – has learnt – how to understand, say, television news) by the application of common-sense practical inferential reasoning (which is the same common-sense reasoning that went into the programme's design). The logic of intentionality we are talking about here *is* the common ground between programme-makers and audiences. Intentionality is not to be understood in some psychological sense (as what the programme-makers have in mind). It is what is shared between participants as a precondition of any kind of social interaction (including the kind that broadcasting represents).

The notion of common ground, as used here, does not in any way imply a consensus about the substance of the interaction (shared values, beliefs, etc.). Nor does it imply a successful 'transfer' of a preferred evaluation of an intended substantial meaning from, say, speaker to hearer, broadcaster to listener. It supposes, most generally, a shared competence in the procedures of practical reasoning and its applications to everyday circumstances and situations (a cross-cultural, universal competence). Within that it supposes a common cultural/linguistic competence, shared knowledges and understandings, so that – for instance – indirect meanings will be perceived as intended: irony will be recognized as irony, etc. And within that it is supposed that in any particular situation (such as a lecture, a football match, going to a movie with a young child, watching news) there will be a historically cumulative common knowledge and understanding of the nature of the occasion, a deepening sense of its biography (it is this that enhances the knowledge/pleasure effect of television soaps). Finally, the notion of common ground does not rule out the failure to find common ground (though it presupposes an effort to reach it), nor routine breakdowns, misunderstandings, etc. within the interactions which

---

[9]    On the 'reflexive monitoring of action', cf. Giddens 1984.

give rise to remedial repair work. On this last point conversation analysis's study of various aspects of 'repair work' in talk-as-interaction (Schegloff et al. 1977) and Goffman's remarks on embarrassment, tact, etc. (1972) are illuminating and helpful.

We can now formulate these arguments by introducing Paul H. Grice's theory of communicative intentionality, which holds that an intended meaning is one that is intended to be recognized as intended by its recipient.[10] The first thing this proposition accomplishes is to distinguish between intended and unintended meaning.[11] But the crucial force of the theory of intentionality is that it distinguishes between meaning and utterance. It does not specify intended meaning as what is said, but as what is intended to be recognized as intended. For instance: I am listening to the evening news on radio and the newsreader says something about a foreign statesman (say, Mr Yeltsin). The next thing I hear is a (hearably) male voice saying something in a foreign language for a few seconds. This then fades down and over it I hear a (hearably) male English voice speaking that is not the voice of the newsreader. . . . Now all this makes perfect sense to me: I *assume* (though I am not told) that the foreign male voice I hear is that of Mr Yeltsin. And I *assume* (though I am not told) that the English voice over that foreign voice is giving me a literal translation of what that foreign voice is saying. But how do I *know* these things? What is it that warrants these inferential assumptions?[12]

Assuming background knowledge, understanding and especially trust of the institutions of broadcast news (i.e. I can take at face value what is going on), I make sense of the transition from newsreader's voice to Mr Yeltsin's by reckoning that I must have enough relevant information from what has immediately gone before to figure out the owner of this strange and unexplained foreign voice.

---

[10]   For a fuller account of Grice's theory, the related conversational maxims and the study of implicatures (implied meanings) as a central concern of linguistic pragmatics, see Levinson (1983), the classic textbook on the subject in which ordinary language philosophy, pragmatics and conversational analysis (CA) are all shown as closely linked to one another. Cf. also Leech (1983), another early pragmatics textbook.

[11]   Unintended meanings are an important phenomenon in their own right, but they lie outside the intended scope of this chapter. Goffman has examined slips of the tongue and other unintended 'bloopers' by broadcasters in his essay on radio talk (Goffman 1981). Rather differently, the question as to whether taken-for-granted ideological assumptions embedded in everyday practices are intended or not is a matter that needs careful consideration.

[12]   The particular practices here described may be specific to British broadcasting, and it is likely that the use of, say, foreign-language inserts in news will be done differently elsewhere. The more general point is that, no matter where, news practices and techniques presuppose that their audiences can and do apply the interpretative logic analysed here. That is, institutional techniques are intelligible (are *meant* to be intelligible) within an analytical frame of communicative intentionality: the practices are meant to be recognized as intended by absent listeners or viewers.

So it must be that of the person referred to in the preceding utterance (I must of course be able to trust the reliability of this inference). Likewise, I assume that the broadcasters assume that 'I' do not understand what Mr Yeltsin is saying and that they are providing 'me' with a word by word translation of his utterance. I cannot regard these assumptions as purely subjective or speculative (i.e. as assumptions peculiar to me). I must regard them as *in* the organizational features of the structured sequence of what I heard, and that it is intentionally structured *in just this way* for me (or anyone) to find out what I need to find out to make sense of the sequence.

But *where*, in the sequence, are the prompts that set me off in search of the correct inferences? They are in the editing process, in those points of transition from voice A to B (a 'cut') and from B to C (a combination of fade and superimposition). These 'invisible' elements in the discourses of radio broadcasting are tokens of an unobtrusive institutional organizing presence, which we attend to without noticing that we do so. That is, editing is a highly effective and efficient, motivated way of conveying meaning without having to say it. It is simply not necessary to supply, at the interstices where the edits are made, a commentary along the lines of 'And here is what Mr Yeltsin had to say himself . . . and here is a translation into English of what he said'. The forms of the edits are designed to do that work and to be recognized as doing it. We can reconstruct those intentions because we can apply a virtual assumption of reciprocal, communicative intentionality to what we hear.

## V

It has so far been argued that broadcast programmes should be considered and analysed as naturally occurring social phenomena and part of a sociology of occasions. Further, that any social occasion – including any radio or television programme – is an organized event that exhibits a communicative intentionality in all its aspects (linguistic, para-linguistic and non-linguistic). We can now formalize what distinguishes radio and television programmes from other occasions. In the first place, they are institutional occasions and, in the second place, they are produced for absent listeners and viewers. Taken together, these two characteristics are the distinguishing features of broadcast occasions and the talk occasioned in them.[13]

Institutional occasions are distinguished from others by virtue of the power of the institution to organize and control the nature of the occasion and to impose its definitions on participants in the occasion. In attending to the institutional features of broadcast occasions we can specify how power works in

---

[13]    I am grateful to John Heritage for showing me the cardinal significance of these two points.

them, by the study of (1) the distribution of communicative entitlements, (2) participatory statuses and performative roles and (3) the organization and control of talk. In particular, we should look at the pre-allocation of interactional roles and statuses – i.e. who has opportunities to speak and under what constraints. Pre-allocated turn-taking at talk, as conversation analysis has shown, is a pervasive feature of institutional talk in many different contexts (in the class-room, in the law-courts, a church service, a television studio interview, etc.). The agents of the institution (broadcasters, teachers, lawyers, priests, etc.) have responsibility for the management of the occasion, for ensuring that it comes off, that it works as a lecture, a church service, an interview, etc. A study of institutional forms of social interaction, and particularly the kinds of talk that go on in them, shows how communicative entitlements are unequally distributed amongst the participants as compared with ordinary, plain talk in non-institutional contexts (face encounters in daily life), where participants have equal discursive rights and responsibilities. A simple demonstration of some of these differences comes from the comparative study of conversational openings and closings in broadcast phone-ins and ordinary phone-calls (Hutchby 1991).

But the peculiar feature that distinguishes institutional interactions on radio and television from other institutional contexts is that they are designed for absent listeners or viewers (Heritage 1985). Given that communicative intentionality in broadcasting is organized and designed for those for whom the programmes are made, we can now begin to consider what shapes the *attitudes* to each other of broadcasters, listeners and viewers. It is not simply that broadcasters, in attending to their audiences, must consider how they address them. They must connect such concerns with considerations of behaviours that are appropriate to the settings and circumstances in which listening and viewing take place. In the early days of radio in Great Britain, broadcasters thought of themselves as 'uninvited guests' in the family living room (Lewis 1924). A growing sensitivity to the implications of the domestic spaces of reception created a conscious readjustment of the forms of talk that radio produced, with a clear aim of being more suitable for 'fireside' listening. Such considerations are crucial to the design of broadcast occasions and the nature of the talk produced therein. Both are pervasively motivated by a communicative ethos of politeness: the form and content of the broadcast occasion is designed with the settings in which it is to be received in mind, and their appropriate forms of social interaction.

It is obvious that in any social occasion participants adjust their behaviours to take each other into account (guided by their assessments of the situation and the others who are present as participants). For behaviour to be communicative a co-operative principle is a necessary entailment. This manifests itself in designed and intended behaviours and utterances that display to others that they have been taken into consideration in the precise form of the displayed behaviour or utterance. We can define politeness in this very fundamental way: not as a matter of social etiquette, but as a matter of consideration for – in Goffman's terms – the face-needs of others. Human beings are sacred objects: that is, they hold themselves entitled, on a reciprocal basis, to due respect and reverence from others (Goffman 1972). Sacred objects can be defiled or desecrated: they can suffer grievous loss of face (Goffman 1968; 1974). Considerations of this kind are among the most far-reaching implications of Goffman's sociology. By a practical–rational principle of do-as-you-would-be-done-by, human beings show respect for each other – co-operate in mutual face-maintenance (avoiding threats to face) – because anyone's self-presentation and performance in any social occasion is (from moment to moment) vulnerable and perishable.

In their classic study of politeness, Brown and Levinson (1987) bring together Goffman's sociology of face and Grice's theory of implicatures. Both form the basis of a theoretically elegant and wide-ranging empirical investigation, via three unrelated languages, of politeness as a universal linguistic category. In the concluding section of the book, they claim that it is possible to generalize from the study of particular interactions, to the overall subtle flavour of interaction in a society (ibid.: 243–53). Paying particular attention to the specific cultural distribution of key social variables such as D (social distance) and P (power), they argue that it is possible to identify the kinds of relationship that prevail in a particular society (dominant ethos). Considerations of P and D particularly determine W, the weight (seriousness) of FTAs (face threatening actions): such considerations regulate the choice of politeness strategies that are typically employed in public situations in a particular society.

The notions of communicative ethos and dominant ethos are particularly useful for catching the quality of broadcast programmes, in their two-fold character as individual items and as sequentially ordered elements in the output of a radio or television channel. In the case of British broadcasting it is possible to show, in the detail of programmes-as-broadcast, that communicative ethos on radio and television has – over 70 years – shifted from distant and authoritative relationships between broadcasters and audiences to more equal, open and accessible relationships (Scannell 1989). Over the years broadcasting has learnt, has had to learn, to create and sustain a sociable ethos between itself and its listeners and viewers. Communicative ethos, even dominant communicative ethos, is thus not some simple, unitary thing. It not only changes in time, but at any one time it will vary across different areas of programme output (authoritative styles being preferred in news, say, informal styles in DJ talk) and within particular areas: the talk produced around classical music is different to that produced around pop music. In studying the character of communicative ethos on radio and television one is studying in effect the character of public discourse, in its unity and diversity, in a modern society.

Broadcasting lies across what in Habermas's terms are called system and lifeworld (Habermas 1989). The peculiarities of broadcasting's ethos lie in the tensions between these two worlds and the play of conflicting rationalities: those that are instrumental and strategically oriented to self-interest and success, and those that are non-instrumental and disinterestedly oriented to playfulness and sociability. The cultures of public and private life today converge and intermingle on radio and television. To study their communicative ethos is to study the organization and characteristics of public life in today's world, since much of what we know and understand as public life is constituted in and by the activities of broadcasting. The study of radio and television output as made up of displayed social interactions in public, with talk at the heart of the analysis, is central to this book and its concern with the analysis of the historically evolving impact and effect of broadcasting on our modern world.

Classic social theory took a disenchanted view of a world that it found to be disenchanted. It saw modernity as drained of meaning and found it meaningless – an iron cage (Weber 1971), a reified world (Lukács 1970), a world of mass deception (Adorno and Horkheimer 1985). The kind of theory presented in this book finds the world (and in particular the world of broadcasting) as enchanted and enchanting, meaningful and full of meaning. This is not a fanciful trope. The language used to describe the invention of radio first and, later, television expressed over and over again a sense of wonder at them as marvellous things, miracles of modern science. Their magic has not vanished. It has simply been absorbed, matter-of-factly, into the fabric of ordinary daily life.

# 2

---

## *Sociability*

The political, the economic, the purposive society of any sort is, to be sure, always 'society'. But only the sociable gathering is 'society' without qualifying adjectives, because it alone presents the pure, abstract play of form, all the specific contents of the one-sided and qualified societies being dissolved away.

(Simmel 1950: 129)

### I

Sociability, as the essence of the social, is like art. It has no purpose, no ulterior motive; that is, no rational self-interest is served by it. As such it is wholly oriented to the interplay of persons in their personable self-presentations. The personal traits of amiability, breeding, cordiality and attractiveness of all kinds determine, says Simmel, the character of purely sociable association. When people enter into each other's company for the sake of sociability they seek nothing more than the pleasure of each other's company, and to create an occasion in which all are at ease with each other. In this respect, as Simmel suggests, sociable occasions are essentially democratic, in that distinctions of wealth, social status, learning and so on are – momentarily – set aside. So, too, are purely personal matters. It is tactless to introduce one's own problems, 'the light and shadow of one's inner life'. And so:

> This world of sociability, the only one in which a democracy of equals is possible without friction, is an *artificial* world, made up of beings who have renounced both the objective and the purely personal features of the intensity and extensiveness of life in order to bring about among themselves a pure inter-action, free of any disturbing material accent. If we now have the conception

that we enter into sociability purely as 'human beings', as that which we really are, lacking all the burdens, the agitations, the inequalities with which real life disturbs the purity of our picture, it is because modern life is over-burdened with objective content and external demands. (Simmel 1950: 130)

If sociability lacks a content (a message, a purposive intention) its medium is conversation, talk for talk's sake: 'in sociability talking is an end in itself; in purely sociable conversation the content is merely the indispensable carrier of the stimulation, which the lively exchange of talk as such unfolds' (ibid.: 136) If sociability is the only kind of social occasion in which talk is a legitimate end in itself, it becomes 'the most adequate fulfilment of a relation which is, so to speak, nothing but relationship, in which that which is otherwise pure form of interaction is its own self-sufficient content' (ibid.: 137)

## II

Sociability is the most fundamental characteristic of broadcasting's commun-icative ethos. The relationship between broadcasters and audiences is a *purely social* one, that lacks any specific content, aim or purpose. This, of course, is not to deny that a very great deal of broadcast output has content, aims and pur-pose. News intends to provide information. Adverts intend to persuade. But even where there is a manifest content with obvious strategic–purposive inten-tions (most obviously, as we shall see, in the propaganda that saturated every area of programming in the Second World War), there is a necessary prior soci-able commitment in the communicative form of every programme. The force of this claim is to undercut any ultimate strategic, manipulative or exploitative purpose in broadcasting. It is not to say such motives do not pervade broad-casting's communicative ethos, but rather that they do not constitute it.

The character of broadcasting as *necessarily* sociable lies in the form of its communicative context, and the broadcasters' lack of control over their audi-ences. The relationship between broadcasters, listeners and viewers is an *unforced* relationship because it is unenforceable. Broadcasters must, before all else, always consider how they shall talk to people who have no particular reason, purpose or intention for turning on the radio or television set. If we ask whether people have a particular reason, a motive, for listening or watching, it seems an implausible question. One could reply, in a highly abstract way, 'for relaxation', or 'for company', or 'to be informed' – but these are not practical, means–ends oriented reasons. Raymond Williams has pointed out that we talk of watching television or listening to the radio, not of watching or listening to something in particular. Of course, within the 'flow' of programme output, people make a point of turning on for the news or a favourite drama serial. But still, it is hard to give good reasons for watching and listening. We do so because we can't find anything else, anything better, to do. In this way, the activities of listeners and viewers appear unmotivated. They are nothing more (or less) than pastimes, ways of spending 'free time'.

Given, then, that you cannot coerce listeners to listen, it would follow – as we have already argued – that you would try to speak to them in ways that they would wish to be spoken to. So that the appropriate expressive idiom for any broadcast is one that fits the contexts in which viewing and listening take place. To describe the communicative manner and style of radio and television as conversational means more than chatty mannerisms and a personalized idiom ('I', 'you' and 'we'). It means orienting to the normative values of ordinary talk in which participants have equal status and equal discursive rights. In short, it is no use talking *at* listeners, or talking *down* to them, for if you do they can simply switch you off. The communicative task that broadcasters faced was to find forms of talk that spoke *to* listeners, modes of address which disclosed that listeners were taken into account in the form of the utterance itself. What this came down to was the discovery that existing public forms of talk were inappropriate for the new medium of radio. The lecture, the sermon, the political speech, all had rhetorical styles that spoke to audiences constituted as a crowd, a mass. But radio must speak to each listener as someone in particular, with the attributes (the face-needs) of a person. The for-anyone-as-someone structure of radio and television's communicative style was first found in the development of friendlier forms of address, a more informal discursive style as markers of a general sociable intent that showed itself in most areas of programme output.

There remains the separate question of what, in broadcasting, is a sociable *occasion*. Although now the answer seems obvious enough, it was not so 60 years ago, and the invention of sociable occasions for radio and television deserves detailed attention. A sociable occasion then, for broadcasting, should exhibit the following characteristics: it should be an 'event' that is original and particular to broadcasting. It should be an event whose object is nothing more (or less) than to produce an interaction between people for its own sake, as something enjoyable and entertaining for listeners. If that is the essence of a sociable occasion, it presents a number of problems for broadcasting. Who shall the speakers be, and how shall they speak? On the one hand, the charm of the sociable is its seeming spontaneity and relaxed naturalness. To achieve this, however, for broadcasting, it will have to be most carefully managed: for the object is not, in the first place, the production of a sociable occasion for the participants in the programme, but for listeners and viewers.

The first programme that sought to create a sociable occasion as its *raison d'être* was a little series broadcast on North Region in 1935, called *Harry Hopeful*. It had a considerable impact and a second short series was produced the following year. The format of the programme was not taken up elsewhere in the BBC and lapsed until the war when, in very different circumstances, it was revived (by its original producer) in the form of factory feature programmes about the workers, most notably in a series called *Billy Welcome*. Finally, after the war, Wilfred Pickles, the wartime presenter of the *Billy Welcome* series (and many others) took up the format again and revised it to produce what was to be the most popular single programme on radio across the fifties – *Have a Go!* Thus, we can explore, through production files, scripts and recordings of the programmes spread over 20 years, the origins and development of a format which, in extended variations, now pervades broadcast entertainment on radio and television: namely chat shows, game shows and quizzes, and – most recently – 'people' programmes along the lines originally developed in the United States by Phil Donahue and Oprah Winfrey.

The essential ingredients of all these programmes – their basic format – is an organized set of social interactions situated in a studio, or some other suitable public space. The members of the occasion consist of (1) a host, (2) participant–performers, (3) a live audience and (4) absent listeners and viewers. The object of the occasion is fun, having a good time. There are, as we shall see, at least three sets of communicative interaction always in play in programmes of this kind: (1) host and participant–performers, (2) host and audience, (3) host and listeners or viewers (sometimes there is an organized interaction between performers and audience). The object of the accounts that follow will be to explore how, in the course of time, such interactions were organized and managed to bring off sociability as an achieved and accomplished effect for listeners and viewers.

### III

## Harry Hopeful (1935–6)

*Harry Hopeful* was an ingenious solution to a policy demand and the limitations of radio technologies at the time. The brief, for all the regional production centres in the mid-thirties, was to reflect the life and variety of the area they served. In Manchester this was interpreted as a mandate to make programmes about the people and places of North Region (Scannell and Cardiff 1991: 333–54). Two areas of programming took the lead in this: Outside Broadcasts and Features. Manchester's Director of Programmes was Archie Harding, an outstanding features producer in London before his 'promotion' to North Region. Harding wanted to emulate the methods of British documentary film makers by creating 'sound-pictures' of Northern life shot on location. There were, however, no sound recording facilities in Manchester

in the mid-thirties, so it would all have to be done in the studio. To realize
the project, Harding recruited an aspiring young poet and writer, Geoffrey
Bridson.

Bridson conceived of an imaginary central character, Harry Hopeful, an out-
of-work glass-blower's assistant on the tramp in search of work, meeting and
talking to real people in the real places he visited in Northern England (Bridson
1971). Bridson was fortunate in finding a 'natural' for the part, Frank Nicholls,
a clock-mender from Irlam who was already a regular performer on Manchester's *Children's Hour*. The locations chosen were well-known beauty spots – the
Peak District, the Yorkshire Dales and North York Moors. Together, Bridson and Nicholls visited these places and talked to the local people whom they
had invited to take part in the show. As Nicholls talked to them (he had that
rare ability to draw people out in conversation) Bridson made detailed notes of
what they said. Later, he worked this material into a script, a copy of which
was sent to each participant. A few weeks later he and Nicholls returned with
portable wireless equipment and a radio engineer. The microphone was then
set up in the homes of the participants and they each rehearsed their part with
Nicholls while Bridson listened on headphones in the car outside. Thus, the
speakers were accustomed to the microphone in familiar surroundings and
adjustments could be made to the script, if necessary, to make the talk sound
more natural and spontaneous. Later the full cast was assembled in Manchester's main studio. After one complete run-through came the live broadcast
itself, performed before an invited audience which included the families and
friends of the participants.

| 1 | *Announcer* | This is the Regional Programme from the North. |
|---|---|---|
| 2 | | For the next fifty minutes we're presenting Cressbrook |
| 3 | | to Ashbourne. |
| 4 | | Or Harry Hopeful's Day in the Dales. |
| 5 | | A Derbyshire itinerary initiated by D. G. Bridson and E. A. Harding |
| 6 | | (.) |
| 7 | | Harry Hopeful's Day in the Derbyshire Dales! |
| 8 | | (*The show's theme tune is faded up, with Hopeful* |
| 9 | | *coming in on the last line . . .* |
| 10 | | My luck mun' change on Monday! hehhehehhe |
| 11 | | (*Cheers and applause* |
| 12 | | eheheh . . . Aa:h well folks, 'ere we are again (.) |
| 13 | | Winter may 'a laid me up but Spring cann't hold me down, |
| 14 | | oo::hh no. |
| 15 | | It takes more than a (?) to put me out of action. |
| 16 | | And seeing as it's nigh on a year sin I made this trip |

| 17 | | be walkin' into Yorkshire[1] I thowt proper to spend me |
| 18 | | Easter in De::rbyshire. |
| 19 | | Eh:::eh but it's a right county that is. |
| 20 | | I must a' bought about half of it back into studio on me |
| 21 | | shoes by t' look on it. |
| 22 | | (*Laughter* |
| 23 | | Are we all 'ere now? |
| 24 | *Audience* | Aye we're all here. |
| 25 | *Hopeful* | Are we all ready then? |
| 26 | *Audience* | Aye we're all ready. |
| 27 | *Hopeful* | Then let 'em have it. One Two Three Four |

|  | *All* | Harry Hopeful is me name |

*All*

Harry Hopeful is me name
Harry Hopeful is me name
Out of work I am the same
Me luck must change o' Monday

Got me cards and off the payroll
Got me cards and off the payroll
Nowt to do is not the same
I mun find work o' Monday

Time to spare is what I've got
Time to spare is what I've got
Sounds alrcct but that it's not
My luck must change o' Monday

Jigger off and see what's doing
Jigger off and see what's doing
I've got nowt while some's a lot
There mun be work o' Monday

Touting round is not me game
Touting round is not me game
Got to do it all the same
If luck's to change o' Monday

If you've something put me to it
If you've something put me to it
Harry Hopeful is my na::me
I *mun* find work o' Monda::y.

(*Laughter from Hopeful, loud cheers from audience*

---

[1]   This is the first programme in the second series (1936). The first series, the previous year, began with a day in the Yorkshire Dales.

The immediate difficulty is that the printed word is not hearable, and it is the hearable properties of what is going on here, and their effects, that I want to discuss: the clipped, precise and mannered voice of the anonymous (young, male) BBC announcer, for instance. Though the programme comes from Manchester, his voice comes from somewhere else where Harry is pronounced 'Herry', Derbyshire is 'Dahbishah' and 'itinerary' has its full five vowels picked out with sugar-tongs. The contrast with Hopeful's voice is striking. How to describe a human voice and its communicable qualities? It is as hard (as absurd) as attempting to put the taste of wine into words. But hearably, let us say, this is a Northern voice, a manly voice, firm and clear and deep with warm, humorous undertones. You would guess the owner of this voice was in his fifties. It is an experienced voice, a welcoming voice, a pleasurable voice to listen to; a voice at ease with itself and with the situation. It greets its audience(s) as if renewing an already established relationship: 'a:h well folks, 'ere we are again'. It immediately puts everything onto a sociable footing.

That this is to be a public, sociable occasion is further underlined by the hearable presence of the studio audience, even before Hopeful's first words of greeting. 'Our' sense (as listeners) of the presence of a studio audience is perhaps the crucial innovation, in *Harry Hopeful*, which lays down the basis for all subsequent variants on its basic format. For the hearable effect of an audience is to constitute what is taking place as a performed *public* event in the presence of an audience drawn from the listening public. Thus, whereas some programmes attempt to enter into the private and domestic spaces in which listening takes place,[2] *Harry Hopeful* and all its successors, invite absent listeners or viewers to enter into the studio (or wherever) as a public space to participate in a publicly constituted occasion.

As we shall see, in the immediate variations on the original, the programme's host takes care, from the start, to distinguish the live and present audience from the absent listening audience. But in *Harry Hopeful* the talk does not immediately establish this distinction. Who is addressed by Hopeful's greeting – 'ah well folks, 'ere we are again'? Who is implicated in the programme's 'we'? Certainly the audience that has already produced laughter-as-greeting for Hopeful. Maybe listeners too, but it's not made clear that they are acknowledged as part of the programme's sociable address. The joke about bringing Derbyshire mud into the studio (18–21) seems to speak particularly to a studio audience of Derbyshire people and so, too, does the prior assertion (19) that 'it's a right county'. However, it is clear that the immediately following little interaction – 'are we all 'ere now?', 'are we all ready?' – is addressed directly to the studio audience, and so too the cry to 'let 'em (i.e. listeners) have it'.

---

[2]    The classic entertainment programme, from this period, which deliberately sought to enter into the 'fireside world' of listeners, and to invoke 'the pleasures of privacy' was *Monday Night at Seven* (see Scannell and Cardiff 1991: 266–8).

This little routine is a standard way of warming up a theatre audience for a bit of direct participation in the show. But the force of 'let 'em have it' is to acknowledge that *this* bit of audience participation (unlike in theatre pantomime, for instance) is not for the present audience, but for absent listeners. So that, in a doubling effect, the routine and the singing of the song establishes what's happening in the studio both as a participatory, public event, but also as one that is produced (first and last) not for the participating studio audience, but for absent listeners. That is, the studio audience are part of a performance produced for absent listeners.

This use of a hearable audience as part of the programme aroused considerable curiosity up in London, when heard for the first time. The Director of Talks, Charles Siepmann, felt it was the nearest thing to real and typical regional performance that he had yet heard. The whole thing had a great air of spontaneity but he wanted to know if the audience was literally there, whether the laughter and applause were real or recorded, and whether they they genuine characters or actors. Such responses point up the inherent ambiguities of the manufactured performance of spontaneity. For a sociable occasion to be a sociable occasion requires an overall effect of being natural, easy and relaxed. Yet as a *public event* intended for absent listeners any studio-based occasion must be most carefully controlled. It is live and in real time, with the ever-present possibility of going wrong. It brings ordinary people into an unfamiliar and intimidating studio, puts them on stage and expects them to produce performances that are appropriate to the occasion. It expects the studio audience to adapt its responses so as not to drown out what's happening at the microphone by unruly behaviour. On the one hand there is the danger of too little control leading to disaster and chaos, on the other there is the danger of too much control leading to an awkward self-consciousness and an air of embarrassment all round. Somewhere in between lies the golden mean of a managed performance that controls with a light touch what's happening in the studio to bring off a collaborative interaction between all present as a sociable occasion produced *by* them *for* absent listeners.

| 1 | *Bill* | And then tha covers it al ower wi' sand and then tha puts |
| 2 | | thee clay in |
| 3 | *Hopeful* | Aye. |
| 4 | *Bill* | And then tha starts a-beatin' it wi' a wooden mallet – |
| 5 | *Hopeful* | Here, hold on, 'old on a minute. How d'you gerrit in? |
| 6 | *Bill* | Well, y'ave to kerry it in. |
| 7 | *Hopeful* | Shovel it in? |
| 8 | *Bill* | Shovel it in, aye. |
| 9 | *Hopeful* | Mix it nice and soft like? |
| 10 | *Bill* | Aye we temper it . . . |
| 12 | *Hopeful* | Temper it. Why is it bad tempered? |
| 13 | | (*Laughter* |

| 14 | *Bill* | Oh aye, yes. Sometimes it's dry and sometimes it's wet. |
| 15 | *Hopeful* | Aye, and you 'it it with that there nice little 'ammer |
| 16 | | I see'd about six foot long. |
| 17 | *Bill* | Aye that's it. Eeh and it does squat you. |
| 18 | | (*Roars of laughter* |
| 19 | | Aye it does squat you. |
| 20 | *Hopeful* | Squatch me! |
| 21 | *Bill* | Aye it squats yer eyes and it covers you all over. . . . |

How shall we characterize this talk about making a clay-bottomed pond in limestone country to stop rainfall draining away immediately? It is hardly an interview since Bill, not Hopeful, leads the talk for the most part. It is scarcely instructive – how to make a clay-bottomed pond in your back garden (anticipating *Gardener's Question Time*). Nor is it private chat, since Hopeful's echoing repetitions, queries and prompts are surely audience-oriented, designed to elicit explanations on behalf of those in the studio and/or absent listeners. Perhaps the closest parallel to this talk is the stand-up double-act that was familiar at the time from variety and music-hall. It is certainly intended to be entertaining and laughter-eliciting.

| 22 | *Hopeful* | And what else d'you do? |
| 23 | *Bill* | You gone on beating it wi' this wi' this 'ere mallet, keep dundging |
| 24 | | (*Laughter* |
| 25 | | it down till it gets solid, till it's |
| 26 | | about seven or eight inches thick, and then it's all nicely |
| 27 | | for putting pitchings on then. |
| 28 | *Hopeful* | Pitchings? |
| 29 | *Bill* | Aye that's what we call pitching it. |
| 30 | *Hopeful* | And what do we put them on for? |
| 31 | *Bill* | That's for to stop cattle creeping in and mekkin |
| 32 | | 'oles in it d'you see? |
| 33 | *Hopeful* | And is it done now? |
| 34 | *Bill* | No it isn't. You want to put webs on it so as weeds does'na |
| 35 | | grow on top and let watter off, go down into t' klee. |

Note that the three points in this talk that draw laughter from the studio audience involve the use of either technical or dialect terms: 'Temper' (12), 'squat' (rhymes with cat: 17) and 'dundging' (23). It seems to me that the overall communicative character of the talk is focused in these moments and expressed in the laughter they elicit. Hearably this is a good humoured, good natured interaction between two 'characters' whose performance involves playing with regional and local identity: that is, a generalizable 'northern' identity and, within that, a more particularly located identity (in this case, Derbyshire). Note that Hopeful invites glosses on Bill's technical terms such as 'temper' or 'pitchings', assuming that both studio and listening audiences might need these things explaining a bit. But everyone is presumed to grasp dialect terms (such as squats or dundging), or meanings (webs = ducks?) or pronunciations (klee = clay), none of which are glossed or queried by Hopeful. Since the studio audience consists of local people and since the listening audience is regional, it is expected that all will understand the language of North Region.

'Northernness' was a specific quality of place and people that the Manchester station sought to capture in all its programmes – in the 'flyting' comic plays of Yorkshire and Lancashire, in dialect tales and poems (Bill goes on, after this conversation, to sing a dialect song of his own invention about two dud racing pigeons), in the regional music (from brass bands and choral societies to the Manchester Hallé or the Liverpool Philharmonic), in countless outside broadcasts and occasional documentaries and features such as this. The 'northernness' on display in *Harry Hopeful* is a performance, a cheerful, humorous assumption of an identity that can be 'turned on' as required. Siepmann had wondered whether those taking part were genuine characters or actors. It is the very clear feeling that we are listening to a performance that gives rise to such uncertainty. What we have, in effect, are ordinary people playing at being themselves, playing it up, remaining in character but being 'a character'. Bill's performance (and I think it's about the best in the whole programme) actually wins a round of applause from the studio audience at the end – the only one in the whole show to do so.

But most of the talk in the programme is not so markedly playing with identity. Consider this interaction between Hopeful and the first person he meets at the beginning of the show – Miss Lydia Lomas, who comes from Cressbrook:

| 1 | *Hopeful* | Cressbrook Mill it was as caught my eye and I thought |
| 2 | | there might be a job going, but no. Same old tale. |
| 3 | *Miss Lomas* | They didn't take you on then? |
| 4 | *Hopeful* | Take me on? Not they! They said you don't have to be |
| 5 | | a glass blower to get a job in a doubling (?) mill. |
| 6 | | [*Laughter* |
| 7 | *Miss Lomas* | You should have applied when it were a peppermint mill. |
| 8 | *Hopeful* | And when were that? |
| 9 | *Miss Lomas* | About a hundred and fifty years ago. They used |
| 10 | | to grow the mint on the hill side. |
| 11 | *Hopeful* | A hundred and fifty year ago – here, 'ow old do you think |

| 12 | | I am? |
| 13 | | [*Laughter* |
| 14 | | ( . . . ) Now look here, how long were you working in t' mill? |
| 15 | *Miss Lomas* | Oh about forty-five years. I started the day after |
| 16 | | I was ten. |
| 17 | *Hopeful* | Day after you were ten! 'Ere, I thowt this were a |
| 18 | | cotton-mill, not a kindergarten. |
| 19 | | [*Laughter* |
| 20 | *Miss Lomas* | Well children used to have to go to work sooner |
| 21 | | i' those days. |
| 22 | *Hopeful* | Aye it seems like it. Things must've been pretty bad |
| 23 | | i' those days. |
| 24 | *Miss Lomas* | Not thee(?) You should've heard tell what happened |
| 25 | | to a friend of mine. She was ninety-five when she died |
| 26 | | and that was fifteen years ago. She was kidnapped when |
| 27 | | she was eight and set to work as an apprentice. |
| 28 | *Hopeful* | Kidnapped did you say? |
| 29 | *Miss Lomas* | Yes. They used to kidnap children to work |
| 30 | | in the mills in those days. And keep 'em at it. |
| 31 | *Hopeful* | But didn't they run away? I know I should've done. |
| 32 | *Miss Lomas* | You wouldn't've got chance. They had sentries |
| 33 | | posted above and below the mill to stop them running away. |
| 34 | *Hopeful* | Sentries. Good Heavens! |
| 35 | *Miss Lomas* | Aye, only one girl was known to escape and she |
| 36 | | had her brother to help her. |
| 37 | *Hopeful* | And what were conditions like i' those days? |
| 38 | *Miss Lomas* | Very bad. The apprentices used to sleep |
| 39 | | in little pens under the rafters. They're still there if |
| 40 | | you want to see them. |
| 41 | *Hopeful* | No I don't know as I do. |
| 42 | *Miss Lomas* | But I believe the food was good and regular. |
| 43 | *Hopeful* | It'd need be I'm thinking. But what were t' food? |
| 44 | *Miss Lomas* | (brightly) Porridge! |
| 45 | *Hopeful* | [eh? |
| 46 | *Miss Lomas* | and I think they had it about |
| 47 | | twenty-one times a week. |
| 48 | | [*Laughter* |
| 49 | *Hopeful* | Twenty-one times a week – ohoh, nice and varied like |
| 50 | | ehehehh |
| 51 | *Miss Lomas* | [ehehehh |
| 52 | | [*Laughter* |
| 53 | *Hopeful* | But look here, did they kidnap all the apprentices? |
| 54 | *Miss Lomas* | No, a lot came from the orphanages and they had to |

| 55 |            | take the mental ones along with the sane ones. |
|----|------------|------------------------------------------------|
| 56 | *Hopeful*  | What, mental ones? Did they 'ave to work as well? |
| 57 | *Miss Lomas* | Yes. And every one for nothing. The owners had charge |
| 58 |            | of them till they was twenty-one years of age. Then |
| 59 |            | they could go where they liked. Most of them married |
| 60 |            | and settled down in Derbyshire and that's how it came |
|    |            | about − |
| 61 | *Hopeful*  | [Ah well, there's no more in Derbyshire than |
| 62 |            | anywhere else |
| 63 |            | [*Laughter* |
| 64 |            | you know, I'm a bit queer |
| 65 |            | meself for that matter |
| 66 |            | [*Laughter* |
| 67 |            | At least I should've been if I 'ad to work 'i those |
| 68 |            | times. By it meks me flesh fair creep to think on it. |
| 69 | *Miss Lomas* | Well. (.) Times have changed now alright. |
| 70 | *Hopeful*  | Aye well Miss Lomas. Let's hope they 'ave. Good night. |
| 71 |            | You're an older hand than I am at t' job. |
| 72 | *Miss Lomas* | Good night Harry. |
| 73 | *Hopeful*  | Good night. |

To understand the character of this talk we might begin by considering what it is that entitles Miss Lomas to speak. Clearly it is to do with what she speaks about − Cressbrook Mill and its history − and her knowledge based on experience that arises from having lived there all her life and having worked in the mill for 40 years. She can thus claim to know what she is talking about, and hence is entitled to talk about it. But this is not a 'documentary' interview in which the primary object is to elicit information on some social topic. In the first place the talk between Hopeful and Miss Lomas has a more conversational feel to it − it is Miss Lomas who initiates the talk and it is not until line 14 that Hopeful initiates a topic change and assumes control of the direction of the talk with an 'interview' question designed to elicit information for a third party − the studio audience and listeners.

It is also good humoured talk, whose humorous qualities lie not so much in the content of what is said, but in how it is said. Consider the laughter produced by the studio audience at lines 52 and 63. Now the subject matter − an unrelieved diet of porridge for the kidnapped child-apprentices, and the use of mentally disturbed orphans as child labour − is hardly funny. It is the manner, the style, in which the information is conveyed, that produces laughter. In both instances Miss Lomas carefully prepares the ground for the presentation of her anecdotes as amusing. It is she who makes a topic change to food (42) in such a way as to invite Hopeful to ask for further clarification (43) enabling her to produce her first surprise, 'Porridge!' It is said with a bright, exclamatory response-inviting force that is met by Hopeful's surprise token, 'eh?'. Her follow-up second surprise (46–7) is that porridge is all they ever had to eat. Note that at this point the audience produces its (unscripted) laughter (48), after which Hopeful produces another exclamatory 'surprise' response to this second piece of information, and then adds his own assessment of the information ('nice and varied like') at which he himself laughs (50) and Miss Lomas produces (hearably) 'polite' laughter (51), which produces a second round of laughter from the studio audience (52).

Now it seems as if the script, which is designed to 'win' laughter, anticipates that the audience's laughter will come at Hopeful's exclamation 'nice and varied like' and that laughter is scripted for this point. The studio audience actually laughs a bit earlier, however, in response to Miss Lomas's second surprise – 'and I think they had it about twenty-one times a week'. The oddity of the laughter produced by Hopeful and Miss Lomas at 50/51 is that it seems superfluous. Coming *after* the audience's laughter it sounds like two people 'privately' laughing at something that everyone else has already responded to. This laughter is hearably 'scripted', and it is this that produces the second burst of laughter from the studio audience. Had this been unscripted, spontaneous studio-talk, Hopeful would have (should have) omitted his own response after the audience's laughter and proceeded to change – or rather to retrieve – the topic, which he does at line 53 ('did they kidnap *all* their apprentices?'), thereby taking up again the topic introduced at 26.

Thus, intentionally and unintentionally, this laughter-seeking talk proclaims itself as designed for public hearing. It is *not* a private conversation but a displayed, performed interaction in public whose overall communicative intentionality is directed towards laughter and sociability. The talk produced by Hopeful and Miss Lomas is not primarily *for* each other: a point that is, so to speak, proved by the odd and awkward quality of the moment when they seem to produce laughter-tokens for each other. Rather both collaborate in a performance designed for receipt by others. That the overall management of this conversation-in-public is primarily for entertainment is further underlined by the strategic position of the laughter-eliciting anecdotes in the overall structure of the interaction. Coming as they do towards the end, and after a long stretch of talk about the exploitation of young children in the first stages of the Industrial Revolution, these anecdotes shift the discourse into a lighter key and signal too a movement towards ending the interaction ('always end on a light note' seems to be a general maxim for story-telling).

This then is talk-in-public. Its object is to entertain. But there is surely a problem here, if we attend to the subject matter of the talk. The period being talked about is the beginnings of the Industrial Revolution in the North of

England, and its impact on people's lives at the time. This was a topic frequently taken up in Manchester's programmes, most notably in Olive Shapley's distinguished documentary, *The Classic Soil* (6 July 1939). Indeed, less than a year after this *Harry Hopeful* programme the topic of child labour in the 1830s was resumed in a feature series called *News of 100 Years Ago*. The third programme dealt with children at that time, the horrors of the ways in which they were educated or put to work at an early age: exactly the same time and topic as Miss Lomas's talk (her friend, if you work it out, started work in the mill in 1830). But the tone in *News of 100 Years Ago* is unremittingly serious, leading to a strangely self-conscious ending in which the authors write themselves into the programme as 'voices'[3] and send a message to the other voices in the script to the effect that they refuse to go on writing:

| | |
|---|---|
| *Voice I* | 'We note what you say about promptly sending the remainder of the script for the "Children" programme in your series. It so happens that we have decided simultaneously that we are unable to go on writing as we had intended and in fact that all we want to do is to go away *and wash*.' |
| *Voice III* | See, ladies and gentlemen? |
| *Voice I* | Yes, er . . . 'We are sorry, but we do not consider the affliction of small children funny . . .' Well, neither do we. |
| *Voice III* | Go on. |
| *Voice I* | Ah, yes er . . . 'Not only that. We do not even consider it dramatic. We consider it merely disgusting.' |

In serious matters we are expected to focus on the serious content of what is said. But as Simmel has argued, in purely sociable conversation 'the content is merely the indispensable carrier of the stimulation which the lively exchange of talk as such unfolds'. It would surely be absurd to propose that the *Harry Hopeful* programme finds the affliction of small children funny. What unfolds, for us, as we listen to this performed talk are revelations not of the horrors

---

[3]    The polyphonic use of anonymous voices in radio features and drama productions goes back to the late 1920s, when it was often used in the so-called 'multiple-studio' productions. The different elements in the programme – sound effects, choir, music, character parts, voices-as-chorus – were placed in different studios all linked to each other and to the dramatic control panel – a state-of-the-art mixing panel at which the programme's producer sat, orchestrating the whole thing (cf. Sieveking 1934). By the late thirties these techniques were becoming, in radio, rather passé and an object of cheerful parody. The same technique was used in agit-prop theatre, particularly in so-called 'living newspaper' productions.

of early industrialization in Derbyshire but of character and personality. And these revelations are not in the things that are said, but the way they are said.

Erving Goffman makes an important distinction between the information that people give out about themselves and that which they give off about themselves. The information that we give out about ourselves is more or less voluntary, intentional and within our control; what we choose to say about ourselves, but also how we choose to present ourselves – our style (our own 'expressive idiom') in clothing, haircut and so forth. The information we give off about ourselves is rather more involuntary: physical attributes (height, fatness or thinness, the colour of our eyes), sweating and other behavioural tics. These are aspects of self that are apparent and from which inferences can be drawn. We can, of course, with an effort of will, modify or control some aspects of these traits, but they appear as by-products rather than intended aspects of our personality.

Voice is one important aspect of an individual that gives off information about the individual's personality. Voices can, as we all know, be beautiful or ugly, hard or soft, warm or cold and much else besides. In every utterance the hearable properties of the voice – irrespective of what the voice is saying – will give rise to inferences about the character and personality of the speaker, their mood, their attitude to what they are saying and to the person they are speaking to. In radio, voice is peculiarly important, since it is the only 'visible' physical quality that is available to listeners as a basis for making assessments of the speaker. Among the things that are easily and reasonably accurately hearable in voices are the age and sex of speakers, while social class and place of origin can often be reasonably inferred. But the more subjective qualities of voice – for every voice is different and bespeaks a unique individual – are more intangible, more likely to be heard differently by others on the basis of their varying personal preconceptions and predispositions.

The words that come to mind to describe Miss Lomas's voice are 'sprightly' and 'cheerful'. I hear, in this talk with Harry Hopeful, the voice of a small, still active, elderly woman who is lively, neat, bright and respectable. I am charmed by this voice. I hear her telling her little anecdotes – by now well-polished with repeated tellings – to old friends over the teacups. Do I hear too much in it? No doubt, but I know this voice touches me, pierces me like a little wound, Barthes' punctum not in an old photograph but in a voice from 60 years ago, a voice from the dead past yet vivid and live to me every time I hear it. Where Bill performs himself as a 'character', Miss Lomas performs herself as herself – that is, to the life. Certainly we can hear that she is reading a script; but equally, we can hear that she puts herself into her self-performance. She gives her self to us. What I hear in this voice, in this performance, is the telling of a lifetime's recollections: memory, gossip, talk with an old friend long dead, a rootedness in time and place, a secure achieved identity. Someone in particular.

## IV

### Billy Welcome (1941 2)

Before the war the working class, both as an audience for whom programmes were made and as a subject about whom programmes were made, was marginalized on national radio and recognized and acknowledged only in the regional service. In the war, however, the working class soon became a major centre of attention for the BBC's morale and propaganda activities on the home front. This sudden change of heart was guided by instrumental, pragmatic considerations. In this first total war, for the British, labour was the nation's ultimate resource. Without the continuous supply of weaponry (and all the necessary back-up resources) the forces on land, sea and air were powerless. So the work front was as important – if not more so – than the fighting front (Cardiff and Scannell 1986).

In the immediate aftermath of Dunkirk, Churchill's government launched a major propaganda drive to back up its switch to a full-scale war economy. A great and sudden upsurge of effort from the workfront was called for by the Ministry of Supply, encapsulated in its propaganda slogan aimed at the workforce, Go To It! Three weeks after the ministry launched its campaign the BBC Features Unit, led by Lawrence Gilliam, began a series of industrial features, Go To It!, to show how the workforce had responded to that appeal. The first in the series (12 July 1940) surveyed the response to the call of workers in Bristol, Glasgow, Newcastle, Birmingham, Belfast and Cardiff. It began and ended with a pep-talk from the Minister of Supply: 'Work is *still* the call. Work at war speed. Once again – till the war is done – Go to it!' The series continued with programmes that showed the workers hard at it in munitions, tank and aircraft production.

A few months later Geoffrey Bridson launched a series called *We Speak for Ourselves* aimed at the working class more generally and intended to be really popular in its format. Bridson, as we have seen, had pioneered entertainment features for and about working-class people in Manchester before the war.[4] He was regarded in the BBC as the one man who knew how to communicate with the working class and was now called on to apply his talents to propaganda

[4]  Not only in *Harry Hopeful*, but in a quartet of features on the major industries of North Region: *Cotton*, *Wool*, *Steel* and *Coal* all made in the late thirties (Scannell and Cardiff 1991: 341–5).

features about the workers, which he willingly did. This is how he described the aims of *We Speak for Ourselves* in an internal BBC memorandum (July 13 1940):

> The life and outlook of the industrial population in wartime is obviously of immense importance. Industrial areas are usually the most vulnerable. Long hours, the blackout, rationing and the loss of recreation have, and will increasingly, add to the strain of their lives in war. Enemy propaganda is directed largely at the working class.[5] For all these reasons programmes which reflect the fighting spirit, cheerfulness and morale of the workers, done by the workers themselves, would be of immense value.

Like the *Harry Hopeful* series, these programmes were pre-scripted, but they were also censored by the Ministry of Information, who deleted all references to place names, the weather, fire services, Lord Haw Haw,[6] etc. Thus the title's claim, and Bridson's statement in the publicity release for the series, that 'the people of the industrial areas of Great Britain will freely express their opinions of the war as they find it', should be taken with a large pinch of salt.

An extract from the script of the first programme indicates the general tone of this series and many subsequent similar ones. Wilfred Pickles[7] presented and compered the show which, like *Harry Hopeful*, began with a communal sing-song from a local choir and the studio audience that faded out to applause, cheers and Pickles:

> *Pickles*        Well done, lads, well done. There's nowt caps a bit of a sing. It's good to hear folks sing these days, now that Goering's doing his level best to shut us traps. All I can say is it takes a *lot* to keep Lancashire quiet, – aye, a lot more than we've had so far! The gradely[8] folk aren't licked yet, – no, nor

[5]    There were worries in the Ministry of Information and elsewhere, at this time, that working-class morale might crack or, worse still, become disaffected. There were Nazi black propaganda stations directed specifically at the British working class. One, calling itself The Workers' Free Radio, called on the rank and file to reject the plutocratic war being waged by the British ruling class, and to dissociate themselves from the Trades Union leaders who were their catspaws.

[6]    The nickname of William Joyce, the Nazi's chief English language broadcaster, who was hanged as a traitor after the war. On Joyce's wartime broadcasts, cf. Calder (1971: 74–5, 156–7) and Briggs (1970 *passim*).

[7]    Pickles, a working-class Yorkshireman, was a brilliant broadcaster who became a household name during, and for many years after, the war. He was, on BBC radio, the voice of Everyman, a typification of the working man – bluff, jovial, friendly and down to earth. He was used as a newsreader, earlier in the war, as part of the BBC's drive to sound more in touch with the majority of its listeners. See Pickles (1949; 1978) for his own accounts of his life on and off the wireless.

[8]    Gradely (dialect): excellent, handsome, comely, real, true, proper.

|            |                                                                                                                                                                                                                                                                                                                                                                                                                |
|------------|--------------------------------------------------------------------------|

Merseyside neither! They won't lick Liverpool all that easily, *nor* Manchester, Salford, Bolton, Rochdale or Blackburn. What about Oldham? Are you licked yet?

*All*          NOOOOO!

*Pickles*      Nay I thought not! But it's funny y'know. You *ought* to be. The Germans think you are. Did you hear what (Haw Haw deleted) they said about you on t'wireless last week? They said there wasn't a smile to be seen in Lancashire; and that they hadn't bothered about Oldham yet because there was nobody lived there but bald-headed, bow-legged minders[9] and consumptive women! (*Roars of laughter from everybody*) . . .

*Pickles*      But what's Oldham got to say about t'war?

*Mrs Truman*  Plenty! We ain't scared o' Hitler. We call him Tashy[10] at home. He seems to think if he could floor London he'd ha' floored all England. He seems to forget there's Lancashire. He won't floor us – any more than he's floored London. (*loud applause*) . . .

                         (and so on and so forth)

For Bridson,

the main thing was to get radio linked up purposefully behind the war effort. . . . At that time a Dunkirk spirit at the workbench was desperately needed if we were to survive. The spirit was there all right, but everyone wanted to hear it at work: thanks to those I brought to the microphone, they did. The programmes were invigorating not because they were saying the right thing but because they were real and genuine. . . . These working people had been allowed to put their emotion into the words they habitually used. (Bridson 1971: 77)

Pickles, in retrospect, took a very different view of the many factory feature programmes he and Bridson made between 1940 and 1943. He loathed going into factories asking such questions as, 'Are we afraid of Hitler?' and 'Can we lick him?' which would be followed by a decisive roar. 'Rank propaganda disguised as entertainment' he called it (Pickles 1949: 126). It is precisely this unholy mix of propaganda and entertainment that makes the wartime factory feature programmes – there were many and those by Pickles and Bridson were far and away the best – so fascinating. For if sociable interactions are

---

[9]   Minders: of the looms in the cotton factories – the staple industry in the industrial Lancashire towns mentioned by Pickles.
[10]  A colloquial reference to Hitler's moustache.

purposeless, that is flatly contradicted by the instrumental purposefulness of propaganda.

| | | |
|---|---|---|
| 1 | *Announcer* | Billy Welcome is on the road again. |
| 2 | | This time he's paying a visit to a large aero engine works |
| 3 | | somewhere in Britain. |

(*Fade up first few bars of Billy Welcome signature tune.*
*Then Pickles's voice comes in leading the audience*:

| | | |
|---|---|---|
| 4 | | Me name is Billy Welcome lads |
| 5 | | And Yorkshire is me father. |
| 6 | | I'm out to do the best I can |
| 7 | | There's nothing that I'd rather. |
| | | |
| 8 | | I'm not a one for sitting back |
| 9 | | You'll never see me quit. |
| 10 | | Whenever I can get a (?) |
| 11 | | I like to do me bit my lads |
| | | |
| 12 | | I like to do my bi::t. |
| 13 | | *Loud cheers etc. from audience* |
| | | |
| 14 | *Pickles* | Well, good evening everybody. This is Billy Welcome |
| 15 | | talking to you from one of the many aero engine works |
| 16 | | making the famous Rolls Royce Merlin engines in Britain. |
| 17 | | We're broadcasting this from a canteen before an audience |
| 18 | | of workers who have just finished their shift. And it's because |
| 19 | | of these highly skilled engineers and technicians |
| 20 | | that you and I can listen to newsreader Frank Phillips |
| 21 | | telling us this. |
| 22 | *Phillips* | Last night Lancasters and Halifaxes of Bomber |
| 23 | | Command made a heavy and concentrated attack on |
| 24 | | Berlin. The weather was clear and reports indicate that |
| 25 | | results were good. Objectives in Western Germany were also bombed. |
| 26 | | The raids closed in dramatic manner the Nazis' celebra- |
| 27 | | tion of Luftwaffe Day. One of the pilots said, |
| 28 | | 'The inner port engine was hit but we managed to get |
| 29 | | back without difficulty'. |
| 30 | *Pickles* | 'But we managed to get back without difficulty'. |
| 31 | | *That's* what these workers like to hear! |
| 32 | | *Loud cheers and applause* |

Billy Welcome is clearly son of Harry Hopeful and the introductory format mimics the prewar programme – a communal sing-song, the reiteration of

Northernness and Yorkshire more particularly (Pickles came from Halifax) –
but here the listening audience is sharply distinguished from the canteen audience. For if Hopeful's opening remarks were addressed primarily to the studio
audience (and by extension to listeners) Pickles speaks first to listeners. The
'everybody' addressed in 'Good evening everybody'(14) is everybody out there
listening. In an obvious sense what he says serves to put in context where,
literally, the programme is coming from, the time of the occasion and the participants in the event. So immediately, time, place and people (the essential
components of any occasion) are established for the listening audience. But so,
too, is the nature of the occasion.

Notice the way in which 'the workers' are produced as an object, as a third
party ('them') in a discourse between I and you and we (17–21). To whom do
these indexical terms refer? 'We' (17) is clearly the BBC *and* Pickles as its
institutional voice. 'You' is the listener, addressed as an individual in a two-
way 'me-and-you' conversation by Pickles's self-referencing 'I' (20). Thus,
Pickles aligns himself with the listener, thereby putting himself outside the
situation from which he speaks. He, so to speak, 'looks' at this occasion from
the point-of-view of the listener. And what does he see (or rather hear)? He
hears (as 'you' do) 'our' newsreader Frank Phillips telling us some 'good' news
about last night's raid on Germany by Bomber Command. Now why is that
insert there? How is *that* relevant to *this* occasion? Or rather, how does bringing that context (the news) into this context (a gathering of workers in a factory
canteen) affect the nature of the occasion? It is there as a kind of proving – a
proof of what had just been claimed – namely that these engineers and workers
are 'highly skilled'. Even though one of the engines was hit, 'we managed to get
back without difficulty': by implication the quality of the remaining engines
enabled them to do so. It is that particular bit in the news story that affirms the
skill of this workforce, and it is that that 'these workers' like to hear.

| 1  | *Pickles* | And now and now I want you to meet some of the |
|----|-----------|------------------------------------------------|
| 2  |           | people who are manufacturing the finest manufacturing |
| 3  |           | engine the world has ever known. Jack Barber, one of the |
| 4  |           | workers, has promised to take me round. He's worked here |
| 5  |           | for a long time (rising intonation) come on Jack! |
| 6  |           | *Cheers. Cries of 'Go on Jack'. Applause.* |
| 7  | *Jack*    | Well Billy |
| 8  |           | how much do you know about an aero engine? |
| 9  | *Billy*   | Well ah (.) ah don't know much |
| 10 |           | (0.7) *Trickle of laughter* |
| 11 |           |                    In fact ah know nowt |
| 12 | *Jack*    | No .hhehh you don't look a- heh |
| 13 |           |                    *Laughter* |

| 14 |       | No you don't look |
|----|-------|-------------------|
| 15 |       | as if you do. (.) Wl yu well you remember the Battle of |
| 16 |       | Britain don't you? |
| 17 | *Billy* | (serious) Ah do. |
| 18 | *Jack* | (gabbling) Our fighters were vastly outnumbered by |
| 19 |       | the horde of enemy bombers but we came through with flying |
| 20 |       | colours. Those Spitfires, Hurricanes and Defiants were |
| 21 |       | pow- powered by the Merlin engine which was the forerunner |
| 22 |       | of the much improved Merlin of today. Our pilots had faith |
| 22 |       | in these engines, because they knew that every one of the |
| 23 |       | ten thousand parts was made and inspected by experts. |
| 24 |       | And here's one of the chaps 's been inspecting such parts |
| 25 |       | for twenty-five year (rising intonation). |
| 26 |       | Staff(?) Humphries |
| 27 |       | (*Cheers, applause* |

Having described the situation, and set up the nature of the occasion, Pickles now begins the introductions. 'We' (the listeners) are to meet some of the people who work 'here' and we begin with Jack Barber. Barber's voice is hearably 'Northern working class', and note that he addresses Pickles as 'Billy' (7). In response to this (the first moment *in* the programme that Pickles has been directly identified as Billy Welcome), Pickles's voice hearably changes into a performed 'stage' Yorkshire voice. He pauses after his first utterance – 'ah don't know much' – for the effect to register and there is a little spillage of laughter acknowledging the effect. The more emphatic follow-on – 'in fact ah know nowt' – is more pronouncedly performed (what have we here? A good-natured, slightly gormless 'tyke'), drawing an amused response from Jack and a burst of laughter from the canteen audience. This change of voice is a change of footing, a shift from his initial alignment with the listening audience to a realignment with the participants and audience in the canteen. Thus, here, and throughout, Pickles has two recognizably distinct voices that indicate which audience he is directly addressing at any one time. There is his 'normal' voice, that he starts the show with, and with which he addresses the listening public at large. This, though hearably Northern, is much lighter, much less thickly Northern than his Billy Welcome voice which he uses in his interactions with the workers.

Harry Hopeful did not distinguish the studio audience from the listening audience because he did not need to: that is, the listening audience was treated as an extension of the studio audience, because this was a programme about Northern people for a Northern radio audience. Pickles, however, is hosting a programme about 'the workers' (and their Northernness helps to identify them *as* workers) for a non-Northern, non-working class audience – the Great British

Public – which was always, at heart, constructed by the BBC as middle class and living a semi-detached existence somewhere south of the River Trent. So Pickles, as host of this event, has two different identities, two different roles to perform. He must align himself with the working people he talks to in the canteen. He must produce himself as one of them. Yet 'they' are being produced for 'us' (the listeners) as proof that 'they' are the ultimate resource on which the war depends. For without the skill and dedication of the workforce – without their labour – the fighting forces are as nothing, for they would have nothing to fight with. So the propaganda task of this and countless other programmes had a double task: on the one hand, to affirm to the workers themselves that their skill and efforts were acknowledged and on the other hand to display to 'the nation' (the authorities, the other classes) that the workforce was in good heart, was battling on with the cheery resilience that was expected of them.

That this was, in Pickles's phrase, 'rank propaganda disguised as entertainment' is palpably so today. And so it was heard to be at the time. By 1942 (two years after the start of such programmes) the news began to filter back to Broadcasting House in London that out there, in the rest of the country, these factory programmes were being listened to with derision. Listener Research was commissioned to investigate and delivered its findings on 11 January 1943. Its report made pungent reading. Programmes about industry were far more popular with middle-class listeners without direct knowledge or experience of wartime factory conditions. Amongst working people, only a minority appreciated them. A range of comments from workers was quoted, all hostile. The programmes were not genuine, sincere or honest. They were obviously manipulative – 'put up jobs' – with a strong smell of propaganda. Their style was sardonically mocked:

> The people who take part in these programmes are badly chosen, and obviously reading tripe from a script. When the chaps in my works get a rotten job, or feel 'browned off' they often mimic these programmes: 'Ho yes, I love my work.' 'Ho no, I never get fed up.' 'Ho yes, I would like to work longer hours', etc.

That the factory programmes *were* propaganda is evident. *How* they were hearably so is rather less self-evident. There is, of course, the simple disparity between the actual facts of factory life, and the picture painted in the programmes, as one radio producer complained to her boss, Lawrence Gilliam, Head of Features, in the summer of 1942:

> The Ministry of Aircraft Production gave me the name of Parnell Aircraft, who were most helpful and co-operative, but unfortunately it is a factory where about 30–40 workers are about to be sacked as redundant. This is

mainly because the factory has to sit around waiting for parts from the west country, and needless to say when I got there I found a great battle going on between management and shop-stewards. When I interviewed Mr Cooney whose name had been given me as 'Worker of the Week', and also spent some time interviewing other people who worked with him, I came finally to the shop-stewards and found they were highly amused and cynical about the whole scheme. They had not been consulted and just laughed at the idea of Cooney as their Worker of the Week.

The Admiralty had suggested she visit BSA Guns:

I went there yesterday morning and found that the Ministry of Labour had just stepped in to sack a number of hooligan shop-stewards who were causing strikes every other week in the factory. There was no possibility of getting the shop-stewards' agreement to a Worker of the Week as they were all up in arms and the whole place bordering on revolution. As the Manager pointed out, it was no time for a sunshine broadcast.

So to anyone who knew about what was going on in the factories, the factory features were a whitewash. But this does not account for the propagandist tone and manner of the programmes. How can we account for how they *work* as propaganda? By definition, propaganda is persuasive (or purposeful): it is motivated, it has an aim in mind, so that what is being said is often a means to some particular end (save fuel, eat more potatoes, don't gossip, work harder). Here the more diffuse propagandist aim is the maintenance of the nation's morale by a display of the cheerful, hardworking reliability of the workforce – the nation's ultimate wartime resource on which all else depends. Propaganda reveals itself *as* propaganda here partly by overstatement: 'the *famous* Rolls Royce engine', the '*highly* skilled engineers', the '*finest* engine the world *has ever known*', etc. Overstatement violates the maxim of quantity and generates the question, why are 'they' talking it up all the time? And this in turn provokes the suspicion that 'they' are trying to sell 'you' a line. And why (in this case)? So 'you' will believe how good British industry is. Now if you happen to know that it's not all roses in the factory you'll see through the propaganda and simply dismiss it as 'tripe'. But even if you don't know that, you'll still have the feeling of being 'got at', and you *may* (but not necessarily) be suspicious, simply on those grounds alone. That is, the tactics of propaganda generate distrust, so that even if what is being claimed cannot be disproved (by a particular recipient) it may well be regarded with scepticism at least, for seemingly making exaggerated claims that go against common-sense expectations and assessments (it can't be *that* good, etc.). And even if you don't distrust it – if you 'buy' the line being put across – you can still see that it *is* propaganda because it's saying more than is necessary.

Furthermore, the introduction of propaganda puts in question the very nature of the occasion. Consider the awkwardness of the topic change at (15) above. After the initial cheery laughter-eliciting interaction between Jack and Billy there is an immediate, sudden switch to a 'serious subject' – the Battle of Britain. There's nothing to laugh at about that and Billy's voice becomes hearably solemn in answering Jack's question. Notice how Jack hesitates and momentarily stumbles (15) as he switches from the sociable routine that seems to be getting under way, to the plug for the Merlin engine which he quickly gabbles his way through, so that what becomes unclear is what exactly *is* the nature of this occasion. Is it entertainment and fun, or is it serious and solemn? Has it got an aim (is it *saying* something) or not?

There were many kinds of morale-and-propaganda programmes aimed at the workers, and it was a constant worry for BBC staff that their entertainment value was constantly undermined by the injection of a pep-talk about lateness, absenteeism, or carelessness on the job. Here is the Head of Variety trying to persuade the Assistant Director of Programmes not to persist with his idea for a two-minute talk to be stuck on the end of *Workers Playtime*:[11]

> Pep talks are an excellent idea, but not actually in the programmes. It would be a grave error to insert propaganda or exhortation into the middle of this entertainment programme. Workers are always thoroughly suspicious of 'welfare' in any shape or form, invariably thinking the employer or the Government is only giving them entertainment or the canteen or whatever the amenity may be, in order to get something out of them.

We have here a fine example of practical reasoning, whereby welfare from the authorities (and we should include the BBC) is perceived as a Greek gift. If the 'natural attitude' to the authorities is to see them as miserly, tight-fisted and exploitative, then their giving of gifts for no apparent reason must prompt a search for a hidden motive. Such acts go against the maxim of quantity (as motivated departures from the normal; as more than the situation requires) and so give rise to the inference that they are only given in order to extract more in return. The presence of propaganda in entertainment cannot conceal the instrumental thinking behind it, and destroys whatever desired effect the programme might have:

> We've had several examples recently where the superintendent or boss or proprietor has come on after the show (*Workers Playtime*) – which has been enthusiastically received – and talked to the men about absenteeism or a fall

[11]   A popular entertainment programme in which stage and radio variety stars performed during the dinner break at a factory canteen 'somewhere in Britain'. The show was produced by the BBC in direct response to a request from Ernest Bevin, the Minister of Labour.

in production. The atmosphere created by the programme has in every instance been completely lost. . . . There is nothing the British Workman loathes more than having good done to him.

Pep-talk is irreconcilable with talk-as-fun. Instrumentally purposive talk cannot mix with talk for no purpose. The prewar Harry Hopeful series had no other motive than to invite a group of people into the studio, for some performed chat, for a singalong, for some home-made, locally produced entertainment (a choir, a dialect poem). These elements are all retained in the wartime Billy Welcome series. So that here, in *Power for the RAF*, we have Ernie Lonsdale the storekeeper, singing *Fishermen of England*; Gladys Marshall, a machine turret operator, playing *You Are My Sunshine* on the accordion with everyone joining in; Sam Hawkins doing a couple of dialect poems, including *The Derby Ram*; the works choir singing *The Jolly Roger* and a quartet from the works brass band playing *The Soldier's Tale*. So the form of the programme borrows, and seeks to reproduce, the sociable character of the prewar series, emphasizing its homely, home-spun character. But that, now, seems deeply manipulative, whereas before (to my mind at least) it had a disarming, innocent charm. For the willingness of ordinary people to play themselves, to have words put into their mouths that are not their *own* words (but tripe from a script) shows how that innocence is used (and abused) to promote an effect of social solidarity and class harmony for an absent (middle-class) audience. There *is* a difference – a hearable difference – between performing yourself, where the scripted words are your own and bespeak you as the author of your discourse, and having things you would never normally say ('ho yes, I like working longer hours') put into your mouth.

But even so, a sense of fun keeps breaking through:

| 1 | *Jack* | Now I want you to meet a lady who works in the stores here. |
| 2 | | Everybody knows her her name is Miss Ethel Hinds |
| 3 | | but she's known to everybody here as Au:ntie! |
| 4 | | *Enthusiastic applause, cheers* |
| 5 | *Pickles* | Well hehh I – I'm very glad to meet you Miss Hinds |
| 6 | | but tell me (.) ah say how did you get the name of Auntie? |
| 7 | *Miss Hinds* | Well I mother all the girls. They bring all their |
| 8 | | troubles to me. Even if they cut their finger they ask |
| 9 | | me to dress it rather than go to the Red Cross room |
| 10 | | so of course I became Auntie to everybody. |
| 11 | *Pickles* | And you er you really enjoy working here? |
| 12 | *Miss Hinds* | I should just say I do. Even if they wanted to sack |

| 13 | | me I shouldn't go! |
| 14 | | *Laughter* |
| 15 | *Pickles* | And how do you like being at the training school? |
| 16 | *Miss Hinds* | I like it very much. Of course some of these young |
| 17 | | lads are a bit of a handful some(.)times. But if they don't |
| 18 | | behave I tell them I shall give them a good sherrocking. |
| 19 | | *Laughter* |
| 20 | *Pickles* | Heh ah well now what on earth's a good sherrocking? |
| 21 | *Tommy* | That means a good kick in the behind. |
| 22 | | *Laughter* |
| 23 | *Pickles* | Oh aye an and 'oo are you? |
| 24 | *Tommy* | I'm Tommy Bowstead one of the lads. |
| 25 | *Pickles* | Oh (.) and 'ow old are yer? |
| 26 | | *Ripple of laughter* |
| 27 | *Tommy* | Ah'm fifteen an' alf. Ah've bin at the tech the training |
| 28 | | school for five months yuh start off by goin in the |
| 29 | | classroom for a week then into the workshop for two |
| 30 | | weeks then back into the classroom again. We have seven |
| 31 | | instructors and about a hundred boys. |
| 32 | *Pickles* | Ah see an' you just practise makin things – |
| 33 | *Tommy* | Are we 'eckers practising we're mckkin real machines |
| 34 | | an we get paid full apprentice wages during the training |
| 35 | | there let me tell you that. |
| 36 | | Pickles (mock irate): 'Ere don't you talk to me like that! |
| 37 | | *Loud laughter, cheers, prolonged* |
| | | *applause* |
| 38 | | You know what 'e wants Jack is a good sherrockin'! |
| 39 | | *Laughter* |

Here, as in *Harry Hopeful*, we have the familiar playing with Northernness. Notice how (like 'squat' and 'dundging') 'a good sherrocking' provokes laughter and further, that in this case, rather than letting it pass unmarked (as Hopeful did in both cases) an explanation is called for (20). Partly this cues the arrival of the 'cheeky' youngster, Tommy, but also it provides a gloss for the non-Northern listening public who cannot be assumed to know what the word might mean (though it's easily guessable from the context). The dialogue between Pickles and Tommy is good knockabout stuff and provokes hearably genuine laughter as distinct from the forced-sounding cheers and applause at other moments (such as when Pickles exclaims '*That's* what these workers like to hear!'). In short, the propaganda can't quite kill the good-natured fun, the sociability of the occasion, though at the end a fighter pilot from the Battle of Britain is brought on to ram home the programme's message. 'And I'm proud to tell you', says Pickles, 'that he's shot down eight Huns'.

| | |
|---|---|
| *Pickles* | Here is Flying Officer Wriggler. |
| | *Cheers, applause* |
| *Wriggler* | Well ladies and gentlemen and fellow workers now I address you as fellow workers because that's exactly what we are. We're fellow workers in the fact that we're all working towards the same end and that is the winning of this war in the shortest space of time. Now I welcome this opportunity of coming amongst you our brothers and sisters in industry just to say thank you for some of these products of yours. I can pay no higher tribute to the efficiency of the Merlin engine than to say I owe my life to it. . . . |

So the social relations of this programme are neatly tied together at the end. The workers are reminded of what and who they're working for. The listeners are reminded that behind the fighter pilot is the skill, hard work and dedication of the workforce. Communal solidarity between the work front, the fighting front and the home front has been manufactured yet again.


V


## Have a Go! (1946–67)

In the aftermath of the war North Region decided to revamp the formula of *Harry Hopeful* and *Billy Welcome*. It came up with a quiz show, in which a selected number of programme-participants engaged in a bit of chat with the show's host before answering a few simple questions that might win them a smallish sum of money. Pickles would host the programme that would go out and about to the towns and cities of the region rather than being – as *Harry Hopeful* had been – studio-bound. The pilot programme and the first series was broadcast in the regional service, but thereafter it was transferred to the Light Programme – the BBC's new, postwar popular channel, an extension of the wartime General Forces Programme. There it remained for 21 years, becoming – at the height of its fame in the mid-fifties – the most popular weekly programme on British radio.

| | |
|---|---|
| 1 | Ladies and Gentlemen we invite you t:o Have a Go! |
| 2 | (*A few bars of the theme song on the piano* |
| 3 | Have a go, Joe |
| 4 | Come out and have a go |
| 4 | You can't lose 'owt, it costs you nowt |
| 5 | To make yourself some dough |

| | | |
|---|---|---|
| 6 | | So hurry up and join with us |
| 7 | | Don't be shy and don't be slow |
| 8 | | Have a go:::o, have a go:::o! |

| | | |
|---|---|---|
| 9 | *Announcer* | And here is Wilfred Pickles! |
| 10 | | *A few bars on the piano. Thunderous cheers and applause* |
| 11 | *Pickles* | [1] Ladies and gentlemen of Ramsbottom (.) |
| 12 | | [2] 'Ow do (.) 'ow are yer? |
| 13 | | *Loud cheers* |
| 14 | | [1] Yes we're back once again with Have a Go. |
| 15 | | And to bring us back we've come to Ramsbottom. |
| 16 | | And you can't go further back than that! |
| 17 | | *Laughter* |
| 18 | | Now Ramsbottom is an industrial town which lies |
| 19 | | between Manchester and Burnley and its chief industries |
| 20 | | are cotton and woollen spinning and weaving. (.) |
| | | Ramsbottom! (.) |
| 21 | | ⌊2⌋ I know its other name as well |
| 22 | | *Howls of laughter* |
| 23 | | [1] Now its a very- very prosperous little town is this. |
| 24 | | Everybody in this district has pots of money, [2] particu- |
| 25 | | larly them 'as lives at Warmsley-cum-Shuttleworth |
| 26 | | *Loud laughter, cheers* |
| 27 | | I'm not joking, I knew a feller 'oo lived at Warmsley- |
| 28 | | cum-Shuttleworth (.) *(titters)* (.) 'Ee made a fortune. |
| 29 | | 'Ee bought 'imself a big 'ouse ( ) out at 't Stubbins |
| 30 | | *(laughter)* [1] and his proudest possession was a big oil |
| 31 | | painting for which he'd paid a thousand pounds. So a pal |
| 32 | | came to see him one day and looking at this huge picture |
| 33 | | he said [2] 'Jo:e' he said, 'tha's been done.' *(titters)* He |
| 34 | | said, 'This picture isn't genuine'. (.) 'Ee said, 'Isn't genu- |
| 35 | | ine? (.) Thee put thee shoulder under it 'nd try and lift it, |
| 36 | | tha'll soon change thee tune!' |
| 37 | | *Loud laughter* |
| 38 | | [1] Well the competitors have just come onto the stage |
| 39 | | and this hall in Ramsbottom is crowded to capacity (.) |
| 40 | | and when I arrived here this evening the first thing that |
| 41 | | was handed to me er was the printed words of this lovely |
| 42 | | song, a song which says 'Welcome to the County Palatine' |
| 43 | | *a couple of bars of music, then Pickles sings:* |
| 44 | | [2] Tha's welcome Wilf, tha's welcome |
| 45 | | Give us the 'and owld chum |
| 46 | | Sit thee down and draw up 't fire |
| 47 | | Just mek theeself at 'ome |
| 48 | | There's luck and there's health |

| 49 | There's joy and there's wealth |
|---|---|
| 50 | If ever tha's passing this way |
| 51 | We shall allus be glad |
| 52 | To see thee old lad |
| 53 | Tha's as welcome as flowers in Ma:::y |
| 54 | *Loud cheers, applause* |

The opening format is by now familiar: the communal singalong, the host's genial introductory greetings and chat. But a key innovation is the abandonment of a script. Wartime propaganda's claims that *We Speak for Ourselves* were hearably phoney. But now everyone – Pickles and all the participants – speak for themselves and as themselves. All collaborate in a celebration of working-class laughter and sentiment. Pickles's opening routine is expertly done: switching back and forth between his two voices – his 'normal' voice for listeners [1] and his folk-voice [2] for the live audience – he smoothly works the listeners into the occasion. His initial greeting in broad Yorkshire (12), with which he starts every show, is directed to the people of Ramsbottom and after their roar of greeting in return he switches briskly into his normal voice to address the listeners and put them in the picture. Evidently Pickles – or the programme's research team – has done his homework and local references are neatly woven into the routine, eliciting loud cheers of approval. Notice how references to place elicit laughter. Ramsbottom, not surprisingly, but why Warmsley-cum-Shuttleworth or Stubbins should provoke merriment is not apparent to us as listeners. The laughter, however, confirms, for us, that these places mean something to local people even if they mean nothing to us. Particularities of place and people anchor the programme as 'a spot of homely fun' – as Pickles calls it at the end of the show.

|   |   | *Loud cheers, applause* |
|---|---|---|
| 1 |  | 'Ow d'you do Wilfred. |
| 2 | *Pickles* | And that brings our first er personality to |
| 3 |  | the microphone and she's a very charming lady with nice |
| 4 |  | grey hair and a very nice grey frock. It's very nice |
| 5 |  | to have you here will you tell me your name? |
| 6 | *Florrie* | Mrs Florence Holt. |
| 7 | *Pickles* | Mrs (.) Florence? |
| 8 | *Florrie* | Yes. |
| 9 | *Pickles* | 'Ave a go Flo! |
| 10 |  | *Shrieks of laughter* |
| 11 | *Pickles* | Mrs Florence Holt and where where |
| 12 |  | d'you live? |
| 13 | *Florrie* | 82 Warmley Road, Shuttleworth. |
| 14 | *Pickles* | Oh you live – oh you live at Shuttleworth do yer? |

| | | |
|---|---|---|
| 15 | *Florrie* | Yes (*over audience titters*) yes. |
| 16 | *Pickles* | Eeh na' then! (.) Well then I know – you're Mrs |
| 17 | | you said didn't yer? – I know there's a lot of women |
| 18 | | in this part of Lancashire and indeed all of Lancashire |
| 19 | | do go out to work as well as being housewives – |
| 20 | *Florrie* | Yes. |
| 21 | *Pickles* | Do you do a job too? |
| 22 | *Florrie* | Yes I'm a bus conductress. |
| 23 | *Pickles* | Are yer? |
| 24 | *Florrie* | Yes. |
| 25 | *Pickles* | An 'ow long 've you been doing that? |
| 26 | *Florrie* | Twelve year. |
| 27 | *Pickles* | Really? |
| 28 | *Florrie* | Yes. |
| 29 | *Pickles* | Well tell me what you er er what where |
| 30 | | where does your bus go to? |
| 31 | *Florrie* | (.) Burley(?) to Rawlstone(?) and then we 'ave |
| 32 | | a little country run Ramsbottom to Shuttleworth. |
| 33 | *Pickles* | heheheheh |
| 34 | *Florrie* |         heh . . . hheh |
| 35 | |            *Audience laughter* |
| 36 | *Florrie* | 'n when 'n when we gets to the terminus there's |
| 37 | | a pub at the end called Duck'th Arms. |
| 38 | *Pickles* | (knowingly) Is there? |
| 39 | |               *Laughter* |
| 40 | *Pickles* | heheheh ee:eh (.) 'n that's where you change your |
| 41 | | trolley? |
| 42 | |            *Roars of laughter* |
| 43 | *Florrie* | We 'ave none o' them now, we've only imitations(?) |
| 44 | |                   *Laughter, shrieks* |
| 45 | *Pickles* | Well now er how d'you manage Flo er Florrie |
| 46 | | I should say do they call you Florrie or Florence? |
| 47 | *Florrie* | Yes, yes Florrie. |
| 48 | *Pickles* | Well then 'ow d'you manage to do your housework |
| 49 | | as well as do a job of work like that? |
| 50 | *Florrie* | Well you see me hubby works on the buses and |
| 51 | | one week he's on early and I'm on late so we (.) |
| 52 | | switch over (*laughter*) kind of thing. |
| 53 | *Pickles* | Sort of fifty-fifty eh? |
| 54 | *Florrie* | Yes yes. |
| 55 | *Pickles* | That's good and er you've 'eard me in in |
| 56 | | Have a Go before ask |
| 57 | *Florrie* | Yes. |
| 58 | *Pickles* | sort of all sorts of questions let's take |
| 59 | | one out of the blue and say is there anything particular |

| 60  |         | er special that you like to eat, Florrie? |
|-----|---------|-------------------------------------------|
| 61  | *Florrie* | (triumphantly) Steak 'nd onions! |
| 62  |         | (*Huge shrieks, laughter* |
| 63  | *Pickles* | Well that's not so bad is it? |
| 64  | *Florrie* | No. |
| 65  | *Pickles* | There's a lot at stake tonight and my name's Pickles! |
| 66  |         | (*Loud laughter, applause* |
| 67  | *Florrie* | Yes. |
| 68  | *Pickles* | What about er (.) now if you work on a bus love |
| 69  |         | you meet a lot of people don't yer? |
| 70  | *Florrie* | Yes. |
| 71  | *Pickles* | Well er eh any sort of embarrassing moments? |
| 72  | *Florrie* | Oo::ooh (*shrieks of laughter*) Yes I've a lot |
| 73  |         | heh (.) heh. For one for instance during the cold |
| 74  |         | weather an old lady gets on the bus 'n she sez to me |
| 75  |         | 'An't yer not cold lass without pants?' Ah sez 'Ah've got |
| 76  |         | them on'. She sez 'No I mean them longg 'uns'. (*titters*) |
| 77  |         | Ah sez 'Oh no:o ah can't fancy meself in them'. She sez |
| 78  |         | 'Well ah'll tell thee what tha wants to do:o'. She sez |
| 79  |         | 'Thee wants to get some comms'. (*shrieks*) She sez |
| 80  |         | 'They go out 'ere and then they come in theyer and then |
| 81  |         | they cover y'ips up and then 't bottom it tightens up |
| 82  |         | and yer tuck that in top o' yer stocking.' (*cries of laughter*) |
| 83  | *Pickles* | (knowingly) Not bad advice. |
| 84  | *Florrie* | No it isn't. |
| 85  | *Pickles* | And have you a sort of er dislike oo:h well |
| 86  |         | as you meet a lot of people shall I say have you got |
| 87  |         | a dislike Florrie about people? |
| 88  | *Florrie* | Yes bad manners. Children sitting in the bus |
| 89  |         | when paren- when adults are stood up. |
| 90  | *Pickles* | Do do yer tick 'em off for that, do yer? |
| 91  | *Florrie* | Yes I try to tell them. |
| 92  | *Pickles* | heheheh it's like that conductor like you were |
| 93  |         | you know that was on 'is bus 'nd a pal went up to him |
| 94  |         | 'n said er – there was an old lady standing – 'n said |
| 95  |         | 'I hate to see an old lady standing, don't you?' Ee said |
| 96  |         | 'Aye, we'll chuck 'er off at the next stop'. (*loud laughter*) |
| 97  |         | 'Ave you ever lo:nged Florrie ever longed to say |
| 98  |         | anything to anybody 'n you just you know you said |
| 99  |         | ooh I daren't do it but I'd like to? |
| 100 | *Florrie* | Yes. Tell him tell Philip Dobson where . . . |
| 102 |         | to put 'is duty sheets. |
| 103 |         | *Shrieks, cheers, applause* |
| 104 | *Pickles* | Well, I (*continuing cheers*) I, I would say in |
| 105 |         | fairness to our listeners we should we should really |

| 106 | | know who Philip Dobson is |
| 107 | *Florrie* | 'E's our Inspector. |
| 108 | *Pickles* | ohohoh is 'e? (*laughter*) I never asked you Flo |
| 109 | | have you any family? |
| 110 | *Florrie* | A daughter, twenty-two. |
| 111 | *Pickles* | Oh very nice too. Is she coortin? |
| 112 | *Florrie* | Yes. |
| 113 | *Pickles* | Is she? Right well now its very nice having |
| 114 | | you Florrie and er I might tell you we're very happy |
| 115 | | to be here in Ramsbottom, and when we arrived here I er |
| 116 | | er the policeman outside when I arrived he said |
| 117 | | 'D'you know we're right glad to ave you ere tonight' |
| 118 | | he said, 'This is the most exciting thing that's happened |
| 119 | | in Ramsbottom since they put the traffic lights in'. |
| 120 | | (*loud laughter, cheers*) So so we're going to give |
| 121 | | you some tune titles – that'll be all right you'll |
| 122 | | guess 'em Florrie – now er er Harry Ansome will play them |
| 123 | | and here's number one Harry number one and they're |
| 124 | | all animals (piano plays *Teddy Bear's Picnic* . . . |

Again – of course – you must *hear* this to catch the full flavour of its communicative, interactive qualities. It is both spontaneous and natural *and* contrived and manufactured. Even the printed transcript shows that what is being said here is not pre-scripted, or not in any literal sense. But in the absence of a script how does this, or any show, work to produce the nature of the occasion as that which it is to be? What stops it (at any moment) from going off the rails? And, given the uncertain terrors of 'live talk' (suppose I can't think of anything to say? suppose I make a fool of myself?) against the reassurances of a script, how does the programme overcome such tensions to generate – as here – a performed and public interaction in which the participant-performers are at ease with themselves, the person they're talking to and the situation in which they find themselves?

Such questions are as relevant for *any* live show today as they were then, and the solutions to the endemic terrors of live broadcasting remain in all essentials the same.[12] The answer is, a lot of backstage work by the production team; a rigidly formulaic structure for the talk-to-be-produced, and last, but not least,

---

[12]  Livingstone and Lunt's report on audience responses to British television talk programmes today (*Kilroy, The Time The Place*) includes accounts from those who took part in such shows. For some it was an uncomfortable experience: 'I was very conscious of making a fool of myself really. And I was also very aware my mum knew I was going to be on it, so I knew certain people knew I was going to be on the show, so that was . . . how I felt' (Livingstone and Lunt 1994: 117; cf. 164–7).

a thoroughly professional, reliable performer to front the whole thing, to hold it all together and bring it off as that which it is meant to be. So of course the people on-stage with Wilfred are carefully preselected. The criteria for selection are varied. They must be, at least potentially, good performers. Again there must be an interesting variety and difference in the half-dozen competitors. So in this show we start with Florrie, who's followed by a gawky lad of 16 (an apprentice librarian), then Alice who's 94 and the oldest lady in Ramsbottom. She 'hadn't got nine years old' when she started work in the spinning-room, and she didn't leave the mill till she was 81. She likes a bit of bread and butter with now and then a beetroot to it, and sometimes a pickled onion. Maureen is 19 – 'a bobby dazzler', a 'cheeky monkey' – and yes, she's coorting. Evelyn is married, has just had her first baby and is glowing with the joy of it. Her pet hate is 'two-faced folk' and she thinks juvenile delinquency begins at home. Lastly – and in a different register – Marian is getting on in years: she's nearly blind, she's seven children (two are dead), seven grandsons and seven granddaughters. Her husband died soon after their marriage and she's worked 'night and day' to bring her children up by herself. 'It's been a hard life. It's been a struggle', says Wilfred sympathetically. It has, Marian agrees, it's been terrible, 'but I'm still here'.

Performers are selected sometimes by special request (Pickles lets us know that he asked the Town Clerk of Ramsbottom to find the town's oldest lady for the show), but more usually from their responses to the *Have a Go* questionnaire, whose preamble spells out what the programme is looking for:

> The following questions are designed to assist us in selecting contestants for the quiz. Our aim is to provide as much variety and interest in the programme as possible and your answers will help us considerably in doing this. We don't expect you to provide an answer to every question but fill in what you can.
>
> If you have had experiences which you think may be amusing or interesting to the public, please mention them. Be assured that we will not make you look foolish in any way; but we need your suggestions and help in making the programme of interest to the listener.

The questionnaire falls into two parts. The first deals with personal matters: name, address, place of birth, occupation, family (are you courting?), hobbies and sport (do you sing?). The second deals with 'general questions' and 'preferences'. There are nearly two dozen questions here that range from 'If you could live your life over again, what changes would you make?' to 'Is there anything you've always longed to say to someone – and dare not?' and 'If you could pass a law to benefit mankind, what would you make a punishable offence?' Preferences are all about your favourite film star, sportsman, food, song or drink. In sum, the content, sequence and structure of the questionnaire is the format and routine for the interaction between Pickles and each and every programme participant.

Thus, if we examine the structure of the interaction between Wilfred and Florrie we find that it falls into two parts that correspond to the two parts of the questionnaire. There is firstly the introductory greetings and self identification (1–54): name (5), address (11–13) and occupation (21). Notice how utterly familiar this routine is, how absolutely standard it has become for these questions to be asked at the start of any interaction in a programme of this sort. Why? Because such questions begin to display the minimal components of any person's identity-kit in our kind of society. We begin to know people by knowing such things about them. We begin to store up the details of their biography. The great virtue of *Have a Go!* – its caritas – rests on the assumption that *anyone* in our society has *something* to say for themself. Anyone can be interesting for anyone else.

Such assumptions are a necessary precondition for the second section of the interaction which explores preferences, tastes and opinions (55–120). The point of homely questions such as 'What do you like to eat?' (60), or 'Any embarrassing moments at work?' (71), or 'Have you a dislike about people?' (87), or 'Is there anything you longed to say to someone but didn't dare?' (97–9) is that they are devices for finding (and displaying) that the other in the conversation is interesting. This is not a natural or inevitable assumption. And if, in the past (or, indeed, today) certain sections of society 'have no voice' it is partly because those who have a say in everything have still not yet managed to find anything worth listening to in the everyday life and everyday talk of those whom they continue to disenfranchise from public speech. So that to find that anyone can be 'amusing or interesting to the public' strikes me as being as much a moral matter as a political matter, as much an act of charity as an act of equality.

The routine character of the show, the ease with which it renews itself on each and every occasion, is not only something carefully planned and worked for, but something that it accumulates by dint of repetition. The show's own past is always a useable resource. Pickles unobtrusively presumes a shared knowledge of the programme's biography in his routines: 'You've heard me before on *Have a Go* ask all sorts of questions', 'Now here's another question I ask on *Have a Go*', 'Looking back on life – and you've heard me ask this question many a time . . .'. This naturally presumed familiarity with the show (and why would anyone appear on it if they didn't know and like it?) is common ground for all members of the occasion. Part of its pleasure is the predictability of the questions and of the answers: both are, in a fairly general way, always already known. So that to reiterate again Simmel's fundamental point: it is not what is said, but how it is said that matters. The small identity-tokens, the ready-made questions and answers are useable for sociable purposes because they are close at hand, easily handled and so produce effects of easy, good-natured fun.


VI


In all the preceding accounts I have tried to hold in focus how such pro-grammes as those discussed produce themselves for absent audiences as that which they intend to be. The popularity of *Have A Go!* was endlessly attested to in Listener Research Reports:

> 'Comment was enthusiastic in the extreme, many said the series had pro-vided the most amusing and human entertainment on the air . . .'
> '. . . frequent expressions of regret at its temporary holiday . . .'
> '. . . most . . . paid tribute to Wilfred Pickles whom they seemed to regard as a personal friend rather than just a favourite broadcaster . . .'
> '. . . the only real complaint . . . was that it was too short . . .'
> '. . . the predominant feeling . . . was gratitude for the cheering influence of the whole series . . .'
> '. . . warm affection for Wilfred Pickles . . .'
> '. . . he makes the show . . .'
> '. . . bubbles with fun . . .'

That *Have a Go!* is found to be entertaining, amusing, warm, cheering and fun is the programme's sought for, worked at, achieved and accomplished inten-tion, an intention that is realized in and by the moment by moment particular-ities of the performed interactions of the participants. What audiences find in programmes is a fact that can only be established by empirical research. But that such things as audiences find in programmes are there *for* them to find in the programmes is what this account has tried to show. In so doing I have, of course, displayed at the same time my own assessments and evaluations of these old programmes and I hope that I have conveyed (for I certainly meant to) my warm admiration and affection for them.

Others, of course, may evaluate them differently. At the time there were those who found *Have a Go!* distasteful: it was mawkishly sentimental and its humour was common and vulgar.[13] More generally it could be, and was, seen

---

[13]     The production files for the programme are littered with hidden battles over the show's content. Pickles was famous for his 'soft heart' and some of the early shows came from hospitals and, on one notorious occasion, from St George's Crypt in Leeds – a night-shelter for the homeless. This and the tendency to include in the show 'blind-girls, mothers of ten and singing grandmothers' at last provoked this explosion from T. W. Chalmers, Head of the

as *too* folksy, too matey, perhaps too self-congratulatory (Hoggart 1962: 82, 169). Rigorous thinkers could find that it was yet another instance of the bourgeois media's false-consciousness, evoking an image of working-class life that did not correspond to 'the real conditions' of their existence. Such responses do not derive from misunderstandings of the show's intentions, but either from a refusal or rejection of them. Certainly the show has a *knowingness* about it – particularly in Pickles's 'stage Northerner' persona – which emphasizes (rather than conceals) that it *is* a performance and that is all it is. It is in the nature of performances – in so far as they are seen as such – that they raise questions about the nature of the relation between performer and performance, and thus may give rise to questions as to motives and intentions and such matters as whether or not the performances are authentic or sincere. What radio and television do – in a very pervasive way – is to render transparent that social life (at least as displayed in all their programmes) is a performance of one sort or another. The more we get used to radio and television as one essential, seen but unnoticed part of our everyday existence, the more we become connoisseurs of performances. The programmes we have been discussing reveal the beginnings of this process.

Light Programme: 'We have now had our bellyfull of the halt, the maimed and blind, not to mention the poor and needy . . . this exploitation of the unfortunates of this life has gone far enough and is indeed a trifle cynical, implying a kind of "give 'em a cripple Barney" and there won't be a dry eye in the house'. 'Vulgar' jokes were another recurring problem, and Pickles was again berated by Chalmers for a young lady whose most embarrassing moment was apparently when she said to her boyfriend, 'I do dislike those people who sit on you and make a convenience of you'. While this would hardly raise an eyebrow today, there were, reportedly, floods of letters to the BBC following the broadcast. Pickles's response to charges of bawdiness and vulgarity was to say that the South didn't understand the North. This, he was told, was nonsense. (All details from Foster 1983, a useful study of the programme).

# 3

---

# *Sincerity*

*Sincere*, adj. pure, unmixed: unadulterated: unfeigned: genuine: free from pretence: the same in reality as appearance.

I

Sincerity involves a performative paradox.[1] If a person's behaviour is perceived by others *as* a performance, it will be judged to be insincere, for sincerity presupposes, as its general condition, the absence of performance. Can one, indeed, asks Niklas Luhmann (1986: 166), communicate one's own sincerity at all, without becoming insincere in the very act of so doing? We must suppose that it is possible, for people are frequently assessed by others as being either sincere or otherwise, so there must be common-sense, recognizable criteria both for the kinds of social contexts in which sincerity is likely to be a performative requirement, and for the kind of performance that will be credited as sincere.

Sincerity is both an attribute of the modern person[2] and a prerequisite of

---

[1]  The notion of performance that underlies this chapter is derived from the sociology of Erving Goffman (1968) and that of Harold Garfinkel (1984) and the ethnomethodologists (see Heritage 1984; Button 1991). It is assumed that even the most seemingly natural of social phenomena, like shyness or – as here – sincerity, have to be 'done': that is, performed according to recognizable criteria in specific social settings.

[2]  For a debate on whether the category of the person is a distinctively modern, Western phenomenon, see Carrithers et al. (1987). See also Taylor (1989). On the emergence of sincerity as a theme in modern literature, see Peyre (1965) and Trilling (1971). Both locate it initially in the great flowering of secular, professional public theatre: in Shakespeare (Trilling), in Molière (Peyre). Self-revelation, in the form of autobiography (above all, in Jean-Jacques Rousseau's *Confessions*) is perhaps the high-water mark of the motif of sincerity in European literature. Kant praised Rousseau for discovering the essence of man, 'for having, better than anyone else, lifted the mask off the face of man' (Peyre 1965: 110).

modern intimate relationships.[3] The basis of intimacy is love, but for love to be true what is required of each participant is true (genuine) self-disclosure to the other. It is not merely that feelings must not be feigned; the personality of the lover must reveal itself in its fullness to the other. Such self-revelation must be spontaneous and genuine, that is, sincere. Sincerity is a form of self-display without concealment, for concealment is a kind of dissembling in which possibly disreputable motives are disguised. To be sincere is to be the genuine article, the real thing.[4] It is a necessary condition for trust in the other, and as the basis of a mutual relationship. Sincerity therefore is prized, above all, as the hallmark of a true person, of one who is reliable in interpersonal relationships. It authenticates intimacy.

In a general sense, then, sincerity is an ordinary expectation in everyday personal life. It is not a requirement in public, impersonal forms of social life.[5] Sincerity is not demanded of a doctor, a teacher or a journalist, for it is not an obviously relevant aspect of how they interact with their respective clients. Of course, professionals are expected to believe in the general efficacy of their professional conduct: a doctor 'believes' that the course of treatment prescribed

[3]   The historical sociology of intimacy is explored in Habermas (1989: 43–51) and more fully in Luhmann (1986). The work of social historians on the themes of the modern family, love and sexuality are reviewed by Lawrence Stone (1987: 311–87). Stone (1979) traces the emergence in the 18th century of 'the companionate marriage' based on mutual affection as the model of modern marriage. See also Davidoff and Hall (1987). The social history of intimacy is to be found in such studies of the emergence of new kinds of relations between marriage partners and their offspring that reconstitute kinship relations in the form of what we now tend to call the nuclear family. For a recent sociological study of 'the transformation of intimacy' in the 20th century, see Giddens (1992), especially ch. 10, 'Intimacy as democracy'. For a very different view of 'the tyranny of intimacy' in modern life, see Sennett (1985).
[4]   The issues at stake here were as much a concern of Shakespeare's view of the world as a stage and all its men and women merely players, as they are of Goffman's dramaturgy of *The Presentation of Self in Everyday Life* and Garfinkel's exploration of performed identity as a case of the genuine article and the real thing. Trilling rightly identifies *Hamlet* as Shakespeare's most profound exploration of the relationship between the 'true' (inner) self and the outer performed self. The complexity of Hamlet's character (quite unlike that of any of the other great tragic 'heroes') lies in this tension between inner and outer self, laid bare in those moments of self-revelation, the so-called soliloquies. The motif of sincerity is most succinctly captured in Polonius's celebrated advice to his son: 'This above all. To thine own self be true, And it doth follow as the night the day, Thou cans't not then be false to any man.' Trilling and Peyre both point to Molière's *Le Misanthrope* as the other major European drama on the theme of sincerity. Alceste, in his desire to present himself as an *honnête homme*, declares his intention of exposing all those who dare *'Egaler l'artifice á la sincérité, Confondre l'apparence avec la vérité'* (Peyre 1965: 54).
[5]   Weber's analysis of the technical, rational character of modern bureaucracies emphasizes their hierarchic and impersonal character. They operate *'sine ira et studio*, without hatred or passion, and hence without affection and enthusiasm. The dominant norms are concepts of straightforward duty without regard to personal considerations' (Weber 1947: 340).

will work, the journalist 'believes' in the facticity of his or her report. It is rather that professionals are not personally committed to what they do as professionals, in that they are not required to deal with others as persons, but rather as clients: as patients, pupils, readers. There are, of course, good practical reasons for the depersonalization of public, institutional life: to treat another as a person is to treat them in their particularity. This would suppose a different medical remedy for each and every patient, a different course of schooling for each and every pupil that took account of their particular abilities and needs. By treating people impersonally (i.e. objectively) objective remedies and programmes can be devised to be applied in all cases. In public institutional life, interactants are deprived of their personal attributes in order that institutional life can function at all. It is in this sense that sincerity – as the hallmark of the personal – is absent from public, institutional systems. It is not that they are insincere, rather that sincerity is irrelevant for their routine operation.


                                     II


So, too, I want to suggest, for the performing arts. Traditionally, sincerity has not been a criterion for assessments of acting and singing until new communicative contexts created by modern technologies and media made it a relevant (indeed a crucial) consideration in the moral assessment of performances in public. To bring out the force of the argument and the wider issues involved, a brief historical sketch of the development of Western singing in public contexts is offered, that tries to account for it as a performance whose character is shaped by the communicative context in which and for which it is produced, and particularly by the architecture of the social space in which it is performed.

Because singing imparts to words a special aura that they do not possess when they are simply spoken, it has always played a vital role in producing the heightened ritual effect of religious ceremony.[6] In the medieval church, which barred women from any active participatory role, singing was restricted to male voices, and the preferred kind of voice was 'high, sweet and strong'. Falsetto singing was common in polyphonic arrangements from about the 14th century, and boys came to be used for the highest parts. There was a tension between adorned and unadorned styles of singing in religious contexts: beautiful singing might give glory to God, but it also contained the seductive perils of sensual

[6]    This account is taken from the invaluable *New Grove Dictionary of Music and Musicians*, Macmillan: 1980. See 'Singing', Volume 17: 338–46.

pleasure for its own sake. Plainsong gradually gave way to more decorative styles of singing from the 16th century, especially in madrigals. In these secular musical arrangements for several parts female voices were, for the first time, included.

The development of opera in the next two centuries profoundly affected the character of singing in Europe and marked its secularization as a public, profane pleasure. The emergence of the professional opera star was accompanied by the wide popularity, in the 18th century, of castrato singing in the bel canto style with a high degree of vocal ornamentation and artifice. Opera in the 19th century added weightier timbres (or voice colours), more brilliant upper registers, more sonorous low notes and greater volume in general. These stylistic innovations were adaptations to the growing size and scale of opera production in larger theatres with larger orchestras. The voice of the singer had more work to do. Jenny Lind, 'the Swedish nightingale' (1820–67) owed her fame partly to her ability to project her voice in large concert halls without abandoning the bel canto style in which tonal intensity was prized over sheer volume. But other singers were pushed to their limit by having to compete against the strength and brilliance of the full-scale Romantic orchestra in vast theatres. Hence, many singers explored new techniques to increase the penetrative power of their voices by strengthening their resonance. More volume, greater dramatic expression, a new sense of grandeur – these were the characteristics of 19th-century 'grand' opera.

Against this, the last century saw an unprecedented intimacy in singing emerge with the German *lieder* tradition of solo singing of lyric poetry set to a piano accompaniment. The two greatest composers for this new kind of singing were Schubert and Schumann. Schubert wrote 600 *lieder*, which were performed in private social gatherings with amateur or professional performers. Few of them were ever published or sung in public in his lifetime. Schubert set to music the poetry of Goethe and Schiller. His arrangements were admired for their beauty of melody and the variety and genuineness of the lyrical moods and feelings expressed in the music. As the 19th century turned away from the bravura style, there arose an ever-increasing appreciation of the subjective element in singing that produced a new class of singer specializing in solo recitals and oratorios.

At the beginning of this century, although experimentation with the voice continued in *Sprechgesang*,[7] the basic technical requirements of the singer had not changed fundamentally since the mid-19th century. All singing was, perforce, live. The dominant public, theatrical style of singing emphasized the

---

[7] *Sprechgesang/stimme* (speech-song/voice): a highly stylized mode of vocal expression, halfway between singing and speaking. Associated particularly with the so-called 2nd Viennese School, beginning with Schönberg's *Pierrot lunaire* (1912).

beauty, resonance and artificiality of the human voice. Extremes of register were valued – the very high female or deep male voice. Opera, on an ever-grander, melodramatic scale, called for ornamentation and decoration of the voice. Against this, *lieder* singing was more intimate and private. The voices of *lieder* singers were lighter, though ornaments and decorations were also characteristics of this style of singing.

In the early 20th century technical innovations in the form of the gramophone and radio profoundly affected the character of every aspect of all musical performance, including singing. Until the 1920s there was no essential difference between classical and popular singing, though a fuller voice and greater technical accomplishment were demanded of opera singers (Grove, vol. 17: 345). Thereafter two separate styles emerged as popular singers used the microphone for which the techniques of voice projection were simply irrelevant. It was harder for sound engineers to damp down a loud, resonant voice than to amplify a soft one and so early radio performers had light, mellow, intimate voices. Singing at the microphone – whether in the ballroom, recording or radio studio – produced a new conversational style of singing, with greater emphasis on the interpretation of the text, that followed the dynamics of speech rather than melody. The higher and lower registers of the voice disappeared on radio; most female voices were and are contralto, while male voices are predominantly baritone. Thus, in all essential respects popular singing in this century diverged sharply from the norms of operatic singing which had defined expectations of what 'real' singing in public was for at least two centuries.

The impact of technical innovation was from the beginning, and in all subsequent developments, deeply controversial. At stake in all the fuss, as Simon Frith has persuasively argued, has been a continuing concern that as older performative styles have been displaced by newer ones, authentic musical values have given way to inauthentic ones (Frith 1986). The authentic is very widely held to be based on relations of presence which radio and recording technologies destroy. They are thus unnatural and false. Britain's first radio singing star was Vera Lynn. When she appeared in stage variety shows she used a microphone, for which she was roundly condemned by the *Birmingham Post*'s critic when she appeared at The Hippodrome in late 1941. He noted the ecstatic reception the singer received from both Forces and civilian members of the packed audience, but went on to say:

> For me the microphone destroys the first principle of the living stage, which is direct contact with the audience. A microphone, and the intervening gadgetry of valves and loudspeakers are necessary to the singer in London who wishes to be heard in Lancashire; but the banishment of the ubiquitous 'mike' from the music-hall would be a service to song. It is impossible to judge whether a singer has any voice at all when the sound produced on

stage reaches the audience from some eyrie above the boxes. Studio is studio and stage is stage. These attempts to make the twain meet are another example of the domination of man by the machine. The microphone has created the crooner and criticism is becoming an electrician's job rather than a task for one who looks to the stage for the first-hand projection of voice and personality. (*Birmingham Post*, 30 December 1941)

Objections of this kind were commonplace at the time. A singer who 'depended' on the microphone to amplify a 'weak' voice was felt to be inferior to so-called 'legitimate' singers.[8] But the microphone is a sensitive device that can only amplify what it 'hears' and exposes good and bad vocal production.

The new style of singing at the microphone – crooning, as it was called – became increasingly popular in the thirties, especially in the United States, and it remained the prevalent style of popular singing until the rock and roll revolution of the fifties. Its pioneers were 'Whispering' Jack Smith, 'Little' Jack Little, Rudee Vallee and above all, Bing Crosby. In the early thirties Crosby began a spectacularly successful singing career in radio, records and film. As the most popular singer of his generation his style, more than anyone else's, articulated the divide between classical and popular singing. His way of seeming to talk or whisper to a melody involved singing less forcefully, passing into the head voice lower than art-song performers, singing on consonants (a practice of black singers shunned by classical artists) and the discreet use of appoggiaturas, mordents and slurs to emphasize the text. Such techniques were emulated by nearly all later popular singers (Grove, vol. 5. 60).

In Britain the development of crooning on the radio was more fraught. Popular music, in the interwar period, was largely synonymous with dance-band music. The singer, or vocalist as he or she was called, had no special status in the band and the pop-song – as we know it – had not yet been born.[9] The voice was treated simply as one of the instruments in the band that had, like the others, its opportunity to do a solo. Since the music of the band was actually for dancing the circumstances militated against close attention to the singer or the song, and vocal numbers were outnumbered by non-vocal numbers in a typical evening's repertoire. The first British crooners were often

---

[8] For instance, Gracie Fields (see footnote 12 below) had 'a powerful voice, carrying to the farthest corner of the great concert halls even before the days of the constant use of the microphone. "She made the Palladium stage her own. She explored parts of it which other singers, rooted to their microphone, never visit," said a *Daily Express* reviewer in 1948' (Moules 1983: 69–70)

[9] The song, that is, as the vehicle of a singer–star. There is a big difference between buying sheet music, and buying the recording of a song. The former serves music to be performed, the latter, music to be listened to. Sheet music finally gives way to the gramophone record as the vehicle of popular songs only after the Second World War.

instrumentalists who also sang: of these the best known was Al Bowlly, the guitarist in Lew Stone's band in the thirties and the only British singer to rival the popularity of the Americans in this country. Bowlly defined the new art of singing at the microphone in terms of the new range of emotions – a smile, a sigh, a frown, a laugh – which crooning allowed the invisible singer to express. Crooning thus, for the first time in *public* singing, was a vehicle for intimacy. Whispering is hearable only within an individual's intimate zone – within a range of two feet, according to Edward Hall's system of proxemics (Hall 1959). Intimate singing is, of course, very ancient and universal, most notably in cradle songs and lullabies, but such a style was physically impossible in any public context before the microphone's amplification of the voice. With crooning intimacy crosses a threshold: what was formerly for and heard by one other person now is simultaneously heard by millions in live radio transmissions or on disc, but each listener experiences it as speaking to him or her alone.[10]

Crooning had been fitfully present on British radio in the early thirties for several years before it came to the notice of BBC policy-makers in Broadcasting House. In early 1936 Cecil Graves, Controller of Programmes, was insisting that 'this particularly odious form of singing' must be stopped right away. But it was not easily done. The Variety Department responded to Graves's directive by playing for time. The Music Department batted it straight back, asking if anyone had produced a definition of crooning. Definition was to prove elusive. The issue was addressed at a Programme Board in late 1936 where it was agreed that it was hard to find a suitable definition of crooning or, more exactly, of the particular kind of crooning that was thought to be objectionable.[11] It depended so much on the words themselves, how they were sung and the artistry of the singer. Graves wanted to insist that a BBC official should always be present at the final rehearsal of light musical combinations using a singer – particularly those with a tendency to improvise their programme at the last minute. But no one wanted to undertake such a hapless task (Scannell and Cardiff 1991: 188–90). There were other more pressing matters facing BBC administrators on the light music front – song-plugging and orchestrations in particular – so the

---

[10]   The audio equivalent of the close-up in film. It has been pointed out that the intimate close-up that cinema offers to millions creates an access to the human face and an exchange of looks that hitherto existed only between lovers or a parent and little child.

[11]   The hatred of crooning – which was not, of course, restricted to the BBC management – was prompted by two quite distinct factors, class and sex. On the one hand, it was vulgar and common – in a word, American – and so destroyed the social distinction of singing. On the other hand, it feminized singing: that is, it brought such feminine values as intimacy and tenderness into the public domain. The expression of such feelings ('emotional slush') appeared as a threat to male identities. Male crooners were labelled effeminate, and there was a clear homophobic strain in the fear and loathing of crooning. In the war, the fear was that crooning would sap the virility of the soldiers, thereby undermining their willingness to kill.

problem of crooning lapsed for the moment, until it returned with renewed ferocity in relation to one of the most popular programmes on wartime radio, *Sincerely Yours, Vera Lynn*, which began in November 1941.

## III

By this time Vera Lynn, in her early twenties, was a professional singer of long standing.[12] She had begun her career at the age of seven in working-men's clubs in the East End of London (she was born in East Ham). As a child performer she sang straightforward sentimental ballads and cornered the market, as she wryly notes, in 'Daddy' numbers: 'Dream Daddy', 'I've Got a Real Daddy Now' and the 22-carat tear-jerker, 'What is a Mammy, Daddy?' (Lewis 1975: 24). At the age of 15 she went fully professional and progressed remarkably quickly as a singer with the top dance bands, at first with Joe Loss and Charlie Kunz and then, in the late thirties, with the premier band of the day, Ambrose's.

All the leading London bands appeared regularly on late-night radio, and so Vera Lynn was a familiar voice by the time war broke out. She was already the most popular singer on radio with British troops, and had a very busy working schedule between singing with Ambrose, performing in revue and making recordings, when she was booked by Howard Thomas at the BBC for a short programme series in late 1941. It was to go in the Forces Programme, aimed at the troops overseas or billeted all over the country. Howard Thomas gave the programme its title and designed its format to fit round Vera Lynn's voice and performative style. It was the first programme on British radio that showcased an individual singer named in the programme title.

Howard Thomas produced it, as he put it, in 'an un-BBC-like way', conceiving it as 'a letter from home in words and music' (Thomas 1977: 96). It was a new perspective on 'personal vehicle' programmes because instead of the usual

---

[12]    The account that follows, unless otherwise indicated, is taken from Vera Lynn's autobiography (Lewis [her married name]: 1975). By way of comparison and contrast with Vera Lynn's success and performative style, there is much of interest in the career of Gracie Fields – perhaps *the* great female, working-class singing star of a slightly earlier period. For a brief but fascinating account of this 'mill girl with *an operatic voice*' (my emphasis), 'with a grand bourgeois voice' see Frith (1988: 67–71). Frith notes, in his analysis of the character of her performance, the complex quality of her voice and her relations with her public, her capacity to 'make conversation sing' (71). Gracie Fields was a great music hall star, in a way that Vera Lynn never was. 'Our Gracie', as she was affectionately known, was public property, because she was a great public performer, whose performance was 'the real thing' – she was herself in public. In contrast, Vera Lynn constructs an intimate one-to-one relationship with listeners. These two singing stars, then, embody the two different aspects of sincerity: on the one hand, as embodied in the genuine, true person and on the other, as embodied in interpersonal intimacy.

crooner's 'direct-from-me-to-you-darling' approach the show had to be designed
for men and women in the Services listening together without causing mutual
embarrassment. Vera Lynn sang, Thomas acknowledged, 'clearly, slowly, unaf-
fectedly and with absolute sincerity'. To accompany her he chose the well-
established Fred Hartley Sextet, who alternated lively instrumental numbers
with the slow numbers sung by Vera Lynn. Each show began with 'Wishing'
and ended with, perhaps, her most famous wartime song, 'We'll Meet Again'.
Thomas wanted to give the programme some novelty, some human touch,
some piece of news from home that would appeal to everyone. He came up
with the idea of a message for an expectant father in the forces that his baby
had arrived safely. The London maternity hospitals were asked to ring in to the
BBC studio on Sunday (the day of the programme) with news of the latest
arrivals. These would be mentioned that evening in the show by Vera Lynn,
with a promise (always kept) to visit the proud mother the next day with a
bouquet of flowers. The weekly letter – written by Thomas in 'an easy, conversational style' – worked in some topical propaganda theme that the BBC
and/or the Ministries were anxious to promote: encouraging middle-aged women
to take up part-time factory work, for instance. Each week Thomas took Vera
Lynn round the factories so that she could faithfully report on what the wives
and mothers back home were doing for the war effort. Vera Lynn thus worked
to link the men abroad and the women at home by sharing their favourite
songs. Requests flooded in at the rate of a thousand a week.

In its concept it was, in Vera Lynn's own words, 'a humble little radio
programme' (Lewis 1975: 109). But it turned out to be, for her, the most
important thing she had ever done. Its appeal lay in her own obvious 'sincerity': on that, all those who liked the show and her singing style, agreed. Again
and again contemporary press comment falls back on praising not only her
'fresh, young voice, but – well, there's no other word for it – it's her sincerity'
(*Woman's Illustrated*, 21 February 1942). Or, 'It's not only her fresh, young
voice – not only the completely natural, unstudied quality about her singing
that reaches out to people's hearts: there's no other word for it – it's her
sincerity' (*Empire News*, 31 March 1942). Or, 'Partly it's that low, caressing
quality of her voice. But also in that voice you catch the simple sincerity of a
humble girl unspoilt' (*Sunday Pictorial*, 1 February 1942). Or – this is Joyce
Grenfell in *The Observer* – 'What is it that Vera Lynn has that the other gals
haven't got? Vitality? No. Glamour? No. Sincerity? Yes, yes a thousand times
yes, and that I think is her power. That, of course, and her gentleness and
simplicity and her homeliness. And I use that in its dictionary meaning: "of
familiar, every-day character; unpretentious" . . .'

Yet Vera Lynn was, by the time of the programme, an accomplished performer at the top of her profession, who viewed her voice and performance
with professional detachment:

A lot of play was made with the word 'sincerity', which is very flattering as long as you remember what it means. On the whole – and it was certainly true in 1941 – a popular singer uses other people's words, and she hasn't necessarily been through the experiences she's describing (in some cases the song-writer himself hasn't, either). So she has to use her imagination, which is not a matter of sincerity so much as conviction. The sincerity comes from the singer's belief that the words are right for what they are trying to say, that they are what she herself would use in those circumstances. If she can believe in the song, it doesn't matter how trite it is as a piece of literature, its message will come across. (Lewis 1975: 93–4)

Sincerity demands not so much that you say what you mean as that you mean what you say. Yet how can this be when your words are not your own, when they are merely learnt? (with difficulty, in Vera Lynn's case: her greatest fear was not remembering the words). There is, as she makes clear, a discrepancy between singer and song. The singer does not author(ize) what she sings. This non-correspondence has the effect of invalidating the experience (the feelings) to which the words of the song lay claim: how *can* you mean what you have not experienced yourself? Inauthentic experience is banal and trite because it lacks the authenticating, validating seal of first-hand experience. Given all this, how can her singing be sincere? Vera Lynn's answer is clear: because she performs as if she believes what she sings.

The effect of Lynn's performance in the first and last instance depends on the quality of her voice, irrespective of what it might actually say – a voice which is *heard* as fresh, natural and true. By implication such a voice is assessed against voices that lack freshness, naturalness and truth; voices that are trained, artful and hence artificial – in other words, the normal criteria by which 'legitimate' singing voices were judged at the time. Lynn herself considered going, in 1940, to a singing coach for voice training. It was not in the hope of acquiring 'a posh voice' that she did this, but in order to extend her vocal range, thereby allowing her a wider selection of material. The singing teacher asked for a little demonstration:

So I just sang, the way I always did.
'Oh', she said, 'that's not your true voice, I'm sure.'
'Well it's the only one I've ever sung with.'
'Haven't you got another voice? Can't you sing higher?'
'Well, I've got my bath voice, when I'm pretending to be in opera.'
I trilled away.
'Ah', she said, beaming with triumphant satisfaction, 'that's the voice I shall train'.
'I'm sorry, that would be useless to me; I've got recording contracts for which I use my ordinary voice.'

'But that's not a true voice, that's a freak voice,' she said, appalled. (Lewis
1975: 95)

And that was as far as Vera Lynn went in having orthodox voice training. Note
the conflicting perceptions of a 'true' voice: what Lynn regards as her ordinary
voice is regarded by the teacher as not true, as a freak. When Lynn puts on a
pretend (opera) voice the teacher accepts it as true. But Lynn knows that to
train her voice in the orthodox way would be to destroy its appeal.

This is not to say that her voice is untrained. Its actual *sound* had been with
her from childhood, and singing 'came naturally' from an early age. It was
always unusual (loud, penetrating, rather low in pitch) and once Lynn became
convinced of its distinctiveness she quite deliberately gave up listening closely
to other singers for fear of being influenced by them. Lynn's voice is untrained
in the sense that it has not been schooled in orthodox singing that filters out
the particularity, the *grain* of the voice, 'the body in the voice as it sings'
(Barthes 1977: 188). This she is careful to protect by avoiding imitation of
other voices, or learning operatic 'trilling'. But she has deliberately adapted her
voice to the microphone, which she first encountered in her teens when she
began singing with the bands. At the microphone she learnt very quickly to
lower the volume, but found this meant lowering her pitch as well. As she
reduced the pressure on her voice it simply dropped into a lower key, thus
extending her vocal range. She found no difficulty in adapting to singing with
the bands, and was glad to discover so early what a microphone could do and
how, as she put it, to make it work for her (Lewis 1975: 40). If her voice had
a natural sound, she worked hard to preserve and develop it, for she recognized
that in so doing she protected her own identity as a singer.

In modern societies voices are treated as recognizable markers of individual
(personal) identities. This is due, in part, to the individualizing power of modern communication systems such as telephone and radio which particularize
rather than generalize voices.[13] The effect of the studio microphone on singing
was to repersonalize the voice; that is, to recapture its expressive character in

---

[13]   Schegloff's (1979) analysis of telephone conversational openings shows clearly how voice
is treated by callers and receivers – in the USA and UK at least – as a mark of personal
identity. Callers phoning people they know well (and to whom they assume they are well
known) – such as friends, family members, etc. – routinely introduce themselves simply with
'hi', 'hello', 'it's me', etc., thereby expecting that they will be recognized by virtue of their
voice alone. Responses such as 'hi', 'hello' or 'hello you' confirm recognition, and reciproc-
ally assume that the respondent is recognizable to caller by virtue of voice sound alone.
Everyone has had the embarrassing experience of not identifying a caller by voice alone, and
of fishing for further identity clues as the talk progresses until either light dawns or one has
to say 'I'm sorry, but I'm not sure who you are'. For further discussion of the relationship
between voice and identity in broadcasting, see chapter six.

interpersonal interaction as an idiom of public communication. Radio reverses the public–private relationship. Because in all its output it speaks to the domestic and private, it has the pervasive effect of bringing the values that attach to the private realm into the public domain. These values are embodied (literally) in performances. For centuries singing voices had demonstrated their ritual, public character by distancing themselves as far as possible from ordinary, everyday voices. The aesthetics of singing valued a depersonalized voice (as the vogue for the castrato voice rather drastically showed) whose beauty had a distinctive 'otherness' that explored the heights and depths of the vocal range. Techniques of mass-performance had to be developed in order to project to large audiences over large orchestras in large auditoriums. All these were instantly reversed by the microphone: instead of loudness, softness; instead of singing to many, singing to one; instead of the impersonal, the personal; instead of extraordinary, ordinary voices. Thus, public performative values were displaced by private performative values that privileged the particular and the personal. In a word, for the singing voice, the microphone, radio and the gramophone record made sincerity the authenticating measure of intimacy as it was transposed from the private into the public domain.

Sincerity mediates intimacy; it is its medium of communication. This, however, is something that has to be proved. It is not enough merely to invoke the sincerity of a voice, especially a public voice, since sincerity can be faked. Proof is required that there is no dissimulation going on. Sincerity's vice is hypocrisy. Hypocrites are insincere because they say one thing and do another and so (if they are discovered) are revealed as not committed to their utterances. Public persons (politicians, for instance) are vulnerable to revelations about their private lives that might discredit their publicly projected personality. Vera Lynn claims she *believes* in the words she sings. Even though the words themselves may be inauthentic her (sincere) belief in them makes the experiences, the emotions they convey, authentic. The emotions are true because she makes them so. There is, in her public performance, no discrepancy between singer and song. Or so we are asked to believe. The common-sense test of such a claim would be to look for evidence that might disprove it, such as a private life at odds with the public performance.

Lynn's personality in *Sincerely Yours* is elaborated round her voice and singing style. She is presented as an ordinary girl, 'the girl next door' who speaks for all the girls at home whose boys are far away:

> Dear Boys, I've been working in the West End all this week and using the tubes and buses a lot. I realized how well some of the girls are doing your job while you're away. On the underground girls shout out 'mind the doors!' At the railway station they unload great parcels. And on the buses they take your money and shout the stops. It's one of the sights of London to see them, cheerful and chatty but getting on with the job. Most of the girls are

married. I had a pleasant surprise when one of them – a girl on the 23 bus
– recognized me. She must have seen a picture of me somewhere. She said
she'll be listening-in tonight, and so will her husband. This letter of mine is
getting to be a sort of rendez-vous where husbands and wives torn apart by
war can be brought together by music. On the wings of these melodies the
sentiments go from me to both of you. From you to her. Here is our song
together tonight . . . [Fade-in 'Night and Day']

The letter is, of course, an intimate form of communication; from one person to
another, private in its contents, loving and sincere in its expression, as 'love' or
'yours sincerely' signals at the end. Lionel Trilling suggests that the trivialization of sincerity (its loss of authenticity) is marked by its epistolary usage
as a standardized farewell (Trilling 1971: 35). Its usage on radio is obviously
problematic, for how can a personal, private form of communication be used
publicly?[14] We might note all the elements in the letter that render it inauthentic
(i.e. not the communication of personal experience). It is written by the producer of the programme and contains fairly obvious propaganda elements (the
girls are doing a grand job). Vera Lynn claims to speak on behalf of the men
away and the girls at home and, more particularly, to bring together wives and
husbands torn apart by war. She, like all the other women for whom she
speaks, is a working girl, who uses public transport and meets other working
women on the buses, etc. She can thus claim to speak for all these women
because she is like them, she knows them, she understands them and their
experiences. They are ordinary, so is she. 'Songs that spoke for very ordinary
people were my chosen means of expression.'

For such a claim to be valid, Vera Lynn must be ordinary too. In some ways,
of course, she is not. *Sincerely Yours* tipped a successful career into the super-
successful category and her market value went through the roof. Ambrose,
who in 1940 was paying her £40 a week was prepared, two years later, to offer
her £500 a week when the average weekly wage was less than £5. And yet her
life-style did not change radically. Her own accounts and contemporary press
reports present her as remarkably untouched by success. 'This rather shy,
demure young lady is quite unspoiled by her phenomenal success' declared
*Film Pictorial* (14 March 1942). 'Her voice sells more gramophone records than
any other star including Deanna Durbin and Bing Crosby . . . yet she is still a
typical Cockney, sincere, warm-hearted and with a sound business sense. The

---

[14]    This problem has been analysed with great subtlety by Montgomery (1991) in his study
of *Our Tune*. This was a regular slot for most of the eighties in a daily DJ programme on
Radio 1, in which a reader's letter (always about personal and domestic crises) was read out
by the DJ. The practical problem for the broadcast reader of the letter was how to 'trans-
late' the private idiom of a letter into the public idiom of radio talk whilst preserving its
authenticity.

sort of "nice little wife" that men dream of having' (*Sunday Pictorial*, 1 February 1942). 'I have never met', writes Jean Merrill du Cane, 'any girl who fitted less into the accepted "star" type. . . . She lives quietly just outside London, is married to Leading Airman Harry Lewis and outside her singing, just devotes herself to planning what they will do when Harry is on leave' (*Empire News*, 31 March 1942). The prevailing public perception of Vera Lynn was that her publicly presented personality and her private life were in harmony with each other. If she appeared to sing like a simple, innocent, unaffected young girl it was because she was all those things.

And yet there was a small but influential body of opinion that deeply disliked her kind of sentimentality. In the letter columns of the *Daily Telegraph*, in the House of Commons and in the War Office objections were raised against the slush, 'flabby amusement' and 'sentimental sloppy muck' on the radio, that was undermining the morale of the fighting troops. Senior management in the BBC shared such views and there was a concerted effort to stamp out 'crooning, sentimental numbers, drivelling words, slush, innuendos, and so on' (Briggs 1970: 577–8). A minute of a Board of Governors meeting (4 December 1941) records '*Sincerely Yours* deplored but popularity noted' (Briggs 1970: 578 n. 5). Howard Thomas was asked by his superiors to respond to such criticisms by some 'general brisking up' of the programme. At the same time the solid popularity of the programme with the ordinary soldier was noted. A. P. Ryan, Controller of Programmes for the Home Services, reported on the impact of the programme after visiting the troops overseas and talking to both officers and men: 'The strange thing was that the morale of the men was not affected adversely. On the contrary, Vera Lynn cheered them up. If we put a stop to Vera Lynn we would be doing harm to the troops, and in their eyes look very foolish.' Howard Thomas's solution was to 'rest' Vera Lynn after her second short series and to try to start a new trend with 'another personality programme, but of the most virile kind. A man-to-man programme, which does for marches and straight songs what Vera Lynn has done for the Charing Cross Road product' (Thomas 1977: 94–100). The trend, however, did not catch on, and no male superstar appeared in the wake of Vera Lynn, to belt out marching songs that would stir the lads to martial valour on the fighting fronts, though Anne Shelton – who had many fans – had a reputation for putting over 'simple marching songs' effectively.

Vera Lynn was also the butt of female satirists. In revue on the London stage Dorothy Dickson burlesqued her in what Eric Bennett described as 'a wickedly funny act. The microphone-enhanced whine of her crooning and the studied monotony of gesture brought the house down' (*Strand Magazine*, November 1942). Within a year or so everyone, it seems, was doing it. Lynn's reaction was one of hurt bewilderment. How *could* anyone mock her own 'sentimental but sincere approach to the fighting services' in whose value and

importance she so passionately believed. Eric Bennett noted 'her almost evan-
gelical belief in the need for the sentiments she expressed. She just does not
understand the people who dislike her songs.' In 1944 she attempted to impose
legal curbs on those she regarded as her 'more spiteful impersonators' (Lewis
1975: 128). Such responses on her part underline the sincerity of her belief in
her own performance. But perhaps the final proof came a few years later when,
in 1949, her regular work with the BBC suddenly stopped. She was abruptly
told, by the new Head of Variety, that her kind of music was finished. Sob stuff
was not wanted and, if she wanted to go on broadcasting, she would have to
change her style. He could not have picked on a line of attack more guaranteed
to infuriate Vera Lynn. 'My style was *me*' (Lewis 1975: 148). She could no
more change her act than she could change herself.[15]

## IV

In his volume on the BBC and the Second World War, Asa Briggs justly remarks:

> The war will be remembered not only for its great broadcasting landmarks,
> moments of shared experience, but for its songs and its slogans, its rhythms
> and its moods. Tommy Handley, Vera Lynn, Dr Joad, J. B. Priestley and
> many others besides left their imprint on social history in a manner that people

[15]    The same is true, though in a very different way, of Gracie Fields. Her obituarist in *The
Times* remarked that 'The excellence of her singing at one time seemed a menace to her
performance, for the sentimental ditties on which she lavished so much artistry were quite
unworthy of her talent. Early in her career she had an entrancing trick of indicating her real
opinion of these tearful ballads by introducing into the middle of her song some ludicrous
trick of voice, or by absentmindedly scratching her back between high notes' (Moules 1983:
202). We might consider this 'trick' rather differently, though. It is as much a social as an
aesthetic distinction to think of sentimental ditties as unworthy of a grand opera voice. Gracie
Fields could have had a career as an opera star (it was suggested to her, but she chose not
to), but that would have been with a quite different (bourgeois) audience and a quite different status (as diva). The deflating trick, which was a hallmark of Gracie Fields's performances, may have been directed more at the voice itself than the words – for it was the singing
style, rather than the sentiments in the words, that might seem la-di-da and over-inflated to
her audience (never a problem, as we have seen, for Vera Lynn). On stage Gracie Fields
presented herself always as what she originally was – a mill-girl from Rochdale with a magnificent voice who was always ready to laugh at life and at herself. This essentially true public
self-presentation, combined with her remarkable voice and skilled performance, was what
endeared her to millions. The sincerity of Gracie Fields's performance was that she was
true to herself and her audience. It was a public and sociable relationship created in direct
interaction with audiences on the stage of music hall that Gracie Fields established, rather
than the intimate and personal one created by Vera Lynn through radio. Thus, in different
ways, the two performers were themselves in their performances (unlike opera singers), while
revealing different aspects of sincerity-as-performance across the boundaries of the public
and private.

who never heard them at the time may well find difficult fully to understand. Recordings of their broadcasts, where they exist, have a Proustian quality which is still capable of stirring the strongest individual feelings. In years ahead, however, they will have to speak for themselves. (Briggs 1970: 73)

In this chapter I have tried to bring to life the quality of a voice that had a powerful, immediate and controversial impact on wartime audiences. I have listened to the one extant recording of *Sincerely Yours, Vera Lynn* many times. Most of it I hear unmoved, and some of it I find embarrassing, but the song with which Vera Lynn ended every show touches me each time I hear it:

We'll meet again, don't know where don't know when
But I know we'll meet again some sunny day.
Keep smiling through just like you always do
Till the blue skies drive the dark clouds far away.

The words are simple, direct and conversational. They speak to the heart of everyone's experience at that time, and they are sung from the heart. Everyone can hear themselves and their own particular circumstances in the words, and everyone can hope for what it promises when the war ends. At the time of its singing that day seemed a very, very distant prospect. The power of the song lies in its truth: the truth of the words, of the way in which they are sung, of the circumstances to which they speak and of the contexts in which they are received. A performance is sincere when it meets such conditions. A performer is sincere who believes in, and is committed to, her performance and provides collateral guarantees of that commitment in a private life in tune with her public role.

Sincerity changes the basis whereby singing is judged. We no longer ask 'is it beautiful?' but 'is it true?' It may be the case that beauty is truth; truth, beauty – but if we emphasize one rather than the other we express a very different sense of the relationship between life and art. To emphasize truth rather than beauty involves a shift from aesthetic to moral judgement. Aesthetic judgement proceeds by immanent criteria: the qualities of, say, the singing voice are *in* the voice itself which can be compared – impersonally – with other voices of that kind. As a matter of *pure* taste, the song can be detached from any singer or any performance: heard melodies are sweet but those unheard are sweeter. It is only a naive taste that attends to the singer rather than the song, that worries about whether the song is *meant*. Aesthetic judgement is pure taste, unsullied by grosser emotions and feelings. 'Taste that requires an added element of charm and emotion . . . has not yet emerged from barbarism', says Kant.[16] If

---

[16] Quoted in Bourdieu (1984: 43), whose sociological critique of Kant's Judgement of Taste supports the themes of this article. See especially his discussion of 'the popular aesthetic', based on the affirmation of the continuity between art and life (32ff.).

we believe in art for art's sake what we mean, simply, is that no criteria enter into judgement other than purely aesthetic ones. Such claims have persistently been used in modern times to ring-fence the arts and literature from ordinary life and experience.

Radio and television tear down the fence: the distinction between life and art is no longer sustainable. The displacement of aesthetic criteria by moral and social criteria is a very pervasive effect of broadcasting and contributes to that common-sense perception of television and radio as lacking artistic value. In assessing radio and television performances listeners and viewers tend to over-look the quality of the performance (unless it fails to *pass* and thereby becomes, in some way remarkable, i.e. a matter of comment). That is, the unobtrusive aesthetics of performance are presumed. Of more immediate concern are moral assessments of the genuineness (or otherwise) of performances, and social assessments as to whether they are enjoyable or boring.

Sincerity is a much more pervasive performative requirement on radio and television than the singular instance considered in this chapter. Vera Lynn's case is particularly interesting since it is a clearly identifiable moment when a new performative style was created, bringing with it changes in the perception and evaluation of performances. But it is part of a much wider process in which performances in public have been restructured through and through by the pressures on broadcasting to adopt the interactive idioms of ordinary, mun-dane, interpersonal life. Sincerity is pervasively a performative requirement, on radio and television, that affects all aspects of performances in both factual and fictional settings.[17] What is expected, in all cases, is the projection and presentation of ordinariness as a case of the real thing, the genuine article. Hence, narratives – both fictional and factual – become increasingly naturalistic in all aspects of their production. In other words, artificial, mannered or styl-ized performances are rejected on radio and television – except as pastiche or as send-ups. Sincerity, we might say, is nowadays one defining characteristic of any person appearing in the public realm who lays claim to ordinariness. It is how you prove you are like the rest of us. This can, occasionally, create difficulties for television performers. William Roache, who plays Ken Barlow in *Coronation Street*, had to go to court not so long ago to prove he was *not* as boring in real life as he was in the lifeworld of the programme (Roache 1993: 212–33) and thus that sincerity – at least in relation to television soap-operas – *is* only a performance and not, as for Vera Lynn, a case of the real thing.

---

[17]     I have not found a succinct account anywhere of changing styles of acting in European theatre across the same period to match that to be found in the *Grove Dictionary of Music*, but Sennett (1985) has a fascinatingly tendentious account of the character of public life in the last three centuries and the connections between acting styles in the theatre and perform-ance on the wider public 'stage'.

# 4

## *Eventfulness*

### I

Jürgen Habermas has argued, in his influential analysis of the formation of the modern (political) public sphere, that the media have contributed to the 'refeudalization' of public life. In pre-modern Europe publicness was a status-attribute of the lords spiritual and temporal. 'They represented their lordship not for but "before" the people' (Habermas 1989: 8) whenever they appeared in public. The people were simply the audiences for such displays. And so, he argues, it is today.[1] 'The public sphere becomes (again) the court *before* whose public, prestige can be displayed – rather than *in* which public critical debate is carried on. . . . In the expanded (i.e. mediatized) public sphere the (political) transactions themselves are stylized into a show. Publicity loses its function in favour of a staged display' (Habermas 1989: 201, 206). We are clearly meant to disapprove of this. The critical tradition, as John Durham Peters notes, has long regarded public ceremony with nothing but suspicion. Theatre, ritual, ceremony – these things are somehow irrational, or if not that, at least an unnecessary distraction from the rational conduct

---

[1]  *The Structural Transformation of the Public Sphere* was published in Germany in 1962 and thus describes the contemporary world of the late 1950s. However, its publication in English in 1989 triggered a major debate in England and America (Calhoun 1992) – powerful testimony to the abiding relevance of the book's central concerns. Habermas, in light of this renewed engagement with his work, has reviewed his attitude today to the theses he developed more than 30 years ago. He still sticks, by and large, with the argument of the second part of the book; namely, that public life in late capitalism has been subverted from its critical functions in early modern Europe and reverted to pre-modern forms of publicness – refeudalization, in short (cf. Habermas in Calhoun 1992: 436–7).

of public life. It is very understandable, in Habermas's case. 'Given the Nazi aestheticization of politics, and (his) lifelong struggle against fascism, it is not hard to imagine why he resists theatre, rhetoric, narrative, festival or pomp from entering into the political' (Peters 1993: 565). But even so, as Peters points out, such a puritan, iconoclastic stance towards public life points to an impoverished understanding of the communicative richness and scope of social life.

It is a widespread attitude. We are supposed to see 'the society of the spectacle' as yet another way in which the ideological veil is drawn over public life. In Habermas's view the only active agents in a 'feudalized' public life are the actors themselves who define and control the occasion. 'The people' function merely as a backdrop, as passive spectators who witness the event and learn their place. As it was in the past, so it is today. The mass media are agents of social control (or integration) whose function shows up in the mediation of public ceremony. But radio and television have restructured publicness through and through by transforming the very conditions of being-in-public. We now live in a world in which the faces of public persons are universally available. Today, everyone 'knows' (in a minimal sense of being able to recognize) royalty, leading politicians, sports men and women, 'stars', 'personalities' and those who are famous for being famous. And this is a world-wide phenomenon. In ways hitherto inconceivable there now exists a domain of publicness in which certain kinds of person routinely appear and thereby are (willingly or not) available to, subject to, the scrutiny of everyone.

Foucault thought the panopticon was a device invented by the authorities for the scrutiny and disciplining of the potentially unruly majority (in prisons, hospitals, schools, etc.), while they themselves remained invisible (Foucault 1977). Perhaps it was so in the last century, but now it is surely the other way round. Those who were once the lords and owners of their faces are no longer, for they can no longer control the terms and conditions of their being-in-public. The management of visibility, in John Thompson's useful phrase, has been thoroughly problematized by modern media (Thompson 1994: 40). In particular, what can no longer be *managed* are the behaviours of the wider listening or viewing publics. And this is because, as we have already argued, the nature of the relationship between broadcasters and listeners or viewers is unforced because it is unenforceable. Public events now occur, simultaneously, in two different places: the place of the event itself and that in which it is watched and heard. Broadcasting mediates *between* these two sites. Events in public thus assume a degree of phenomenal complexity they did not hitherto possess, and this has consequences for the character of the events themselves. We can begin to explore these issues by retracing the presentation, by radio and television, of public events involving royalty.

## II

In 1923 the infant BBC wanted to present the fast-growing audience for radio with a new kind of experience, namely direct, live access to a royal wedding. Permission was sought to allow coverage of the wedding of Lady Elizabeth Bowes-Lyon (the present Queen Mother) to the Duke of York (George VI, the present Queen's late father). In the end permission was refused because the Dean of Westminster feared that 'men in public houses might listen with their hats on' (Wolfe 1984: 79). If this seems a more than faintly ludicrous objection today, it was entirely correct in anticipating the implications for sacred events of their live coverage by radio and television. What the Dean rightly foresaw as a fundamental difficulty for the authorities (for those in charge of the management of such events) was the impossibility of controlling the behaviours of an absent audience of listeners.

This problem showed up in the reactions of listeners to the coronation of the same Duke of York, some 14 years later, when he was anointed King George VI in the same Abbey of Westminster on 12 May 1937. Mass Observation's documentary account of the day shows a very wide range of responses to hearing the coronation on radio:

1    The other people in the office come in to listen. The Abbey service is going on. They first make jokes with the children and William (the dog) and talk, but gradually get quiet and thoughtful and I find I have to hush the children and dog as they are listening intently. Feel I must not smoke. My aunt has already left us for a basement room also with a loudspeaker, where she can listen undisturbed and as if in Church to the service. She has a book of the words. (London: 125)

2    Lansdowne Theatre. Sixpence to hear relay of the Abbey ceremony. Small cinema about one third full. The relay says: 'The Queen, attended by her two bishops, approaches the seat of the Almighty.' The voice of the commentator is unctuous. 'The Queen kneels with her two bishops.' In the seat in front of me a coloured man with small-pox bitten nose is apparently sleeping. Behind me three Americans (or at any rate wealthy visitors) are listening attentively. Elsewhere one young man has his arm around another. (London: 126–7)

3    After lunch got into conversation with proprietress of café. She turned on the 'wireless' for us and we listened in from 1.20 to 2.20. This was mostly from within the Abbey. While the prayer 'Wherefore with Angels and Archangels and all the Company of Heaven' was proceeding, there was much clamping around in the kitchen and at the 'Sursum Corda' there was more bustling and banging. While the Archbishop was reciting

passages in the Holy Communion – 'Hear what St John saith' – a customer came into the outer shop and give his order in the same ecclesiastical tones, for tobacco. (South Devon: 281–2)

4   Morning. Listened in to part of commentary on ceremony in common room with 9 people (4 conservatives, 3 liberals, 1 fascist, 1 fabian). General reaction: embarrassed grins, and outright laughter when the commentator was outstandingly loyal. Fascist stood for National Anthem. Conservative remarked 'bloody fool!' It was generally agreed that the Coronation was a good thing because it improved trade, gave ruling class prestige and broke down class barriers. (Cambridge: 283)

5   My hairdresser on Saturday, after asking if I'd been to London on the 12th said they'd listened in to the Service. They'd had the wireless on from half-past ten to half-past four – 'And you should have seen my mother – she sat in front of it all day – and all through the service while he was being crowned and that, the tears were pouring down her face and she kept moaning "*Oh*, it ought to be Edward – it – it – it ought to be Edward" – My mother's a scream!' (Nottingham: 280) (All quotes from Jennings and Madge 1987)

What shows up in these accounts is the wide range of possible responses to the event-as-broadcast, and this variety is directly connected with the circumstances in which listening takes place, and the problem of 'involvement'. The problem points in two different directions: should what is being broadcast adapt itself to, and seek to enter into, the contexts in which it is being heard; in which case it must fit in, in some way, with those involvements. Or, alternatively, should listeners put aside their own involvements and seek to enter into the context and circumstances of what is being broadcast. The latter disposition is expected from those who listen in to sacred events.

To succeed in this requires some effort at disengagement from the involvements of the circumstances in which listening is taking place. Thus, we can see that for one woman to create what for her is a properly reverential involvement with the event she feels she must go to a basement room where she will not be disturbed by the comings and goings of others and can follow the service closely from a book specially bought for that purpose (1). Or, if you are close to the radio, and in a private space, then a high involvement with the event can be achieved as is shown up by the emotions of the hairdresser's mother, an ardent fan (apparently) of Edward VIII whose abdication, the previous year, promoted his younger brother, George, to the throne (5). Elsewhere we can see that in spite of an environment which presumably creates the possibility of focused involvements (such as a cinema) it is possible, while some listen attentively, for others to fall asleep or perhaps have other more intimate involvements (2). In other settings, such as a café, the distractions are such that they

continuously intrude upon the sacred event which becomes, for someone coming in to the outer shop to buy tobacco, a momentary background to his concerns which he mimics when making his purchase (3). Finally, in the mixed
and 'open' context of an undergraduate common room, responses range from
loyal (or defiant) involvements on the part of the 'fascist' and embarrassed
laughter on occasion from the rest (4).

What shows up quite clearly in this sample is the impossibility, as the Dean
of Westminster foresaw, of controlling the behaviours of listeners to a solemn
sacred event. They could listen, if they so wished, in pubs with their hats on,
or in their bath with nothing on for that matter. Those present in a sacred
event (a coronation, or any religious service) are a self-selected or invited public whose behaviours are strongly expected to conform to the proprieties of
the occasion. They are expected to produce, at the least, outward and visible
tokens of involvement in the ceremonial events by arranging their demeanour
to match the occasion as it unfolds from moment to moment. Inwardly they
may be elsewhere, but outwardly they must give off the impression of being
there as a participant–supporter of the event. After all, in so far as they have
chosen (or been chosen) to be there, it is to be supposed that their disposition
is to take part, to be involved, in the successful 'bringing off' of the event.

None of these requirements falls upon absent listeners. The nature of the
occasion  so strongly binding in gatherings when all are in each others' presence – cannot impose itself on absent audiences who are free to listen (or
watch) in a wide range of possible settings and with a correspondingly wide
range of possible dispositions and demeanours. What shows up in many of
Mass Observation's reports on the day are real anxieties and uncertainties
about what is appropriate behaviour while listening to a sacred event. Was it
permissible to engage in other activities while listening: was it right and proper
to eat or drink, to smoke, to knit, to write letters, to talk to others? Should one
sit or stand or kneel at solemn moments? These are real dilemmas that arise
when an event goes beyond its own situation and enters into others. It becomes
something else or, more exactly, it has two independent existences at the same
time, in which one has strong behavioural constraints and the other does not.
Knowing how to behave is always knowing how to behave 'as the occasion
requires'. The uncertainties and anxieties of some listeners on 12 May 1937
arose from their finding themselves in a peculiar set of circumstances: one in
which two occasions (each with quite different demeanours) collided, creating
real doubts about what was the appropriate thing to do.

In its own context (its own time and place) any event creates and sustains
its own being, its own world. In its extended, relayed, mediated form it
simultaneously enters into other worlds and their ways of being. The event is
thus 'doubled': there is the event-in-situ, and (at the same time) the event-as-
broadcast, the former being embedded in the latter. It is not that broadcasting

creates the event that it transmits, but that in broadcasting the event it creates a new event – the event as broadcast. The locales of these two events are radically different. Each locale has its own circumstances and involvements. Broadcasting is *in* the locale of the event, but its there-being is for absent audiences in their locales. Its task is to re-présent the event in such a way as to proximate its eventfulness for those who are not there. What then are the dispositions of broadcasting (what are its involvements) as it goes about such a task? What is its *attitude* to the event?

III

'Attitude' here means stance, disposition or bearing, rather than any set of beliefs or values. It is what shows up in ways of doing. Thus, *how* the BBC (or any other broadcasting institution) does the job, the business, of covering an event reveals its attitude both to the event *and* to its audience. The coronation of 1953 is widely regarded, in retrospect, as having 'made' the BBC's television service. It was for television, as the coronation of 1937 had been for radio (Wood 1979), far and away the most ambitious and complex single broadcast ever undertaken. Its planning took over a year (Briggs 1979) and involved, initially, difficult negotiations with the royal household and its advisers, leaders of the Anglican church and the Conservative government about what kind of coverage might be allowed and on what terms.

'The Palace', writes Jonathan Dimbleby, 'was deeply suspicious of television, regarding it as a potentially vulgar intruder whose uncouth cameras and cables would destroy the dignity of the day' (Dimbleby 1975: 229). The Primates of Canterbury and York (who would conduct the ceremony) had grave doubts about the presence of television. Geoffrey Fisher, Archbishop of Canterbury, thought the television camera would be 'too enquiring'. After an initial refusal to allow television to be there at all in the Abbey, the Duke of Norfolk (the Earl Marshal, and responsible for organizing the whole of the coronation) conceded that television cameras would be allowed positions in the Abbey west of the screen, while cinema newsreel companies (Warner-Pathé and Gaumont British) could have camera positions east of the screen.

The significance of these decisions must be understood in relation to the architecture of Westminster Abbey:

> In Anglican as well as Roman Catholic liturgical spaces the congregation are often architecturally separated from the sacred priestly activities at the altar. Westminster Abbey is an excellent example: the screen supports the organ and access through it is rather small. It is the same in many cathedrals . . . and

it is important to notice that the sacred activities east of such screens cannot usually be seen by any large congregation. In Westminster Abbey the choir space is rather large and can house a substantial congregation as well as the singers, but if they are in great numbers, the (lay) congregation is all placed west of the screen. (Wolfe 1984: 493)

So it was to be for the coronation. The television cameras would be restricted to the west nave where the assembled dignitaries were to be seated. They would have no visible access to the ceremony taking place east of the screen. But why had the newsreel cameras been given such privileged access? Because they, unlike the television camera, would not violate what Fisher called 'the rightful intimacy of the service'. Film cameras, as Kenneth Wolfe points out, 'did not carry the watchful, curious eye of the public at their sets' (ibid.: 498). A more respectful attitude to the event could be induced in the darkness of the cinema. And finally (and conclusively), film could be edited later if those in charge so wished. The last thing Fisher did, on Coronation Day, was to approve the edited filmed version of the ceremony, hastily put together by the newsreel companies.

Fisher's initial attitude to television chimed in with that of the Prime Minister. In the House of Commons Churchill declared that while 'modern mechanical arrangements' (he meant television) should be used to enable the public to see into the Abbey, they should only be able to show what the distinguished congregation there could see, and not what was seen by 'high ecclesiastical dignitaries and state functionaries . . . whose duties require them to be close to the Sovereign'. It was not fitting that the ceremony should be presented as if it were a theatrical performance (ibid.: 497). But that, of course, is exactly what it was. What it amounted to was that the authorities disliked the idea of the general public having a more privileged access to the event than the privileged few in the Abbey itself. Churchill did not want the population at large to have a better view than he had. And added to this was an underlying fear that the presence of television would undermine the sacredness, the mystery, of the occasion.

The BBC's attitude was that it was essential that the young queen be crowned before all the people. It would give a new kind of legitimacy, one without any historical precedent, to her coronation. Their stance was thus, in the first instance, on behalf of their viewers and listeners for whom they claimed a right of access to the event as a whole. They had, of course, other motives, not the least of which was the amount of time, effort and expense that they had committed to the coverage of the day on radio and television. They were also well aware that their own performance on the day could enormously enhance their institutional prestige as well as displaying the potency of the new medium of television. But first and last in this, as in all claims made by broadcasting of a right to cover public events, access to which had hitherto been restricted to those present at the event itself, the interests of the listening and viewing publics were advocated and advanced by the broadcasters.

In the event, after several months of intensive lobbying by the BBC (including a large-scale demonstration in the Abbey, for the Archbishop of Canterbury and the Duke of Norfolk, of how television would cover the event, east and west of the screen), permission was granted for full coverage of the ceremony. The way the event would be covered by the television cameras (there were to be five in the Abbey, four to the east of the screen) was now meticulously planned. It had been agreed with the authorities that there should be no close-ups of any person during the ceremony. Furthermore, there would be no picture of any person during (a) the anointing, (b) the communion prayers or (c) of anyone kneeling in worship. A distinction was made between ordinary and symbolic shots. The latter would be used during such moments as the anointing and would focus on available features in the Abbey such as 'the altar cross, the Coronation Plate, or some Abbey stonework'. The whole service would be shot in a mix of mid-shot, long shot and symbolic shot – the latter, it was estimated, might amount to at least a third of the total coverage of the service (Chaney 1986: 132).

If, in the first place, the struggle over access to the event was one fought by the BBC with the authorities on behalf of its audience, there was no subsequent disagreement between the broadcasters and the powers-that-were about the presentation of the ceremony in particular and the day as a whole. Something of the care with which the BBC planned its coverage shows up in the detailed plans of the camera shots to be used in the service. But this is merely a single instance of the thought that went into broadcasting's preparations for the day as a whole. That the day was a triumph for television was testified to by press comments at the time. For Peter Black of the *Daily Mail*, the coronation in the Abbey was 'a sublime experience'. For *The Times* the television coverage showed up 'for the first time the true nature of the occasion'. In the *Sunday Times* Maurice Wiggin hailed 'Tuesday's magnificent broadcast' which, amongst other things, served to expose the initial suspicions of the authorities towards the presence of television as a historical anachronism. He went on to offer this deeply perceptive analysis of the implications of the new medium of television for public life:

> Television introduces a new and revolutionary element into the art or craft of reporting. Even now one has not fully appreciated the nature of this element, which is often called 'actuality'. On Tuesday it was possible to catch myself wondering if this deeply significant ceremonial were *really* taking place as one watched, or if it were just a film. Almost too good to be true. The power of 'being' in two places at once is the newest that man has

wrested from reluctant nature. . . . The social implications of the miracle are endlessly debatable. No doubt it is possible to have too much of a good thing: but although a nation of onlookers would be a bad consummation, against that danger must be balanced the advantage of a vastly heightened awareness of other people's ways of life. (Quoted in Dimbleby 1975: 238)

The double articulation of an event – its power of being in two places at once – is mediated through the revolutionary 'art or craft' of actuality reporting. This, too, has a double articulation: it is both a showing and a telling. The camera 'shows', the commentator 'tells'. How do they combine to produce an event as the kind of thing that it is found to be? If something (a coronation) shows up as sublime and magnificent, as an apotheosis of 'earthly splendour' – how is this, in part, an effect of the way of its showing-and-telling? Any event, in the manner of its doing, reveals the nature and the extent of the care, concern, thought and attention that has gone into making it that which it shows up as being. A coronation is not, in any 'natural' way, a magnificent occasion. It could be a rackety, shambolic affair, as was the coronation of the young Queen Victoria in 1837. 'It was completely unrehearsed; the clergy lost their place in the order of the service; the choir was pitifully inadequate; the Archbishop of Canterbury put the ring on a finger that was too big for it; and two of the trainbearers talked throughout the ceremony' (Cannadine 1983: 118). The monarchy in the 19th century was merely the symbolic head of aristocratic 'society'. In the 20th century it became the symbolic head of the whole society, of the nation at large. It became so by virtue, in part, of the new kind of publicness with which it was invested by modern media and especially radio and television. The coronation of Elizabeth II was the most singular incident in this process of transformation. It depended on close collaboration with those responsible for the management of the event in the Abbey, but that event was distinct from the event as shown and told by television.

Richard Dimbleby, whose commentary on the ceremony in the Abbey was universally praised at the time, returned there later in the evening for a reflective postscript on the day. He observed, to his dismay, the mess left behind in the triforium by the nobility:

It seemed to me amazing that even on this occasion we could not break ourselves of one of our worst national habits. Tiers and tiers of stalls on which the peers had been sitting were covered with sandwich wrappings, sandwiches, morning newspapers, fruit peel, sweets and even a few empty miniature bottles. (Dimbleby 1975: 235)

He made, of course, no mention of this in his retrospective thoughts on the day which brought to a close television's coverage of the coronation. Nor did such things show up in his commentary, or on camera, during the ceremony itself. Rather, the focused attentiveness of both cameras and commentary was painstakingly planned to screen out the possibility of anything untoward, anything that might mar the occasion, showing up in the live unfolding of the event.

A year's work went into the BBC's planning for Coronation Day. All its immense resources – for both radio and television – were fully deployed. There were 95 sound commentary positions along the route and in the Abbey (in 1937 there had been 17). There were 21 cameras (in 1937 there had been three), 16 of them at different points along the route from the Palace to the Abbey. The sheer weight of the resources deployed contributed to establishing a sense of the significance (the weightiness) of the occasion. If the BBC was, as it claimed to be, a *national* institution, such a claim was, as it well knew, to be tried and tested on great national occasions such as a coronation. At the very least the BBC showed that it had the technical resources to do justice to the nature and scale of the day. But it needed, of course, to do much more than that.

The *liveness* of broadcast coverage is the key to its impact, since it offers the real sense of access to an event in its moment-by-moment unfolding. This *presencing*, this re-présenting of a present occasion to an absent audience, can powerfully produce the effect of being-there, of being involved (caught up) in the here-and-now of the occasion. This being in the moment, especially in its 'unfolding', creates the mood of expectancy: what's happening? what's next? The 'edged' character of live broadcasting is shared by all social occasions – the ever-present danger of being on the edge of the possibility of going wrong, of the event being, in some way, derailed. It is this that creates an underlying mood of excitement and anticipation: will it, won't it, come off? There is always an element of risk or daring in any human, social occasion, the measure of whose success is offset against the known possibilities of how far it might have failed. The greater the aspiration, the greater the calamity of failure. And of course, the greater the triumph if it succeeds – especially if it should succeed 'beyond all expectations'.

This is by way of beginning to suggest why one day's broadcasting might require a whole year's planning to bring it off as not just another day, but as rare and special. For it to be such, it must be seemingly effortlessly accomplished as such. For it to be found by anyone and everyone as special it must appear as 'naturally' so. If the effort 'shows' then the sought-for effect will fail. It must be obviously, transparently the thing that it is. Thus, the labour of bringing it off as such must not show *as* laboured. This does not mean that the effort does not show, rather that – if well-done – the effort is subsumed into the event as constitutive of it; so that the event 'really and truly' shows up as that which it is meant to be. The mark of professionalism in broadcasting is the way in which the thought, effort and care that goes into pre-production appears in the moment of production as 'natural', as apt for the occasion, whose nature is thereby established in whatever way – as magnificent, for instance, in the case of the coronation.

Richard Dimbleby spent six months preparing for his commentary on the coronation. His notes still survive:

Pages of carefully prepared commentary, phrases and sentences worked at again and again, words crossed out and reinserted, and crossed out again. The days of rehearsal, exact notes about the precise length of each section of the ceremony, allowed him . . . to write much of his commentary beforehand, and then deliver it, with only minor variations, at the proper moment. . . . The art of the commentary (and he was never in any doubt, as he frequently insisted, that it was 'an art') on this occasion was for it to become in essence part of the ceremony:

| Richard Dimbleby: | 'Her Majesty returns the orb and the Archbishop now places upon the fourth finger of her right hand the ring, the ring whereupon is set a sapphire and on it a ruby cross, this is often called the ring of England.' |
|---|---|
| Archbishop: | 'Receive the ring of kingly dignity and the seal of catholic faith and as thou art this day consecrated head and prince so may you continue steadfastly as the defender of Christ's religion that being rich in faith and blessed in all good works you may reign with him who is the king of kings to whom be the glory for ever and ever. Amen.' |
| Richard Dimbleby: | 'Now the Dean of Westminster brings to the Archbishop the sceptre with the cross and the rod with the diamond while the Chancellor of the Duchy of Lancaster offers to the Queen the traditional glove of white kid lined with silk embroidered with thistles, shamrocks and English oak leaves and acorns.' |
| Archbishop: | 'Receive the royal sceptre, the ensign of kingly power and justice, receive the rod of equity.' |

(Dimbleby 1975: 233–4)

The effect, of course, is not simply in the words, but in the voice. Dimbleby's voice – measured, dignified, even-toned, solemn – was already well established as the voice of the BBC on ceremonial, state occasions. His voice established a particular mood, a disposition, an attitude to the event of which it spoke. By the time of the coronation, as Jonathan Dimbleby remarks in his ever-perceptive biography of his father, Richard Dimbleby's attitude to the monarchy had developed into an 'absolute but considered devotion. . . . His belief in the monarchy was not dispassionate; it was to partake in an emotional experience *in which his whole being was involved*' (ibid.: 225, 227; emphasis added). It was this involvement that showed up for millions in his commentary on the coronation, an involvement that was more than merely personal, for Dimbleby *was* the BBC on such occasions. So that what spoke through his voice was not just, or even primarily, Richard Dimbleby's thoughts and feelings, but a whole institutional disposition or mood – a mood that was found by the vast majority of viewers to have been utterly and entirely appropriate to the nature of this particular occasion.

But not all institutional dispositions on that day were found to be so appropriate. There was much indignation, after the event, about American network television's coverage of the coronation. It was not possible, in 1953, for live coverage to be transmitted to the United States, or elsewhere round the world. The BBC made simultaneous 'telerecordings' of the event-as-broadcast and, as soon as it was finished, five hours of telerecordings were dispatched, via 'operation pony express' (the RAF's codename for the exercise), to Goose Bay in Newfoundland. There they were picked up by two of the major networks – NBC and ABC – who raced to be the first to bring the coronation to American viewers. An estimated 85 million people in the United States watched the coronation programmes.

The networks had promised not to interrupt the Abbey service with advertisements and, in general, to conduct their coronation broadcasts 'with the greatest dignity and good taste'. Such pledges were hard to maintain in practice. Ed Murrow's CBS programme was interrupted by a large number of commercials (for which the *New York Times* apologized in a leader, two days later), including one which made play with the fact that a car could be called a 'queen'. But it was NBC's coverage that created uproar in Britain. Their *Coronation Coverage* began at 5.30 a.m. New York time. It was broken into for spot announcements, news items and an interview with W. V. Kaltenbourn, one of the most influential political commentators in American broadcasting, who had made his name during the Munich crisis of 1938. Assessing the significance of the event, Kaltenbourn wondered whether this was a 'show put on by the British for a psychological boost to their somewhat shaky empire'. There was worse to come. A one-minute spot for a deodorant was introduced just before the network returned to BBC coverage of the anointing. And worst of all, in the middle of the communion service, NBC had a mock interview with J. Fred Muggs (the network's mascot – 'a charismatic chimpanzee') who was solemnly asked, 'Do they have a coronation where you come from?' Great was the indignation in the British press at these irrefutable proofs of the awfulness of American culture and commercial television in particular. It was a nasty setback for the enthusiastic lobby in Britain who were urging forward the introduction, in the UK, of commercial television supported by spot advertising (all details from Briggs 1979: 470–3).

## IV

By 1958 commercial television was well and truly established in Britain, so that when permission was given by the Prime Minister (Harold Macmillan) for the first live television coverage of the State Opening of Parliament, it was granted to both the BBC and ITV. In allowing television to present, live, for the first time the Queen's speech from the throne in the Palace of Westminster, Macmillan made it clear that it was to be treated as a ceremonial occasion and not a political event (Dimbleby 1975: 326). The BBC's Outside Broadcasting Unit would provide visual coverage of the event for both the BBC and ITV. Each, however, would provide its own commentary: Richard Dimbleby, of course, for the BBC, and Robin Day for ITV. Thus, exactly the same event – in visual terms – on both channels would have a different spoken commentary on each.

Here are the two commentaries on the closing stages of the event as the Queen left the Great Hall of Westminster having delivered her speech from the throne:

Dimbleby: Later today, in the Commons, the debate and doubtless the argument over the Government's programme will begin. But for now, as her Majesty returns to the Robing Rooms and thence to Buckingham Palace, she leaves behind in all of us, a memory of a State Occasion at its most magnificent.

Day: The Queen will go back to Buckingham Palace. The Crown will go back to the Tower of London. All the scarlet and ermine will go back to wherever they came from. And Parliament will go back to work.

The final shot was of that symbolic variety first developed for the coverage of the coronation. Over a medium close-up of the empty throne, and as suitably solemn music was faded up, the last words of Dimbleby and Day were as follows:

Dimbleby: The Throne remains, rich and shining, near and yet remote; the symbol of this rare meeting of the Queen, the Lords and Commons – the Three Estates of Parliament. And so begins, with ceremony that springs from the very roots of our democratic history, the fourth session of the three hundredth Parliament of the Realm.

Day: Everyone is wondering at Westminster what Government will write the next speech from this Throne. Before Her Majesty sits on it again there may be a General Election. That is when

we have our say. And what Her Majesty reads from this Throne
depends on what we put in the ballot box.
(Dimbleby 1975: 328–9)

The same event as visually displayed: two quite different dispositions and
demeanours *towards* it, displayed in the spoken commentaries of Dimbleby for
the BBC, Day for ITV. What shows up in these differences? Most immediately,
perhaps, the deference of the BBC to the pomp and ceremony, the outward
signs of authority; the brisk indifference of the new commercial television
service to such things. The disposition of the BBC is towards the state; that
of ITV is towards its viewers. Their alignments in respect of the event are
different. They pick out different phenomena. They point up, remark upon
and notice different things and interpret them differently because each has a
different for-the-sake-of-which: for the BBC the audience-as-nation, for ITV
the audience-as-citizens.

It is not that one of these versions of the event is more true than the other.
Both illuminate different truths about the event, truths that are not external to
it (i.e. simply in the commentaries) but there-to-be-found in the event itself.
Dimbleby's auratic interpretation takes it at face value and agrees with the
event's self-presentation. Day's 'post-auratic' interpretation sees the same thing
but situates it differently. Day sets this event against the routine daily life of
parliament which he interprets as its *real* business. These differences can not
be reconciled, but neither do they cancel each other out. Taken together they
point up a sea-change in public attitudes. Historical studies always try to catch
what's variously called the spirit of the age (the *Zeitgeist*), the climate of opinion, the structure of feeling, the signs of the times. None of these expressions
quite catches the phenomenon of *mood*. Mood is 'how it is', where 'it' is something like historical temporality (the mood of the times) as manifest in occasions and things, and in collective and individual dispositions and behaviours.
We think of mood as subjective (being in a mood), but for anyone to have the
kinds of mood they do rests on their being publicly available to have (how else
would one – or anyone else – recognize that one *was* in a mood?). That is, mood
in the first instance is public in character. Mood is revelatory or disclosing. It
shows the climate of feelings, opinions or attitudes. What is revealed in this
particular case is a transition from an older, deeply rooted unquestioning mood
of deference towards authority to a newer, more questioning and democratic
mood. In broadcasting, as always, there is a double disclosure: of the attitudes
of those *in* the event and of broadcasting towards the event. These two sets of
attitudes do not *necessarily* coincide. Whether they do or not, in the 'age of
television' that is coming into being at this time, public mood begins to show
up in such ways as are revealed in broadcast commentaries on public events.
What shows up here is not an isolated 'moment', but an aspect of a wider,

pervasive change in the public climate – the atmosphere, the 'feel' of publicly available (sayable) opinion.


## V


One of Heidegger's many remarkable 'rediscoveries' in *Being and Time* is that of the situated, experiential character of time and space. He reminds us that both 'show up' for us always in relation to our situated being-in-the-world. We experience, assess and 'measure' time and space proximally in relation to our own here-and-now, so that both show up, on a scale of 'more-or-less', as near or far from where we presently are: 'here' and 'there', 'now' and 'then'. It is an important part of historical, 'human' geography to recapture the proximal experience of time and space as it has been at different moments in the past. Cannadine observes that, in the early 19th century, the absence of anything like modern media made even the greatest of royal ceremony something of a mystery to all but the most literate and wealthy. In particular, there was no cheap, pictorial press to circulate and make available images of the monarch. Under such circumstances 'great royal ceremonies were not so much shared, corporate events as remote, inaccessible group rites, performed for the benefit of the few rather than the edification of the many' (Cannadine 1983: 111). I have wondered how the public world was experienced at the time that broadcasting intervened in the world. How 'far' was public life from ordinary situated existence? What difference did radio and television make to the 'space' between public and private existence?

One can glean an answer to such a question from what scraps remain of how people felt about the impact of a radio set on their lives, back in the early days of broadcasting. Here is a prize-winning essay written in 1923 for a newspaper competition on 'What radio has meant to me':

> I live in a dull, drab colliery village as far removed from real country as from real city life, a bus ride from third rate entertainments and a considerable journey from any educational, musical or social advantages of a first class sort. In such an atmosphere life becomes rusty and apathetic. Into this monotony comes a good radio set and my little world is transformed.

And here, a few years later, is a letter to *Radio Times*:

> Many of your readers must be office workers. They must know what sort of a life is that of a clerk in a provincial city – a tram-ride to the office, lunch in a tea-shop or saloon bar, a tram-ride home. You daren't spend much on amusements – the pictures and that – because you've got your holidays to

think of. We have no Trade Unions and we don't grumble, but it's not an easy life. Please don't think I'm complaining. I'm only writing to say how much wireless means to me and thousands of the same sort. It's a real magic carpet. Before it was a fortnight at Rhyl, and that was all the travelling I did that wasn't on a tram. Now I hear the Boat Race and the Derby, and the opening of the Menai Bridge. There are football matches some Saturdays, and talks by famous men and women who have travelled and can tell us about places.

The sense of radio as magical, as lighting up lives bounded by monotonous and narrow routines is palpable. Whereas the public world beforehand was over the hills and far away, now it is close at hand and graspable. Its eventfulness enters into uneventful lives giving them new texture and substance. Walter Benjamin, in the 1930s, tried to analyse the impact of 'mechanical reproduction' on traditional art. He argued that its effect was to destroy their 'aura', that halo which surrounds the art-object investing it with authenticity. This authenticity, Benjamin argued, was partly the effect of its rootedness in tradition and partly of its uniqueness and distance from everyday experience. All are undermined by modern media (he had in mind particularly photography and cinema) that multiply the image and 'pry it out of its shell', bringing it into the world and closer to people, so that they no longer have to 'go' to the object – it comes to them. Thus, art becomes intrinsically more available both by its multiplication and by its greatly valorized accessibility (Benjamin 1973). If the same can be said for public events and persons, do they lose their aura by becoming not just available, but available in an unlimited, unbounded way?

Benjamin's attitude to modern media is free of nostalgia. He does not regard them as inauthentic by comparison with older, traditional 'authentic' cultural forms. The aura that modern media destroy is that of mystique: that process whereby art sought to preserve its dignity and worth – to maintain its purity – by withdrawing from the 'bad reality' of the world (art for art's sake). This process of withdrawal is a phenomenological distancing – of putting 'space' between the art-object (and its producer) and the situated character of everyday life – thereby declaring that the concerns of art and of daily life are no longer interconnected. In a similar way the mystique of sacred events may be destroyed by the prying eye of television – or so the authorities worried, who wanted to be able to control behaviours, to enforce respect for the occasion.

We have shown how this was impossible, and how a wide range of responses from the reverent to the frankly irreverent were all permissible, because radio and television create the possibility of participation without involvement for people who are neither present at nor necessarily committed to the event in any way. But, at the same time, we have seen how the aura of events is powerfully enhanced by the *liveness* of radio and television. The aura of *presence* is that edged halo of expectation and anticipation that includes the build-up to an occasion and that runs right through to its conclusion. It is this that marks it *as* an occasion, that makes it stand out as eventful. In attending to the care-structure of broadcast occasions we have shown how the production of them as occasions makes them so. If they are outstandingly eventful it is because they show up as such against a backdrop of humdrum everyday existence as mediated routinely in broadcasting's daily output. It is the one-off, exceptional character of great occasions that helps to make them so, and that contributes to the aura with which they are invested.

In the end, we have shown, it is a question of attitude; of demeanours and dispositions, of behaviours that are or are not *towards* the production of a human occasion as that which it aspires to be. It is, of course, a question, too, of resources and their availability (or not) that help to make an occasion so *memorable* that it stays forever with those who took part in it. Work on social memory shows that in our kind of world the things that people remember are of this sort. For most British people like me, in middle age, our first memory of television is the coronation. Everyone remembers the assassination and funeral of John F. Kennedy. And so on. Even if only for the duration of the moment in which they are produced, radio and television create events as singularities that are part of a common, collective, available, shareable public life. They are marked up not only on the public calendar of 'history' but also on the private calendars of people's lives.

Such broadcast events may be truly magical by virtue of that impossible possibility which they create, and which Maurice Wiggin noted as he watched the coronation – the power of being in two places at once. It is not just that radio and television *compress* time and space. They create new possibilities of being: of being in two places at once, or two times at once. This magic *shows* most clearly for us when we experience mediated occasions in the fullness of what they presence for us. This will vary from one person to another. For me it was watching The Masters from Augusta a few years ago. It is the one event in television's sporting calendar that I watch 'religiously' each year. Golf tournaments are played over four days and the build-up to the climax is slow but relentless. It all comes down, as they say, to the last nine holes on the last day. On this occasion, Sandy Lyle was tied for the lead coming into the final hole on the final day. I held my breath as he drove – into the bunker on the left, 180 yards from the pin. I was sure he'd blown it. He needed a par to go into a play-off, a birdie to win. Surely impossible. Lyle stepped into the bunker with a seven iron – I could hardly bear to watch – and hit the shot of a life-time. He picked the ball up cleanly, sweetly from the sand and it soared to the heart of the sloping green, pitched 20 feet past the hole, stopped and slowly rolled back to within ten feet. He had *done* it, and I wept with relief, excitement and sheer joy at the mastery of that moment. Minutes later Lyle holed out and became the first British golfer to win The Masters. I can see it, feel it, I am *there*, now, as I write. *That*, for me, was magical. It was an experience that I still *own*; that is part of my ownmost being. Not – to tell the truth – *such* a big deal, but nevertheless something that was and is 'for me'; an experience that I possess, a cherishable, unforgettable memory. And so it is, in different ways, for everyone, by virtue of broadcasting's power of re-presencing. The liveness of events is their *dasein*: their magical, edged, unfolding, self-disclosing, unpredictable, mood-creating being. It is this that is made available in quite new ways, for me or anyone, by the care structures of radio and television.

# 5

---

## *Authenticity*

A witness says what is and what is true.
(Hans–Georg Gadamer 1994: 61)

I

In broadcasting, communicative entitlements can be sorted into those that entitle speakers to their opinions and those that entitle them to their experiences. The former are allowed only to public persons by virtue of their status as politicians, experts, pundits, etc., but the latter are more democratic. Experiences are permitted to anyone, because they can happen to any kind of person (public or private) so long as they can talk about them. For to have an experience is, among other things, to be entitled to talk about it, to have something tellable. Harvey Sacks suggests that, for some teenage Americans, the point of kissing is to be able later to describe it to friends ('kiss and tell'), and everyone knows that in some 'epic' moment one of the things one finds oneself thinking is that this will make a good story if (hopefully) one 'lives to tell the tale'.

Sacks develops his notion of communicative entitlement within the context of ordinary, daily life and the routine business of, as he puts it, 'doing being ordinary':

> Among the ways you go about doing 'being an ordinary person' is to spend your time in usual ways, having ordinary thoughts, usual interests, so that all you have to do to be an ordinary person in the evening is turn on the TV set. Now, the trick is to see that it is not that it *happens* that you are doing what lots of ordinary people are doing, but that you know that the way to do 'having a usual evening' for anybody, is to do that. It is not that you happen

to decide, gee, I'll watch TV tonight, but that you are making a job of, and finding an answer to how to do 'being ordinary' tonight. . . . One part of the job is that you have to know what anybody/everybody is doing; doing ordinarily. Further, you have to have that available to do. There are people who do not have that that available to do (e.g. prisoners), and who specifically cannot be ordinary. (Sacks 1992 vol. 2: 216)

Now the 'awesome, overwhelming fact' is that ordinary life and ordinary experience have no storyable features. There is, literally, nothing to say about it. 'What did you do at work/home/school/the office today?' 'Nothing.' It is not, of course, that in some cosmic, existential sense, *nothing* happened, but that what happened was in every way usual, routine and ordinary. There is nothing to say about all this because it is known and understood between the speakers that all that has happened has happened umpteen times before. And if you did try to make more of that question than the occasion warranted you could end up in difficulties:

> If you come home and report what the grass looked like along the freeway; that there were four noticeable shades of green, some of which just appeared yesterday because of the rain, then there may well be some tightening up on the part of your recipient. And if you were to do it routinely, then people might figure that there is something odd about you; that you are pretentious. You might find them jealous of you. You might lose friends. That is to say, you might want to check out the costs of venturing into making your life an epic. (Ibid.: 219)

George Eliot makes the same point in *Middlemarch*: 'If we had a keen vision of all ordinary life it would be like hearing the grass grow and the squirrel's heartbeat, and we should die of that roar which lies on the other side of silence'. It is essential for ordinary existence that the meaningful background remains *as* the background in order to preserve everyday life as an environment in which each and everyone of us can operate effectively by virtue of its utterly normal, taken-for-granted, known-and-familiar, yet deeply meaningful character. This meaningfulness *must* appear, in effect, as its opposite. If we could grasp it in its fullness its roar would overwhelm us.

Thus, in everyday existence, it is only when something out of the ordinary takes place that experiences (which are thus, by definition, extraordinary) happen to people and subsequently and consequently they become entitled (if they wish) to talk about it. But even then they will talk about it in such a way as to make the extraordinary, ordinary; the disastrous, mundane. 'It is really remarkable', says Sacks, 'to see people's efforts to achieve the "nothing happened" sense of really catastrophic events', taking, by way of illustration, newspaper reports of what aeroplane passengers think when a hijacking takes place:

I was walking up towards the front of the airplane and I saw the stewardess standing facing the cabin and a fellow standing with a gun in her back. And my first thought was he's showing her the gun, and then I realized that couldn't be, and then it turned out he was hijacking the plane. (Ibid.: 220)

Imagine, says Sacks, rewriting the monumental events of the Old Testament with ordinary people having gone through them.


## II


Broadcasting is a very-much taken-for-granted part of the orderly, unremarkable ordinariness of everyday life: no more than the usual programmes at their usual times on any particular day. For broadcasting to appear in this way – as part of the seen but unnoticed background of day-to-day life – it must follow that it does the job of being ordinary very well, and that even if, on radio and television, people are laying claim to extraordinary things that have happened to them, or that they witnessed, they do so in unremarkable ways as people ordinarily do in ordinary life. So that a disaster in the news will be an ordinary disaster by virtue of the ways in which it is talked about by those caught up in it, by reporters and eyewitnesses. And it may be the case, that if by chance you happen to be a witness of a disaster, you will want later to check out if it was on radio or television, simply to confirm that it was the disaster that you thought it to be:

A:  Say did you see anything in the paper last night or hear anything on the local radio, .hh Ruth Henderson and I drove, down, to Ventura yesterday

B:  Mm hm

A:  And on the way home we saw the – most gosh awful wreck

B:  Oh:::

A:  we have ev- I've ever seen. I've never seen a car smashed into sm- uch a small space

B:  Oh:::

A:  It was smashed – .hh from the front and back both. It must have been in- caught in between two car::s

B:  Mm hm, uh huh

A:  Must have run into a car and then another car smashed into it and there were people laid out and covered on the pavement

B:  Mm

A:  We were parked there for quite a while. But I was going to, listen to the local r-news and haven't done it

B:  No I haven't had my radio on either

A:   Well I had my television on, but I was listening to the blast off you
     know
B:   Mm hm
A:   The uh ah astronauts
B:   Yeah
A:   And I didn't get any local news
B:   Uh huh
A:   And I wondered
B:   Uh huh, no, I haven't had it on. . . .[1]

                                                     (Ibid.: 241)

Consider the common-sense attitudes to the media that are embedded in this
brief exchange. There is first of all the natural assumption that any ordinary
person these days has quite routine access to the press, radio and television and
hence that what is in or on them is an utterly unproblematic conversational
resource. Further, caller has a clear sense of what are, for the media, newsworthy
topics and how they 'rate' as news stories. For it is taken for granted that car
wrecks *are* newsworthy, and that this kind of car wreck will be reported in *local*
as distinct from national news. Thus, caller is quite specific that she intended
to 'listen to the local r-news' because she knew (again quite unproblematically)
that this would be the most likely place to find reports of what she had witnessed.
All this is common ground between caller and receiver, whose affirmative and
affiliative response-tokens (mm uhuh) indicate an unproblematic acceptance
of the implicit assumptions and evaluations in what caller is saying.

But the focal point I would like to consider is the way in which caller uses
the media to validate her own personal assessment of her experience. It may
be, as Sacks suggests, that the media are used by caller to get into the topic of
the crash because she can simply presume them as part of the common stock
of knowledge between herself and receiver. But this is not sufficient to account
for why caller should, as she concludes her story, make a point of the efforts
she made to check out whether what she saw was reported in the local press:

A:   And I didn't get any local news
B:   Uh huh
A:   And I wondered
B:   Uh huh, no, I haven't had it on and I don't uh get the paper, and uhm
A:   It wasn't in the paper last night, I looked
B:   Uh huh

---

[1]   This fragment of talk between two Californian women in the late sixties is discussed at
some length by Sacks (1992: 229–41). It occurs some way into the phone-call and Sacks uses
it to explore his thoughts on witnessing and communicative entitlements, including the
question of who 'owns' an experience (i.e. is it transferable?).

The media are, I suggest, a crucial support for speaker's claim that what she saw was 'the most gosh awful wreck' she had ever seen. This, after all, is only a subjective assessment, but it takes on an objective character if it can be shown (if speaker is able to say) that it made the local news as a news story. *That* is proof that it was an awful crash. For there is a scale for disasters, as there is for most newsworthy things, that runs from the purely personal to the global. 'I saw it and I thought it was bad. Later I checked the radio and the papers and they reported it. So it was as bad as I thought it was.' And yet it wasn't *that* bad.

Notice how, although caller claims it was the worst wreck she had ever seen, there is absolutely nothing to suggest that this was in any way the worst experience she herself has ever had. We have seen that caller treats the wreck as a routine wreck within a scalar ranking of events of this kind. She knows to look for it in local, not national media. At the same time she has adjusted, quite unselfconsciously, the scale of the event in her own life. It was not the most pressing thing she had in mind in making the call (if it were, she would have mentioned it first: just as television reports the most pressing news first and saves the lighter items for later). The event happened yesterday ('did you see anything in the paper last night'), whereas if it were *that* important you would ring immediately to check if other people knew about it (as they did when the news flashes reported the shooting of President Kennedy). And thus the event, although it was the worst of its kind in the experience of caller (and fateful for those caught up in it), had only a minor significance in her life. And it didn't even make the local papers when it should have done if it were to rank as a newsworthy story (i.e. last night). It was a background event in caller's own life and more generally unremarkable as the fall of Icarus was in Brueghel's painting and in Auden's poem *Musée des Beaux Arts:*

About suffering they were never wrong,
The Old Masters: how well they understood
Its human position; how it takes place
While someone else is eating or opening a window or just walking dully
    along; . . .

In Brueghel's *Icarus*, for instance: how everything turns away
Quite leisurely from the disaster; the ploughman may
Have heard the splash, the forsaken cry,
But for him it was not an important failure; the sun shone
As it had to on the white legs disappearing into the green
Water; and the expensive delicate ship that must have seen
Something amazing, a boy falling out of the sky,
Had somewhere to get to and sailed calmly on.

Thus art, it would seem, takes the same natural stance to disasters (to newsworthy or tellable events) that we ordinarily do in our ordinary daily life. Caller not only got to, but returned from Ventura, and the crash, awful though it was, was but one of the things that happened in her yesterday.

In a lecture two weeks later Sacks begins with the following fragment of talk which continues where the previous left off:

A:    Boy it was a bad one though
B:    Well that's too bad
A:    Kinda // (freak)-
B:    You know, I looked and looked in the paper- I think I told you f- for
      that uh f-fall over at the Bowl that night. And I never saw a thing about
      it, and I // looked in the next couple of evenings
A:    Mm hm
      (1.0)
B:    Never saw a th- a mention of it
A:    I didn't see that either.[2]

Sacks was interested, in this lecture, 'in doing provings. For example provings of what someone heard, or provings of that (*sic*) a story is similar' (Sacks 1992, vol. 2: 252). Clearly, one of the things that both women are doing, in this and the preceding fragment, is proving (testing) their own personal assessments of the newsworthiness (the tellability) of events by checking for them in news-papers, or radio or television to back them up. Newsworthiness here means that the event is worthy of telling: i.e. that you can make a moral claim upon the attention of another because of the weightiness (the worthwhileness) of what you have to tell. In our kind of society the media are a proof (a confirma-tion) of the seriousness of a witnessed event. But more than this: it is almost as if the speakers are uncertain about the validity of their own assessments with-out the media to confirm them.[3] If this is so, then we might see that for these ordinary people, in their ordinary talk, the media serve to authenticate their own assessments of what they have experienced. And it is surely part of every-one's experience that, after having been present as participant or spectator at some kind of event (a play, a football match, a protest march for instance), one tends to look out, in the media, for reviews or reports or replays to confirm that whatever-it-was was as good or as bad or in general as one had experienced it (with a corresponding sense of let-down, disbelief or anger if this should con-tradict one's own assessment).

---

[2]    Lecture 5. '"First" and "second" stories; Topical coherence; Storing and recalling experi-ences' (Sacks 1992, vol. 2: 249).

[3]    For why else would they make a point – as they both do – of scanning their local newspa-pers for reports on what they saw (though it's not conclusive that the speaker in the second fragment saw the fall at the Bowl)? We don't usually make a commitment to scan the news in this way. We simply monitor it in a non-committal way.

## III

A distinction should be made, at this point, between experience in general and in particular. Experience is what accumulates to individuals in the course of a lifetime as know-how, practical knowledge or wisdom. To be experienced is, in this sense, to be able to draw on knowledge from past actions and doings and to apply it in present circumstances.

1    There were other houses and persons were in there.
2    And one of them was a quarter mast- a quartermaster sergeant
3    in the national army-
4    in the free state army, and an experienced person.
5    And he was looking out the window and he saw Jim's body.
6    And he saw four soldiers (.) come into the (.)
7    through the alley-way he could see them coming.
8    He saw one soldier (.) move to the left (.)
9    and the other three .hh came in through the (.) opening.
10   And Mr (.) Porter, the quartermaster sergeant,
11   he was watching and after a couple of minutes,
12   after they walked out he saw Jim raise his head
13   and look towards them.
14   And he says 'my God that young fellow doesn't know
15   there's another soldier behind him.'
16   And he saw Jim's body (*claps hands twice*) jump twice.
17   The soldier from a distance of five foot behind
18   fired two further bullets into his back
19   and then walked over and kicked his body into the gutter.

(*Creggan*: ITV 1980)

The story concerns the killing of one of the 13 Derry men and boys shot dead by the British army during a civil rights march in the city on what came to be called Bloody Sunday, 31 January 1972. It is told by one of the people who took part in the march on that day, but who did not actually see Jim's death. That was seen by Mr Porter, a soldier in the Irish ('free state') army whose story of what he saw is retold by the narrator. We may reasonably assume that the narrator has heard the story first-hand from Mr Porter, since he is quoted directly (14–15). But why should the narrator (who is retelling another person's story for television) make the point that Mr Porter was *an experienced person* (4)? In what sense is he experienced and how is that relevant for the story?

The phrase is strategically placed at the start of the story not just to validate the authority of Mr Porter's account, but to cue us (as recipients of the story) to see and understand what happens through Mr Porter's eyes. In particular, it cues us to make sense of Mr Porter's exclamation when he sees Jim (already shot and injured) raise his head. Why, on seeing this, should he say 'My God, that young fellow doesn't know there's another soldier behind him'? It is, I suggest, because he sees the whole event 'as an experienced person' which (in this very particular context) means 'as a soldier would see it': an experienced soldier, 'a quartermaster sergeant', mind you, not a raw young squaddy. So how does an experienced person see and understand the scene? What does he know that Jim (so tragically inexperienced in such a situation) does not know? We may reconstruct Mr Porter's knowledge as follows. He understands the soldiers' movements as described in 6–9. He knows that soldiers, when operating in the streets in hostile shoot-to-kill situations, move in set formations – with some going ahead while others, behind, cover their rear to protect them. This, we may infer, is what Mr Porter knows, and Jim doesn't know. If Jim knew what Mr Porter knew he would not raise his head. Mr Porter's exclamation anticipates the inevitable consequence of Jim's movement. The soldier who stayed back (8) interprets it as a possibly hostile threat to his three companions ahead and shoots Jim dead.

Are all these warrantable inferences on the basis of (a) the information that Mr Porter is an experienced person, and (b) his exclamation? I think so. For in telling us that Mr Porter *is* an experienced person we are invited to figure out *how* he is experienced and how that experience is relevant to our understanding of his (reported) account of what happened and particularly his directly quoted exclamation. For *only an experienced person* would have, or could have, said what Mr Porter said. What he said both recognized what was happening and anticipated what would happen next. The experienced person knew. The inexperienced person did not. Knowledge-as-experience can be, as in this case, a matter of life and death.

By contrast, *an* experience, as a singular thing, is a particular happening. It is eventful and perhaps fateful for the subsequent course of an individual life. While everyone accumulates experience in a general sense, it does not fall to everyone to have experiences in a particular sense. Most lives are uneventful, i.e. lacking in 'rich' experiences,[4] but if something happens it can happen in a number of ways, including the things that happen to you, and the things that you happen to witness.[5] In the former case a person might get to be injured

---

[4]    Consider, for instance, Benjamin's remarks on Baudelaire as 'the poet of no experience'. See 'Some motifs in Baudelaire' in Benjamin (1973).

[5]    A third kind of experience, not considered here, is that which you make for yourself. A very common kind of experience in this category is the journey. Benjamin's (1973) essay on 'The Storyteller' focuses on experiences of this kind. It is not unusual for people to organize a journey in order to write it or film it – another case of experiences being set up in order to be told in the form of a novel, travel book, television or radio documentary, etc. Michael Palin's television journeys are experiences of this kind.

by a bomb blast. In the latter case a person might get to see the bomb blast (including people injured by it). Television routinely uses the experiences of both victims and witnesses, but the only kind of experience that viewers can get of television is that of being witnesses (unless the television set blows up as you're watching it, in which case you get to be a victim of television). The experience of being a witness is not less of an experience than being a victim. In either case you are entitled to talk either about what happened to yourself or about what you saw happening. But you do stand in a different relation to what happened. It's the difference between direct and indirect involvement, between something happening to oneself and seeing something happen to some others. So that to be a victim is to have a self-related experience, but to be a witness is to have an other-related experience. There are different feelings at stake here: in a self-related experience you get to feel joyful or sorrowful or angry in and for yourself. In an other-related experience you get to feel such things for and on behalf of others.

A man (I) has seen a young boy being shot dead. Shortly afterwards he is interviewed by a television reporter (R):

I: They just came in firing.
   There was no provocation whatsoever er they
R: Firing what? Rubber bullets?
I: No it was lead bullets they fired.
   They seemed to fire in all directions.
   .hh::hh. There was some rubber bullets too.
   They didn't even seem to fire gas (.)
   .hhh it was just it was completely disgraceful.
   They call themselves an army. It's outrageous.
   It's utterly disgraceful.
R: Are you quite sure th- that nothing was fired at them first?
I: There was *noth*ing fired at them first.
   I'm absolutely certain of that.
   I can speak of this ah without any difficulty whatsoever because I was *there*.
   I was standing at the flats where the Saracens[6] came first of all and there was *noth*ing fired at them.
   Positively nothing fired at them whatsoever.
   There weren't even stones thrown.
   People ran in all directions when they opened fire.
   Most people had their backs to them when they opened fire at the time.
                    (*The Troubles*: Thames Television 1981)

---

[6]  Saracens: British armoured army vehicles in common use on the streets of Northern Ireland.

The interviewee (a Catholic priest) is quite certain of his entitlement to say what he saw because he saw it and had no doubt that he saw it. Now you, as the recipient of this story, may have doubts about what the narrator-as-witness claims to have seen so clearly. You may wish to question those claims (as the television interviewer does), since witnesses are known to be potentially unreliable, but what you cannot do is to make the same kind of claims, to the experience of having seen at first hand, as the witness did. And if you tell a story that you have been told by someone else, this is something that you will make plain, as does the narrator of Mr Porter's story. You will not claim the story you tell as your own experience, though it may have less force as a third-person rather than first-person narrative.

The experiential and communicative claims of the witnesses to events on Bloody Sunday were made for television. But is it possible for listeners and viewers to make similar claims in relation to what they see and hear? Can viewing or listening to something on television or radio be an experience in itself that gives rise to communicative claims and entitlements? We have already seen that the media can be used to authenticate the personal experience of an event, and particularly to warrant its tellability *as* a newsworthy event. If something is believable, by virtue of having been seen or heard on radio or television, it can become part of personal experience to be reliably used as the basis for moral, social or political assessments of that and other matters. What is seen and heard on radio and television thus becomes discussable, talkable about, in a general public, social, sociable sense. From such discussion what we call public opinion may emerge. So that the extent of the reliability, the believability or trustworthiness of broadcasting is the basis of its claims to provide audiences with experiences that carry communicative entitlements.

IV

For every experience, it is tempting to say, there are expected ways of performing 'having had the experience', and if your performance does not measure up to expectations it may be that others will doubt whether you had the experience you have laid claim to. In the British television documentary series *Police*, a woman is shown being interviewed by Thames Valley police officers investigating a complaint of rape that she has made.[7] It soon becomes clear that the police do not believe her story. This is partly because they, unlike most of us,

---

[7]    *Police* was a six-part documentary series, produced by Roger Graef and shown on BBC 1 in 1982. 'A Complaint of Rape' was the third programme in the series.

are inclined – as a matter of principle – to disbelieve stories, or at least stories told in police stations:

| | |
|---|---|
| Detective Inspector: | People come into a police station. They say all sorts of things they make up all sorts of stories. |
| Woman: | huh (.) em huh huh you wouldn' make up a story like I huhuh I tell you. |
| DI: | But people do you know. |
| Woman: | heh |
| DI: | For lots of reasons. |

At the start of the programme we see two uniformed police officers (one female, one male) taking preliminary details, in an interview room, from the woman. They leave the room to confer with plain-clothes colleagues who will take over the investigation of the complaint that the woman is making. The woman police officer offers the view that the woman 'might have concocted this rape story', a view that defines the police's initial attitude. The police have several different grounds for treating her story with circumspection. There is their general, principled attitude of mistrust: is this true, or not? People *make up* all sorts of stories in police stations: story-telling then, for the police, means a lying narrative rather than a true one. In this particular case, the person telling the story is well known to some of the local police. She has a history of mental illness. Her husband used to beat her up. They divorced, she had a nervous breakdown. She received hospital treatment, including electro-convulsive therapy. She was picked up on a couple of occasions by the police on the beat for shouting and screaming in the street.[8] All this prior knowledge which the police have weighs against any simple acceptance by them of the woman's story. Moreover, a cardinal consideration, for the police, is whether or not a story will stand up in court, and that – crucially – depends (irrespective of the truth of the matter) on how the complainant performs in the witness box. Here again they have reasonable grounds for thinking this witness will not do well against a hostile cross-examination by counsel for the defence of the three men whom, she alleges, have raped her. The police are reluctant to investigate a case that, if it went to court, is not likely to result in a conviction. It would be a difficult story to prove, since there is another side to it (the three men would tell a different tale) and the police fear that the woman's performance in the witness box would not be convincing.

Why do they think this? Because they are not convinced by the performance she produces for them in the telling of what happened. What emerges in the

---

[8]   All these details emerge in the course of the interview from comments or questions put by the police to the woman.

course of the interview is that she is not behaving – in the eyes of the police officers – like someone who has *really* been raped.

| | |
|---|---|
| Police Officer(1): | After all this happened who was the first person you complained to about rape? |
| Woman: | I told my boyfriend. |
| PO(1): | What time did you tell him? |
| Woman: | When he came home from work. |
| PO(1): | Yes what time was that? Six, five, four? |
| Woman: | Quarter to six. |
| PO(2): | Quarter to six. What time did you get away from these fellers? |
| Woman: | Er I've no idea. I went to the Job Centre. It must've been about |
| PO(2): | Why didn't you say anything to somebody in the Job Centre (.) Surely |
| Woman: | I was too scared. |
| PO(2): | Surely rape is the next – as far as a woman is concerned rape is the next thing to death isn't it? |
| Woman: | huh well I w's [??] he they said |
| PO(2): | Well if a woman's gonna be raped it's like sticking a knife into somebody it's that serious. |
| Woman: | ehhh it felt like it well they raped me I tell you I've got a pain in my stomach now from it. |
| PO(1): | You then went to the Job Centre. |
| Woman: | Yeh I was looking for a job I I knew I had to get a job. |
| PO(1): | So you went through with the activity of going to the Job Centre looking for a job then you came out. |
| Woman: | Yeh got a bus home. |
| PO(1): | Got a bus home your boyfriend eventually arrived then you tell him. |
| Woman: | Well I thought I thought about it when I got home I was gonna ring the police 'n then I thought better of it I waz'n gonna ring you I thought I'd better. |
| PO(2): | What didn't you think first of all Oh God I've been raped. |
| Woman: | I did I felt dirty. |
| PO(2): | Why don't I I should go to the police station and report it why didn't you do that? |
| Woman: | I felt too unclean I didn't want to go through all the process I'm going through now I didn't want my boyfriend to ring up the police but he insisted. |
| | (Pause) |
| PO(2): | All right if you've been raped we will deal with it as a rape. |

The Detective Inspector leaves the interview-room shortly afterwards and the other two detective officers continue the interview. They take the woman through a pretty gruelling account of what happened to her and then offer their assessments of the story. In the view of one of them, it's 'the biggest load of bollocks I've ever heard'. His colleague's response is more measured but he too thinks it a 'fairy tale' because the woman did not put up a struggle and does not now seem to be upset by it all. 'No seriously. You're not upset by it' . . .

PO(2):     What's to stop you shouting and screaming in the street when you think you're gonna get raped? You're not frightened at all. You walk in there quite blasé you're not frightened at all.

Woman:    I was frightened.

PO(2):     You weren't you're showing no sign of emotion every now and then we have a little tear . . .

Why on earth didn't you scream and shout when you come out of the car? Or when you went into the car. . . . When you got out of the car there's always people about. Why didn't you scream and shout?

So the woman's story is disbelieved on two grounds: one, in terms of how she behaved before, during and after the rape and two, in terms of how she is behaving now in telling of what happened to her. In neither case it seems, did she or is she behaving *seriously*. She does not produce an appropriate performance of having been raped either at the time or, subsequently, in the telling of it. It is this performative failure that clinches all the other reasons the police have for doubting her story. So the moral of all this seems to be – and any good story has a moral, i.e. offers practical, useful tips for the conduct of one's life – that if you have been raped you had better produce the correct performance of having been raped if you want to be believed by the police.

Now this moral, which is readily available to viewers, is not available to the police, for it is the moral of a different story to the one they have heard. It is partly that viewers start with a different disposition towards stories. In ordinary circumstances we are inclined to take at face value the truth claims of storytellers unless or until we begin to have good grounds for suspicion. It is a rule of daily life that you take things at face value – on trust – unless or until you begin to feel doubtful.[9] So we and the police start off on a different footing in relation to stories in general. But, more particularly, we, as viewers, experience a different story to that which the police experience. For the police respond

---

[9]    This is the point of Garfinkel's celebrated 'breaching' experiments that aim to disturb that trust in the normality of everyday life which members ordinarily bring to their experiences of and dealings with each other. The experiments undermine that trust in the known and taken-for-granted obviousness of the conduct of social interaction which functions as its general necessary precondition (Garfinkel 1984: 35–75).

directly to the woman's story, whereas viewers respond to *the telling* of her story (and the police are part of that story). So there are two storyable things here: what had happened to the woman, *and* what is happening to her now as she tells what had happened to her. The police attend to the former, whereas viewers attend to the latter. In attending to what is happening to the woman as she tells what happened to her, viewers attend to how the police respond to her for that *is* what is happening to her. Or, to say the same thing differently, it is impossible for viewers not to attend to how the police respond to the woman's story because that is how television presents the situation. There is the story of having been raped which the woman tells to the police, and that is embedded in the situation with which the viewing audience is presented, of her telling that story to the disbelieving audience of the police.


V


Any situation has a multiplicity of possible points of view, or positions, from which what is going on could be experienced by participants in the event. In any event the number of possible positions is drastically reduced by the difficulties for present participants of occupying more than one position at any one time and beyond that, by the ways in which the definition of many situations allocates in advance the positions to be taken up by participants and imposes sanctionable restrictions on them if they should stray too far from the positions allotted to them. Thus, in any kind of interview, where and how the interviewer(s) and interviewee(s) sit in relation to each other is predefined, and movement outside those positions is severely restricted. Now it is open to television to choose what stance(s) it will take up in relation to its presentation of interviews to viewers. Typically, in the studio (a setting dedicated to televised displays) a menu of several shots is always available at any time from which the producer(s) may select the one they deem most appropriate, from moment to moment, as the interaction unfolds. Documentary makers do not have the (expensive) luxury of being able to send several crews to cover the same event, on location and *in situ*, from different perspectives to allow the producer, in post-production, to pick and choose from a range of different points of view *vis-à-vis* the (pre-recorded) situation.[10] Typically there is only one recording crew at work on

---

[10]    The crude gesture in this direction is the so-called 'noddy shot', done after the interview in which a few shots are taken of the interviewer nodding, as if in response to what the interviewee is saying, which may be subsequently edited into the interview. The noddy shot is there to 'prove' that speakers are not talking to thin air or themselves but to someone: i.e. they establish that what is being witnessed by viewers is a real conversation between two people.

location and therefore it records an event (e.g. an interview) from one position at a time, though it may have greater mobility in relation to the event than the participants in the event.

But the point of view taken up by the camera in *A Complaint of Rape* is severely restricted. The whole interview, from beginning to end, is filmed from immediately behind the seated woman, looking towards the police officers seated or standing on the other side of the table, which takes up most of the space in the interview room. It is so small, in fact, that a television camera cannot comfortably zoom in and out of a close-up of one of the police officers to a mid- or long shot of them both. So all the viewers have to look at as they attend to what's going on are mainly close-ups of the upper half of the police officers and/or shots from behind of the seated woman. Now after a while this becomes noticeable, giving rise to speculations as to why shots of the woman's face are being withheld, as they would obviously help in our assessment of the authenticity (the truthfulness) of her performance. Since it is obvious that anyone in this situation would want to see the woman as she tells her story we wonder why the police can but we can't. And gradually it becomes clear that it must be intentional (for this is a common-sense thing that any viewer can figure out if they put their mind to it). It is to protect the woman's identity. There are other things that television has done that support such an inference. When particular streets or places (the hospital at which she received treatment, for instance) are mentioned in the course of the interview these have been bleeped out in post-production. And any viewer can figure that there must be a reason for bleeping out these references, and go on to work out what might be a plausible reason for doing such a thing. Thus, there are common-sense explanations implicated in the observable fact that the point of view is the reverse of what you would normally expect in a story-telling: not a view of the story-teller, but of the audience for the story-teller's tale.[11]

Now it does not follow that because viewers see it from the woman's point of view they necessarily believe her story. What I do think follows is that viewers get a pretty good sense of what is happening to the woman as she tells her story. They get a pretty good feel of what her audience response is like. The police only get to experience and make assessments of one thing, the

---

[11]   Or, to put this more formally: the behaviour of the camera must be treated as motivated. That is, it *chooses* to see what it sees and — by extension — what it does not see. Further, such choices are treatable as having reasons rather than as being random. For such assumptions to be warrantable (more than purely subjective) it must be presupposed that they were intended to be recognized as intended (as argued in chapter one). In this instance its behaviour is treatable as a motivated departure from the normal expectations of how to show a story-telling (show the story-teller). As such, the camera generates inferences that are retrievable (by anyone, not just the analyst–critic) via common-sense, practical reasoning. These inferences confirm the behaviour of the camera as reasonable (accountable).

woman's story. But the television audience get to experience and make assessments of two things: the woman's story (which they hear) *and* the response of her audience (which they see and hear), and what I am suggesting is that the restricted point of view forced upon the programme (and hence upon the viewer) has the effect of focusing attention on the response of the police to what she says. Viewers hear her story, but all the time they are monitoring the way she's being treated, and that lies wholly in the responses of the police to her story. The primary concern of the police is her story, but the primary concern of viewers is what's happening as she tells it. That is, that she is having a hard time and that her fears about going to the police to make a complaint of rape in the first place have been amply borne out by the experience that she is seen to be having. In short, viewers might reasonably doubt aspects of the woman's story as told to the police. What they have less doubts about is her treatment by the police. Television has provided viewers with an experience of the telling of a story as an epic experience, and this is how television itself is storyable, or talkable-about. You *can* have an experience watching television. It, too, has its authentic moments.


## VI


After the woman has gone through her account of the rape and the two police officers have expressed their disbelieving opinions of her story, she is asked whether she still wishes to make her complaint. With considerable reluctance and hesitation she chooses to withdraw it. One of the officers begins to wrap things up. He tells the woman that he'll now go and speak to his Inspector:

| 1 | 1. MCU of PO(2), right of frame. | I'll tell him what's happening. |
| 2 | Back of woman's head in left (L) | We'll take a statement off you. |
| 3 | foreground. | Then you're free to leave the |
| 4 | Starts to rise. | police station. |
| 5 | | Woman: mm. |
| | Leaves through door. | |
| | As it closes, CUT TO / | |
| | | |
| 6 | 2. MCU PO(1), R. Back | |
| | of woman's | PO(1): What's that for? |
| 7 | head, L foreground. | Woman: I don't want to end |
| 8 | | up in the river that's all. |
| 9 | | PO(1): Ah:: c'm on. |
| 10 | Rising from chair. | This is Reading 1980. |
| 11 | Standing, turning to door. | S'not bloody Starsky and Hutch. |

| | |
|---|---|
| 12 | Leaving through door. | End up in the river? |
| 13 | With his back to her as he shuts door. CUT TO / | What's the matter with you? |

12 Leaving through door.   End up in the river?
13 With his back to her as he  What's the matter with you?
  shuts door. CUT TO /

14 3. Back of woman's head, centre Woman: Honestly!
15 frame. Seemingly looking to    (1.0)
  door. CUT TO /

16 4. From same position CU of Woman: They haven't met some
17 woman's lower body. Her foot of the people I know.
18 in focus swinging gently.    (2.0)
19   CUT TO /  See

20 5. Back of woman's head, what people mean by you know
21 slightly R of centre,  it's easier not to say anything . . .
22 looking R.   than go through all this lark.
23     Muffled voice (off mike, out
24     of shot): For sure.
25 Her head turns back to You know what I mean?
  look down, slightly L,
26 towards door.*   (2.0)
27     .hh I was definitely raped.
28     (2.0)
29 Head turns R again. .hh I've got a stomach ache
30     to prove it.
31 Camera starts to PAN R . . . 'nd I can prove it to the doctor
32     as well.
33 . . . to show Soundman
  against wall    (.)
34 with recording equipment. They'd've got a doctor in 'nd
35 He nods as she speaks . . . done it straight away it'd've
36     been much easier.
37     ( )
38 Camera begins to PAN back . . . Why don't they
39 as woman turns head back to do the physical first?
40 centre as at* (26 above). Then you c'd prove it one way
41     or the other.
42     (.)
43     'n then, nhn I'll prove it
44   CUT TO / to them.

45 6. Door opens and PO(1) returns.
  As he does so holds out something
46 to her (a packet of cigarettes). Oh thanks.

(PO(1) now gets her to make a statement withdrawing her complaint then checks it over with her and gets her to sign it.)

What's of central interest here is the camera pan (31–8) to show the sound recordist doing his job. It is of interest for it is not the kind of material that is normally within the frame of reference of this naturalistic documentary style. Moreover, having said that the shot itself is odd, it is even odder that it has been included in the programme as broadcast. Why this shot in the first place, and why it was not edited out, are matters that must be accounted for. This motivated departure from the normal (i.e. from documentary norms) generates inferences that reveal much of the communicative intentionality of this kind of programme.

A central claim, from very early on, that social documentary[12] made about what it was trying to do was that its subject matter should be allowed – as far as possible – 'to speak for itself'. Thus, the aim of documentary is to uphold the right (and create the entitlement) of its subjects to tell their story in their own way and with their own words. Documentary thus wishes to minimalize its own responsibility for the telling of the story (one obvious way of doing this is to refuse to have an institutional story-teller: *A Complaint of Rape* has no narrative voice-over at all). In this respect, documentary is at the opposite pole of news where it is always made quite clear throughout, that the institutions of broadcasting take responsibility for the news that they tell and the manner of the telling.

By contrast, the narrative methods of documentary are intentionally self-effacing. The institution of television is – as far as possible – made to take second place to the experience(s) of the subject(s) of the programme. The effect that is sought for is a kind of truthfulness, of authenticity, that is held to reside in what it is that the subject has to say. And this truth, this authenticity, rests upon their entitlement to speak about something that has happened to them, or that they have witnessed, and which they thus *know* about (knowledge-as-experience). These assumptions are not, as we have seen, in any way peculiar to the institutions of broadcasting. They come from deeply taken-for-granted assumptions of communicative entitlements in everyday life and ordinary experience. The organizational logic of broadcast documentary springs from these sources and shapes its practices.

One way of seeing how this is extended into the very fabric of 'actuality' broadcasting[13] is to consider how this general communicative intentionality has

---

[12]  For a discussion of what 'social' means in this context see Scannell (1979).

[13]  This term was first used by broadcasters in the mid-thirties to describe new kinds of programmes about actual (real) people and places (Scannell and Cardiff 1991: 145–7). There was then, and has been ever since, a particular emphasis on making programmes *in situ*: the actual people in their own spaces and settings. The use of 'locations' (as distinct from putting real people in the studio, or recreating their habituses in the studio) was felt to be a powerful guarantor of the truth of what speaker had to say and of his or her right to say it.

shaped technological developments designed to release the broadcaster from the studio and into the everyday world as a participant witness of what's going on. A crucial, long-sought for facility was portable recording equipment; first for radio, later for television. The hand-held ciné or video cameras currently in use are designed to be held at eye-level and have the same mobility as the human eye, and thus their effect is human-like rather than machine-like. That is, as a recording device, they record what the eye sees and as the eye behaves, the seeing eye of a particular person. Thus, the eye/I of the camera produces not only the effect of being there, but of seeing the scene humanly (cf. Kuhn 1978). It monitors or scans the scene as we ordinarily do in the situations in which we find ourselves. Thus, the camera-eye tends to focus on who is speaking and monitors speaker's face for evidence of the relationship between speaker and utterance. If someone else speaks the camera-I naturally does a flash-pan to the new speaker. In other words the camera behaves as I-or-anyone would in any circumstances, keeping an eye on what's going on and alert to, and registering, any change. In so doing the camera-eye(I) acts, in its being-there, as if it were there for me-or-anyone. This is in direct contrast to the machine-like gaze of, for instance, surveillance cameras in a store or shopping mall, which cannot react to changes in the environment, but repeatedly sweep their prescribed environment and record what they see to a preset programme.

Part of the basic believability of much 'actuality' television material comes from the 'natural' and 'human' feel of the point-of-view of the hand-held camera and the way in which it seemingly spontaneously 'edits' what it sees (as the eye does) as it records the scene. The camera is 'doing witnessing' in the same way that any person does witnessing and thus produces the effects for each viewer of being there as a person. It is not that the actual monitoring behaviour of the camera *in situ* necessarily adopts from moment to moment some optimum point of view acceptable for all persons. It is rather that, in a seen but unnoticed way, the camera exhibits ('naturally', 'spontaneously' – and thereby generating such effects) a palpable, human intentionality. This intentionality is evidenced by the sustained, focused attentiveness of the camera. By contrast, there is no focused attentiveness in the mechanical record of an automatic surveillance camera. Hence, what it records cannot be regarded as motivated, though it can be treated as evidence.

Let us now consider the brief scene transcribed above. The woman's remark at (14) appears to be addressed to the departing policeman, and her follow-on (16–17) could be regarded as addressed to herself. In both utterances her body posture, and particularly the position of her head, suggests that the remarks are addressed towards the door. But what comes next – 'See what people mean . . . (19–22) is evidently addressed to a somebody, to another 'you' ('you know'). It is not merely the form of the utterance, but also that her head is clearly tilted towards the right, implicating an invisible other person (or persons) off-screen right. That there is someone else in the room is confirmed by the muffled off-mike response at (24). It is not a difficult inference that this response comes from the recording team responsible for the programme we are watching. Who else could it be? Up to this point there has been no indication that there was anyone in the interview room other than the police and the woman. Unless it is someone who is there for reasons that are beyond conjecture (and that is implausible), it must be someone who has a reason to be there and who (when we think of it) must be there – the television crew. Now it would be natural, for the camera as observer, to look in the same direction as the woman and to pick out the person who produces the response ('for sure'). It would be natural because we operate on the assumption that people engaged in interaction face each other and look at each other (people do not, as a rule, converse with their backs to each other in a focused interaction). The fact that the camera does not behave in this way therefore generates inferences: we might say the camera pointedly ignores the person addressed by the woman. But what is the point of this ignoring? What does it mean?[14]

In the first place, we can note that it is not the woman who is doing the ignoring, but the camera. And this suggests that what opens up here, for the first time, is a conflict between what's happening and the recording of what's happening. What is happening here is that the woman has changed the nature of the event. By talking to the crew she makes the crew part of the event, thereby implicating television (as institution) in it. The crew is invited to share her assessment of what's happened in the light of her (taken-for-granted) knowledge that they have seen what has happened to her and can be assumed to have views (opinions) about what happened to her. Evidently this invitation is refused – the minimal verbal response (and hearably it is said as a minimal response) and the refusal to look. Now, ordinarily, such a refusal would be markedly impolite for, when troubles are being told, hearers are expected to play a supportive role (cf. Jefferson 1984). There is a conflict here between such considerations of ordinary courtesy and the need to maintain the position of television as disinterested witness on behalf of viewers. For the woman seeks to draw the crew into her point of view and that must be refused in order to maintain a neutral (uncommitted) position for viewers. It is important to keep the two stories separate: the woman's story (told to the police) and the story of

[14]    There is a background assumption, in all this, that an intended function of the camera, throughout, is that of 'being there for me'. That is, it functions as a non-intervening, participatory observer of the occasion. 'Non-intervening' because the camera does not act on its own behalf, but only for me. 'Participatory' because the camera displays a continuing focused attentiveness to the occasion. It does not show signs of boredom, inattention, wandering off the point, etc. Again, this routinely maintained attentiveness is 'for me'. Such assumptions form part of the complex communicative intentionality that is implicated in all aspects of the programme-as-broadcast.

that telling (told by television to its viewers). Television's commitment is to a presentation of the event, not an assessment of it – that is for viewers. Television can have no opinions on the matter, viewers may have. It is a question of entitlements: for an entitlement to an experience (and hence to opinions) is something created by broadcasting not for itself, nor on behalf of the subjects in the programme, but on behalf of its viewers and listeners.

However, when the woman persists in speaking to the soundman (29) after a pause of several seconds the camera this time pans right (31–3) to show him nodding in acknowledgement that she is speaking to him and of what she says. As the woman turns away from the soundman the camera pans back centre (38–40). So why does the camera do this now, when it did not the first time? Well, one answer would be that you can ignore something once, but it's hard to ignore it twice. Another reason, suggested by students in discussion after viewing the programme, has been that otherwise it might confirm the impression (in the interview) that the woman was a bit simple (common-sense opinion has it that talking to yourself is a sign you're a mental case). But perhaps the final reason is that, like it or not, the crew has momentarily become part of the event and thus must acknowledge itself as part of the event and so record itself.

But if this goes against the normal practices of this kind of film-making, it should normally be cut in post-production. So why isn't it? There were other moments, in the course of filming the event, when the crew became implicated in it,[15] but these intrusive occasions have been cut from the event-as-shown in its final, broadcast version. However, the scene discussed above is relevant to the story-as-seen thus far: for it adds a significant gloss on what has preceded it; namely that, having reluctantly withdrawn her complaint of rape under pressure from the police, the woman reasserts that claim ('I was definitely raped') once they have departed, and at the same time comments on her treatment at their hands. There is a conflict of interest (for the documentary makers) here: on the one hand the integrity of their recording methods, on the other hand the integrity of the event recorded by those methods. Gavin Miller has remarked (apropos of this series) that technique and morality are indivisible in documentary.[16] But where they come up against each other – as here – it is a proof of the programme's overall moral honesty that a concern for the integrity of the event takes precedence over considerations of technique. For

[15] On two occasions when the woman was in tears the police asked her if she minded the presence of the camera crew. When she replied that she did the police asked them to leave, which they did. On both occasions Graef, as he put it, negotiated the crew back in: 'When one of the cops came out I would go back in and simply say look do you mind if we come back, and she said no I don't mind. So I mean we kind of negotiated back in if you like' (Williamson 1984: Graef interview, p. 2).

[16] *Arena*, BBC 2, 8 February 1982. Transcribed by Williamson (1984): see Appendix 14: p. 20.

the little scene between the woman and the soundman (it lasts much less than a minute) has considerable weight for viewers in terms of their moral assessments of what they have seen and heard. It does not prove the truth of her story, but it does prove that she feels she has been talked out of her reasons for telling it and that she still believes it to be true despite the disbelief of the police.

## VII

A woman goes to a police station and complains that she has been raped. The police don't believe her. In the end she drops her complaint. Nothing happens. The woman has had two bad experiences. She is entitled to tell either or both. But her stories have no force, no consequences. A woman goes to a police station and complains that she has been raped. The police don't believe her. In the end she drops her complaint. But it happens that a television crew is there recording the ordinary, routine activities of the police. They record her interview. Later it is broadcast in a prime-time evening slot on a major national television channel. Seven million people watch it. Each viewer gets to have the experience of her telling her story to the police. Each viewer has a communicative entitlement to an opinion by virtue of their experience. The trick that television has performed has been to objectify a subjective experience. This is how a private experience gets changed into a public experience that generates the formation of many opinions into public opinion. In this case, a public opinion on such a matter as how the police deal with and attend to rape victims has been entitled by virtue of television, for there was no opinion to be had, because there was no experience to be had, without it.[17] Thus, we can see that a first-person private narrative (this is my story and this is what happened to me) has a different direction and force to a third-person public narrative (this is what happened to x, and this is x's story). What runs in tandem, in *A Complaint of Rape*, is a first-person narrative of a self-related experience and a third-person narrative of an other-related experience, the former being embedded in the latter.

It is tempting to make a gross generalization that television *always* exhibits

[17]    There was enormous public outcry and considerable press comment on *A Complaint of Rape*. It was widely assumed that the programme showed the way in which the police routinely handled such complaints (an assumption rejected by many in the police force). As a result of the programme the police revised its practices in respect of such complaints, setting up special units (that included women officers) to deal with such matters. It should be noted that the topic (of rape) was very much in the public domain at the time of the programme's transmission, which considerably heightened its impact.

this narrative reflexivity: that there is always a happening and the presentation of that happening, that the happening will be a first-person story, that television's telling of the story will be a third-person story. This unobtrusive doubling of the narrative frequently gives rise to confusions about who owns the story (whose story is it that is being told?) and on whose behalf it is being told. Participants in programmes ostensibly about themselves often imagine that the story is theirs and is told on their behalf. But it isn't. The story is television's and is told for viewers. Thus, it is a common experience of participants in television programmes that they have been 'used', and indeed they have.[18] Their interests are never the first and last consideration of programme-makers who want something that is storyable for viewers.

If we ask where is the story in *A Complaint of Rape* the answer is that, to a considerable extent, it lies in the event which contains clearly identifiable storyable characteristics. It has a clear narrative structure for instance: a beginning (the woman comes to the station and makes a complaint); a middle (she tells her story to the police); and an end (she drops her complaint). Like any good story it has a clear moral to it. Television did not make up this story, nor cause any part of it to happen. Rather, it made recordings of an unsolicited event of which it had no foreknowledge, and over whose course it had no control. It was a witnessing of a happening with storyable elements in it, which, subsequently tidied up and made tellable, could be presented to viewers as an experience.[19] The point of view and behaviour of the camera, and the unobtrusive continuity editing,[20] preserved those effects of liveness and of being there which help to create and sustain the effect of witnessing for viewers.

Opinions about stories are of various sorts. Some opinions concern feelings

---

[18]   Thus, for two of the police who took part in *A Complaint of Rape*, the experience of television's showing of the programme was quite traumatic and, for one of them, disastrous. He withheld his consent to a repeat of the series which, as a result, has never been shown again on television. The woman, whose identity is so carefully concealed in the programme, was traced by press-hounds and offered £5,000 for an exclusive on her life-story by the *News of the World*.

[19]   When questioned about how much was left out of the original full recordings of the rape programme, the editor (Charles Aldridge) replied: 'Well there were three boxes of sync rushes of that particular story, when I tell you some of the others had 24 boxes you can see the difference and I should think we took out of it all the boards for a start, some irrelevancies when she went off on a long story which was quite irrelevant, and bits to tidy it up and a few bits to protect her like names and places. And I should think that must have been, what, one and a half to one, something like that or whatever'. Graef claimed that 'there's less left out of that interview than the whole series' (Williamson 1984: Appendix 14, p. 10).

[20]   In the little scene transcribed above, when the woman talks to the crew, there are six edits, most of which are barely noticeable. Their effect is to preserve the sense of what's happening as a continuously unfolding event, preserving the effect of the recording as one continuing take.

(it was sad, or moving or funny); others concern aesthetic judgements (it was a good or bad story; it was well, or badly, told or acted), while others concern moral assessments of the doings in the story (they behaved well or badly). Now if, as is often the case, one of these kinds of opinion tends to be the predominant kind of response, it must be because the way of telling the story gives rise to that kind of response. So it is not accidental that by the end of, say, *King Lear*, you feel pretty gloomy. Moral assessments have a different force to emotional and aesthetic responses in that they look at what's going on in the story to produce assessments that may have applications outside the story (that is why the moral of a story is always practical): so that one might say something like 'this behaviour is disgraceful and something ought to be done about it'.[21] This was a common response to *A Complaint of Rape* in the national and local press, and in letters from readers to both (see Williamson 1984: 30–3).

It is not hard to see that although the story was (largely) in the event recorded by television, the moral was in its re-presentation by television. Overwhelmingly the moral assessments of the programme concerned not the woman herself or her story, but how she was (disgracefully) treated by the police. That such was the predominant opinion produced by the programme depends on a trust in the reliability of what was seen and heard as the basis for such a judgement.[22] If a documentary succeeds in securing such a trust, then it is embodied in the fine details of its presentational methods, in its seen but unnoticed communicative intentionality. It is not being suggested that *A Complaint of Rape* deliberately sought to generate the particular opinions to which it gave rise. Rather, that such opinions were warrantable on the basis of the story as told – not the woman's story, but television's tale of what happened when she told her story.

---

[21]    Such an attitude is not restricted to non-fictional stories. Fictions, too, can give rise to moral indignation, demands that something be done, etc. The classic example on British television is, of course, *Cathy Come Home*.

[22]    On the reliability of television as an institution see Scannell (1993). Charles Stewart, the chief cameraman in the series, noted that when most people first realized they were being filmed they 'were very suspicious believing that we were the police and (that) we were using police cameras and we often had to prove that we were from the BBC and most people's reaction to it changed immediately' (Williamson 1984: interview with Stewart, p. 13).

# 6

---

# *Identity*

For Graham Brand[1]

1

Certain kinds of career are histrionic. Teachers, preachers and politicians and media entertainers all make a living that is, to a greater or lesser extent, dependent on performing in public. This may involve the projection of a carefully crafted identity and the management and maintenance of that identity in and through time. One such class of performers on radio is the disc jockey. It is an unremarkable feature of the job of being a DJ that, like most jobs, those that take it up as a career often stick at it. Terry Wogan, for instance, did the early morning show on Radio 2 for ten years before switching to hosting Britain's best-known television chat show. John Peel has been doing his kind of music for many years on Radio 1. And Tony Blackburn is one of the longest-running DJs in the business with a career going back to the mid-1960s – a 'living legend' in his own eyes at least.

Most pop music programmes are known by the name of their DJ, and they make use of recurrent devices for reiterating the identity of the station, the

---

[1]    This chapter was originally published as a jointly written article by Graham Brand and myself in Scannell (1991a). It is based on Graham's dissertation on *The Tony Blackburn Show* which he wrote as part of his final year's work on the BA in Media Studies at the then Polytechnic of Central London (Brand 1987). I revised and edited it extensively for publication, adding some extra material in the process. It was Graham's careful analysis of Tony Blackburn's different voices which showed me the true importance of voice for understanding the communicative character of radio. Graham's untimely death was a source of much sorrow to his family and friends and those who knew him at PCL. This chapter is dedicated to his memory.

programme and the presenter. Institutional identity is mediated through that of the show's host, and his or her identity is mediated very largely through talk. In the accounts that follow we wish to show how the production and mainten- ance of programme/presenter identity is routinely accomplished through the talk of the DJ. We wish to bring out the double articulation of identity as routine by highlighting the discursive formats recursively deployed across par- ticular morning transmissions of *The Tony Blackburn Show* and repeatedly across a ten-week recorded sample of the programme.

We offer an account of the discursive world of *The Tony Blackburn Show* with a view to displaying its communicative ethos, its expressive idiom. With the concept of a discursive world we draw attention to the *limits* of discourse, to what is ruled out (what can *not* be said) in order to maintain the consistency of the programme's 'line' or identity. As such it has an inside and an outside which is known and understood by the audience who demonstrate, when they phone in, their knowledge and competence as they routinely reproduce not merely a particular discursive content but a communicative manner and style that embodies the show's ethos. That ethos, is, as we shall see, defined and firmly controlled by Blackburn himself through his 'philosophy' of radio and his expressive idiom which embodies it.

Blackburn is well aware that 'behind a microphone you can become exactly what you would like to be' and, from the beginning of his career, he worked hard to carve out an identity for himself that would make him familiar to and popular with radio audiences. That identity is part of the 'personality sys- tem' of broadcasting (Langer 1981; Tolson 1991). What is on display is 'Tony Blackburn' as a public institution rather than Tony Blackburn the private individual. Up to a point. For Blackburn, as we shall see, routinely draws on his own past – his career in broadcasting and his private life – in his talk on the programme. He has, in fact, produced an account of this career, 'as told to Cheryl Garnsey', in *Tony Blackburn, 'The Living Legend': An Autobiography* (Blackburn 1985), and we offer a thumb-nail sketch of that biography as part of the texture of relevances that make up Blackburn's self-projection in *The Tony Blackburn Show*.


## II


Tony Blackburn began broadcasting in 1964 as a DJ on the offshore pirate ship, Radio Caroline, and quickly established himself as the station's best known and most popular broadcaster. From the start he appreciated the importance of creating an identity that would distinguish him from the other DJs and make his audience remember him. He was the pioneer of those 'identity marks' that have become the DJ's stock-in-trade. The corny gag for instance:

On board Caroline I began to tell jokes as something to say between records, but then I made my great discovery. My jokes marked me out. The public became aware of me because of them . . . I was on my way to achieving the crown as the king of corn. Love me or hate me, the public would never in future be indifferent to me. My jokes are my way of seeing the public doesn't forget me. (Blackburn 1985: 19)

Or the personalized jingle. These were already in use as identity devices by the pirate stations and one day Blackburn noticed a driver listening to Caroline's rival, Radio London, and singing along with the station's jingles:

In a sudden flash of inspiration it came to me that if a radio station could brainwash an audience, why not a DJ? So I booked a studio and musicians in Tin Pan Alley and had them make up my own personalised Tony Blackburn jingles. Every DJ in the country now has his own jingles of course, but I was the first. (Blackburn 1985: 35–6)

Other innovations included 'Arnold the Dog', a 'woofing' sound effect that also became part of his studio identikit.

In 1966, Blackburn jumped ship and joined Radio London. It was a short-lived move, for the following year the Marine Broadcasting (Offences) Act was introduced which, in effect, ended the pirate radio era. But the pirates had shown there was a huge audience for pop music to which the BBC responded by setting up, in 1967, Radio 1 – Britain's first, legal pop music station. Blackburn was recruited to host the peak-time Radio 1 breakfast show and felt he was offered this plum job because of the success of his already established broadcasting style. He was the first voice to be heard on the new station when it went on air, greeting the new audience with 'Welcome to the exciting sound of Radio 1'. Later he would construe this distinction as giving him general warrant and authority to comment on Radio 1 and pop radio in general. In his own mind he was 'the voice of Radio 1'.

When he joined the BBC Blackburn brought with him, as his dowry, Arnold the dog and his stock of jingles. 'Tony Blackburn is Number One!' he informed listeners after every record, convinced that when they voted for their favourite DJ in the popularity polls, listeners would remember that it was Tony Blackburn who was number one. Blackburn's marriage, in 1972, to the actress Tessa Wyatt and the birth of their son, brought a new dimension to his radio performance as he began to talk about his personal life on his radio programme. To the performed personality of 'Tony Blackburn', the chattering DJ, was added the 'real' Tony Blackburn, the private individual. The dividing line between a professional and a personal identity began to erode.

Blackburn and Wyatt divorced in 1976, Blackburn experiencing a nervous breakdown in the process. This, too, became part of his on-air talk:

I eased my suffering by sharing my pain with the listeners. Where once I had regaled them with stories of my happy home life with Tessa and Simon, now I told them about my broken marriage. I played a love song by R. and J. Stone called 'We've Thrown It All Away' and dedicated it to 'the person who will always be very special to me'. I followed that with a 1964 hit by Peter and Gordon called 'A World Without Love'. That should have been enough but once the dam of misery broke I found I couldn't stop. I bored the listeners to death with details of my sorrows. I gave interview after interview on the subject of man abandoned by wicked woman. (Blackburn 1985: 121)

This collapse signalled the start of a disastrous period with the BBC. It was not so much the public airing of his private misery that brought Blackburn into conflict with BBC policy, as the gradual intrusion, in his on-air talk, of his views on social and political issues. Blackburn's sister, Jackie, had been unable to walk from infancy and his experiences of, for instance, trying to take her in her wheelchair to a West End show, showed him how little provision was made in Britain for handicapped people. In 1976, when the government decided to stop the issue of special cars to the handicapped, Blackburn read out a letter from a disabled listener and congratulated him on his demonstration against the decision. This provoked a letter of complaint to the BBC from an MP and a warning from the Controller of Radio 1.

But having started Blackburn was not going to be put off airing his views on issues that included strikes, Northern Ireland, racism, blood sports and the divorce laws. He was warned again, taken off air for a two-week spell and finally threatened with the sack. That did not happen, but he was shunted from the morning to the afternoon and then from one show to another, finally ending up with *Junior Choice* on Saturday mornings and *The Top 40 Programme* on Sunday afternoons. Neither of these allowed any opportunity for venting views and feelings on air and in 1984, after 17 years with Radio 1, he moved to BBC Radio London to present *The Tony Blackburn Show*.

The programme ran for five years as Radio London's morning show from 9 a.m. to noon, Monday to Friday. In the space of three hours Blackburn would play between 30 and 35 records punctuated by news and weather reports on the hour, and travel and traffic updates approximately every half-hour. In the first ten minutes Blackburn performs a number of ritual introductions. Listeners are welcomed to the show and offered a run-down of features to come. Listeners' messages are read out. He may comment on newspaper stories, usually of the jokey or human interest variety or to do with TV soap-operas. These will serve as topic initiators for the programme's first phone-in.

Every day there are two or three phone-in features. The first one or two are flexible, though often focusing on Blackburn's preselected newspaper topic. The last, which always comes in the final 20 minutes of the show, is for birthday and anniversary dedications. There are special phone-ins on particular days of the week: Dial-a-Date is on Wednesdays and Sex and Sympathy on Fridays. Midway through each programme there is a 'teabreak' of about ten minutes in which Blackburn reads out listeners' letters, chats to them and offers his beliefs and opinions on this and that. There may be competitions which are usually included at the expense of the third phone-in. In the last quarter of an hour Blackburn produces ritual closing-down signals. The next day's programme features will be mentioned and farewells and renewals offered. The routine, recursive character of all the elements of the show is endlessly, unobtrusively underlined:

> It's birthdays and anniversaries time. That time has come round again. (12 September 1986)
>
> We will be having, as always, birthdays and anniversaries. (1 August 1986)
>
> And we'll have all the regular features for you at the same time as well. (16 July 1986)
>
> And that tune tells us once again that it's time for Sex and Sympathy. (18 July 1986)

### III

Blackburn's past diffusely pervades his Radio London show and helps to 'make sense' of his performance. The weight of experience, and its claims to authority, may be invoked both in respect to his career in broadcasting and his personal life:

> National radio is in a terrible state. Believe me. I've been in broadcasting for ?? years. On the pirate ships, on Radio 1 and now here on Radio London. I've seen it all. I know what I'm talking about. (21 July 1986)
>
> Radio 1 is a station that is regrettably out of touch and one that I opened up many years ago. It plays naff music and is filled with banal characters. My ambition is to close it down and to get the radio system working. (30 July 1986)
>
> (*TB is advising a teenager on a personal problem.*) As you get older, Nicola, and I'm speaking from experience . . . (18 July 1986)
>
> (*To caller*) Don't worry about being yourself Lorraine. It's great. I've had ten years of divorce and it's wonderful. (19 August 1986)

The troubled past is often referred to and, on occasion, assumes an epic dimension as an aspect of Blackburn's heroic self-thematization:

I have never been a yes man. The BBC hierarchy don't like people speaking their minds. They play safe with rather banal and inane characters. I'm not safe. I speak my mind. That's why I left Radio 1. They couldn't cope with my not being safe. I was always in trouble. (19 August 1986)

Your Leader loves you. A man barely alive. A man who refuses to be beaten by the establishment. A man who wouldn't go away. A man who refused to shut up and, though half dead, refuses to die. (25 July 1986)

The mythification of the past is encoded in frequent self-reference to 'The Living Legend' and in jingles such as 'Tony Blackburn. Older and Bigger than Stonehenge' or 'Tony Blackburn. Preserve your National Heritage'. If the thrust of Blackburn's thematization of his biography is his 'struggle' for broadcasting freedom, then his arrival at Radio London is the victorious triumph.

You know something, gang? One great thing about working here at Radio London is I pick all the music for you. But for 22 years I've been with you and now this is the very first programme where I can literally come on the air in the morning and know that I definitely have the best music for you. And it's really terrific for me to know that and to know that I'm bringing you the very best in music. There is no better music I can bring you. It's taken me 22 years to be able to do that. I tell you. (17 July 1986)

Part of this new-found freedom finds expression in the free play of his opinions. Of course, as he admits, 'radio is not a platform for a DJ's political beliefs. But we are frequently criticized for being inane and if we are forbidden to talk about life around us, what is there left?' (Blackburn 1985: 140–1):

There must be room on radio for a bit of serious discussion. If we can't talk about life around us, and people's problems and the real world what is there left? I mean, you can't have people coming on the whole time and just saying 'Isn't the weather wonderful' and 'I went out and I've got some blue socks on today and I've got a great big medallion dangling round my neck' God Almighty. We must have come on a little bit from there. (12 August 1986)

The following are a representative sample of Blackburn's views on political and social matters, and his way of expressing them:

I think the divorce laws are mad. (27 July 1986)

I think people who resent other people because of their colour are just being ignorant. (18 July 1986)

Politicians are all a load of old fools who don't know what's going on. (1 August 1986)

Fool's Paradise. A good name for the Houses of Parliament. (25 July 1986)

Here's a message for you Mrs Thatcher. When the hell are you going to introduce sanctions? (16 July 1986)

Whenever Blackburn reads from newspapers he invariably quotes from the *Daily Mirror* or the *Sun* (which wrote an editorial lamenting his departure from Radio 1 – Blackburn 1985: 159), and the way in which he delivers his opinions echoes their editorial style. His philosophy of radio is entirely consonant with the ethos of the tabloid press:

> If I was asked about broadcasting, my philosophy on radio would be . . . it's very Americanized really . . . it's fun radio. It's creating a Disneyworld for everybody that they can escape into. It's creating a nice atmosphere for people to have fun in. (BBC Radio 1, *The Broadcasters*, 15 November 1985)

In the same radio programme Blackburn said that he saw his Radio London show as being the radio equivalent of a holiday camp (though in his autobiography, speaking of his time at boarding-school, he says, 'My idea of hell is a holiday at a Butlins camp and school gave me the same feeling of organized fun', 1985: 7). Throughout each morning run the show is permeated with a variety of audio images – jingles, sound effects and slogans – that emphasize the values of fun and entertainment. This mélange of sound creates a specific audio environment of 'fun' which Blackburn himself endlessly reiterates:

> Good morning, gang. This is where the fun begins. (15 July 1986)
>
> Welcome to Fun Radio. (1 September 1986)
>
> The Tony Blackburn Show. Pioneering new parameters of fun. (27 August 1986)

Within this world of fun radio, Blackburn has strong views about the kind of music that is appropriate for it:

> I'm the one DJ who actually *does* listen to the music. (1 August 1986)
>
> Let me give you a word of advice. Stick with me and not the inferior rubbish like Radio 1. We only play the best in soul music, the type of music that we like. You won't hear bland rubbish like on the other stations. You'll only hear proper music. (18 July 1986)

'Soul music is fun music' (25 July 1986) and embodies the Blackburn notion of fun radio. Soul music is sexual and, in an interview in *Melody Maker* (22 November 1986: 21), Blackburn declared that the show 'is geared around "sex and soul". . . . All the lewd connotations go along with the music which is very sensual and suggestive'. Those lewd connotations are another pervasive feature of every show – 'the show that's proud of its naughty bits and at every opportunity flaunts it' (25 July 1986):

> What's the weather like? Never mind the thermometer. Let's do the nipple test. Thrust your breasts out of the window and if the nipples are erect, then presumably it's chilly. (16 July 1986)
>
> (*Jingle: Sexy female voice.*) *The Tony Blackburn Show.* The only programme that asks 'When was the last time you got it?' (30 July 1986)
>
> (*Jingle.*) Tony Blackburn plays great soul music to bonk to. (1 August 1986)

The discursive world of Blackburn's show in multiple ways – his 'editorial' comment, his preoccupation with sex as fun, his phone-ins, dating service (London Love) and competitions – creates a tabloid radio equivalent of the *Sun.*

## IV

Within this world Blackburn thematizes himself in a number of different ways, but always quite self-consciously. On a Radio 1 documentary programme Blackburn admitted that behind a microphone you can become exactly what you would like to be. 'If I'm talking to a microphone and I want to be a macho, butch Sylvester Stallone type, I can be that person. If I want to be a buffoon talking nonsense, I can be that person. I can be a giant-sized person, or what I want to be' (BBC Radio 1, *The Broadcasters*, 15 November 1985). In *The Tony Blackburn Show* he can, within minutes, assume totally opposing identities:

> I'm a big, butch and magnificent macho man. (9 July 1986)
>
> I'm wearing my pink frock today and carrying a matching handbag. (9 July 1986)

Lest anyone should mistakenly take this kind of thing at face value Blackburn is at pains to spell out the nature of his performance:

> You may have noticed that most of the things I do actually say are meant as a send-up. And, er (pause) I don't mean a lot of what I say, I talk a load of nonsense, I'm aware of that. (15 July 1986)

Send-up, particularly of himself, has been part of Blackburn's style from the start. On Caroline, lying in his bunk, he would jot down his corny gags in a notebook and not a few of them were turned against himself:

My mother had me at home, but when she saw me they had to rush her to hospital.

My parents never really liked me. When I came home from school they moved.

Even my mother rejected me. She always wrapped my sandwiches in a roadmap. (Blackburn 1985: 20)

If Blackburn's performance is intended to be recognized by listeners as a performance, what are the markers that might make his intentions apparent? One crucial resource is voice, and it is not difficult to hear several different voices routinely deployed by Blackburn to signal momentary changes of footing in his own discourse or in his interactions with audience members on the phone.

Changes of voice are heard as motivated departures from the base-line of a standard, or 'natural' voice that is returned to when speaking 'normally'. The *standard voice*, though seemingly natural, can be modified or adjusted to achieve particular effects. Mrs Thatcher, early in her premiership, adjusted her voice to a lower pitch, at the same time slowing down her rate of speaking, to sound less shrill and 'bossy' (Atkinson 1984: 112–14). Blackburn, at an early point in his career, decided to adjust his 'normal' voice after being teased, by fellow pirates on Radio London, for having a voice that was 'too high pitched':

After a night of being sent-up in the mess with doubts being cast on my sexuality, I disappeared from the studio and recorded myself just to check that my hormones weren't playing tricks on me. I decided my voice was a bit high, so after that I worked to lower it to the warm attractive tone listeners hear today. (Blackburn 1985: 39)

Blackburn's ordinary speaking voice is heard both in monologue chat – during 'tea-breaks' for instance and in telephone conversation. It tends to merge at times into his *DJ voice*, characterized by a tendency to end an utterance with a rising pitch where a falling pitch would normally be heard. It is common, in performing professions (singers, clerics or actors, for instance) for performers to have a distinctive professional voice as a trade mark. The hyped-up, upbeat DJ voice is used routinely for station and self-identifications, for record introductions, competitions and announcements of future programme events. An occasional *authoritative* voice is used to assert technical knowledge (of radio or music in particular) or to reassert distance in telephone conversations with audience members (if they are tending to get out of control) or for giving advice or instruction either in monologue or in conversation with audience members. In telephone conversation Blackburn will often switch to an *empathetic* voice that imitates the voice of the other speaker in order to establish intimacy or shared point of view. Finally, Blackburn has a number of *camp* or *send-up* voices that may signal a switch to macho man, transvestite queen, Casanova or whoever.

The following bit of telephone talk illustrates some routine voice changes (TB stands for Tony Blackburn and C stands for Caller):

| 1 | *TB* | You could always come on holiday with me Sandra. |
|---|------|---------------------------------------------------|
| 2 |      | I'd look after you. |
| 3 | *C*  | I have to stay at home to look after the kids. |
| 4 |      | They're a problem. |
| 5 | *TB* | Us mums have got our hands full haven't we? |
| 6 |      | Hubbies don't understand our problems. |
| 7 |      | (*Pause*) |
| 8 |      | Never mind. Hope you have a nice day, Sandra. |

A favourite Blackburn gambit with callers is to pursue a line of humorous 'slightly risqué chat' (Blackburn 1985: 141). This is usually underlined by a 'chat-up' voice which is here turned on for Sandra (lines 1 and 2). She, however, refuses to enter the fantasy game and instead asserts the mundane reality – her kids. Blackburn, as we will see later, persistently filters out of his world the problems of day-to-day life and, when they are introduced by callers, he will ignore or bypass them in a variety of ways. Here he turns it into a game – his empathy game in which he identifies with the caller and changes his voice again to register the positional shift (5–6). But again Sandra refuses to play along (perhaps she doesn't know how. We will see, in a moment, how listeners show they know the rules of the game). The pause (7) is an invitation to make an appropriate response but it is declined. Blackburn, realizing he is not going to get anywhere with this co–conversationalist, decides to close it down. Reverting to his 'normal' voice (8) he briskly wraps the call up.

In a rather more complex case Blackburn has one conversation nested in another and, in the middle of this, an address to the general listening audience.

| 1 | *TB* | [1]→ | You went to a screening did you, Suzanne? |
|---|------|------|--------------------------------------------|
| 2 | *C*  |      | Yeah. |
| 3 | *TB* |      | I see. What was the film? |
| 4 | *C*  |      | Erm, What was it? *Girls Just Want to Have Fun.* |
| 5 | *TB* | [2]→ | We are taking people to a screening on Monday, is |
| 6 |      |      | that right, Ms Garnsey? |
| 7 |      |      | (*Pause*) |
| 8 |      |      | I wonder if I can get a little reaction here. |
| 9 |      |      | Are we going to a screening on Monday? |
| 10 |     |      | (*Pause*) |
| 11 |     | [3]→ | We have a screening on Monday. |
| 12 |     |      | We're going to be taking everybody too and we're |
| 13 |     |      | giving away the tickets on Monday. All right? |

| 14 | *C* | Mmmm. |
|---|---|---|
| 15 | *TB* | So we're going to do that. So if you want to come |
| 16 | | along and see a film with me on Monday. |
| 17 | *C* | Mmmm. |
| 18 | *TB* | Er, not you Suzanne, because you've been to one, |
| 19 | | all right? |
| 20 | | But I'm just saying to everybody listen out on Monday |
| 21 | | morning and we'll be giving away tickets, all right? |
| 22 | | (*Pause*) |
| 23 | [1]→ | OK, Suzanne. Who did you ring up for? |

Blackburn is in his usual chat-up mode on the phone with Suzanne, who offers him (4) a classic opening to develop a line of lewd chat. This, however, is not pursued and, quite unpredictably, Blackburn switches (5) to a backstage conversation with his producer Cheryl Garnsey. Evidently the caller's talk of the screening she went to see courtesy of *The Tony Blackburn Show* (cf. 18) reminds Blackburn to check if he can announce that there are tickets available for a screening next Monday. This is confirmed by the studio in the pause at line (10) (there is a muffled, off-mike 'yes'), whereupon Blackburn, now switching to his professional DJ role, goes into an announcement, directed at the listening audience in general, that tickets *will* be available on Monday (12–16). Suzanne, still on the line and under the impression that Blackburn is talking to her, produces response tokens at lines (14) and (17). Blackburn overlooks the first but, interpreting the second as a personal acceptance by her of a general offer he is making to listeners, clarifies for Suzanne in the first place (18–19) and then everybody else who's listening (20), just who it is that he's talking to at this point. Finally, after a brief pause (22) he returns to Suzanne and their telephone chat.

Here we have Blackburn shuttling in and out of three different roles: chat-up artist on the phone with Suzanne, professional broadcaster consulting the studio and DJ showbusiness presenter to the listening audience. The switches between these front- and back-stage roles are cued by modulations in voice tone that indicate changes of footing from talking to a caller in voice (1), to conversation with the studio in voice (2) to an address to listeners in voice (3) and finally back to voice (1) and the original caller and conversation.

## V

It is routinely made explicit that this programme exists for its audience:

*The Tony Blackburn Show.* The show that makes *you* become part of the programme. (8 August 1986)

This is your programme, gang, and you can choose the records. Let's open up the Power Line for your Power Line requests. (27 August 1986)

Blackburn, however, is in charge of his gang, as he makes plain in a variety of ways:

How's everything in the furthest corners of my kingdom this morning? What's it like out there in Wimbledon, or Bromley, or Deptford? Good morning to you wherever you are. (25 July 1986)

Good morning gang. Your leader loves you. (8 July 1986)

Power, in this kingdom, is sometimes exercised with ruthless authority:

>       (*Caller tries changing topic.*)
> TB  Hang on a minute Susan. This is *my* programme.
>       I'll decide what we talk about. (1 August 1986)
>
>       (*Caller is talking. Blackburn cuts in.*)
> TB  I'm getting bored with you Paula (*cuts her off* ).
>       Jonathan is in Willesden.
>       (*Continues conversation with Jonathan*) (27 August 1986)
>
>       (*Blackburn has been talking to caller for nearly a minute about EastEnders*)

| | | |
|---|---|---|
| 1 | TB | OK Mandy. So you think it was stupid of the BBC |
| 2 | | to kill off Andy? |
| 3 | C | Yes I do. Can I say hello to a few people? |
| 4 | | I'd like to say |
| 5 | TB | Hold it. Hang on. You're not going to do |
| 6 | | a load of boring dedications are you? |
| 7 | C | I just |
| 8 | TB | We only allow dedications at the end of the show and |
| 9 | | then only birthdays and anniversaries. OK? |
| 10 | C | Yes. I'm sorry. |
| 11 | TB | OK. |
| 12 | | (*Pause*) |
| 13 | | So you think it was wrong of the BBC . . . (*conversation continues*) (9 July 1986) |

This is a show for its audience so long as audience members remember that Tony Blackburn is in charge and play along with the rules of the game in his world of fun radio. One basic rule is to confirm Blackburn's own frequently asserted self-assessment that he is 'the best':

> TB  There's no other good broadcasters around, are there?
> C   No that's true.

| | | | |
|---|---|---|---|
| *TB* | | | I suppose there's Robby Vincent, but he's not such a genius, is he though? |
| *C* | | | No, you're the genius. |
| *TB* | | | Exactly. I'm the best. |
| *C* | | | You are the best, Tony and we wish you were on the radio all day. (11 September 1986) |

This caller, who we may infer is a regular listener, knows how to play the role of courtier. Note caller's assumption of a plural mode and a presumption to speak on behalf of a community of listeners ('*we* wish you were on the radio all day'). Callers who know the game may begin their conversation with supportive remarks such as 'Hello Leader' or 'This is a thrilling honour to talk to you Tony'. Such remarks may be seen as sacrificial offerings to win acceptance and entry into Blackburn's discursive kingdom. Those who fail to sustain such a line are usually summarily dispatched:

| | | | |
|---|---|---|---|
| 1 | *TB* | [1]→ | Why don't you leave him for me. He sounds miserable. |
| 2 | *C* | | Well maybe when I've finished with him I'll come to see you. |
| 3 | *TB* | | Oh thanks. Treating me as second best now, are you? |
| 4 | *C* | | Well you are a bit. |
| 5 | *TB* | [2]→ | Thanks! Oh thank you very much. Thank you ve- so much! |
| 6 | | [3]→ | Joy's on the line from Streatham. |
| 7 | *TB* | [1]→ | Hello Joy. |
| 8 | *C* | | Hello Tony. |
| 9 | *TB* | | Did you hear that? |
| 10 | *C* | | I did. |
| 11 | *TB* | | How insulting. You're not going to give me any of |
| 12 | | | that are you? |
| 13 | *C* | | Oh no, you are the best Tony. |
| 14 | *TB* | | Well exactly, Joy. You're on the same wave length as |
| 15 | | | me. (*Conversation continues*) (18 August 1986) |

Blackburn as usual, is in his chat-up mode (1, Voice (1)), but caller isn't exactly playing along. Blackburn tries to sustain his line and offers (3) another chance to play the game by affirming that he's the best, not second-best. This gambit is refused and Blackburn now switches to a voice (5, Voice (2)) of heavy irony, immediately drops the caller and switches to his professional voice (6, Voice (3)) as he announces the next caller to listeners. Assuming an outraged voice (9), he makes it plain (11) that Joy had better play along and, when he receives her ritual unction (13, 'You *are* the best'), conversation continues in the normal chat-up mode. How much this is all a game is hearably uncertain. It seems that Blackburn is put out of face by first caller's put-down at line (4), and momentarily loses fluency as he stumbles, a trifle incoherently, in his heavily

ironic response (5). But the flow is quickly restored and the indignation is
hearably put on.

Only rarely does the Leader lose control, and that is when the talk goes seriously off course. The following is from a call during a Birthdays and Anniversaries phone-in. Blackburn has been chatting to caller for about a minute:

| 1 | C | I'm not at all shy Tony. Can you do me a quick |
| 2 | | favour? |
| 3 | TB | No I can't (*knowing laugh*) I wouldn't have time. |
| 4 | C | Oh go on. |
| 5 | TB | I have more (*laughs*) staying power than |
| 6 | C | Just a quick favour. Just say hello to my |
| 7 | | boyfriend, Brian. |
| 8 | TB | Oh, why? |
| 9 | C | Well, because he's been acting very funny lately. |
| 10 | TB | He's been acting very funny! Has he been |
| 11 | | wearing women's clothes or something? |
| 12 | C | I think I might be pregnant. |
| 13 | TB | Has he, err (*nervous giggle*) |
| 14 | | I was just err (*inaudible mumble*) |
| 15 | | (*nervous giggle*) I bet he does wear women's clothes. |
| 16 | C | He doesn't. |
| 17 | TB | He's probably a transvestite who's kept it from you. |
| 18 | | That's why he's been acting strangely. |
| 19 | C | He's not talking to me very nicely. |
| 20 | TB | Well. It's his tendencies. |
| 21 | | Anyway Simone I hope very much indeed that everything |
| 22 | | turns out all right. |
| 23 | | OK. John's in Tottenham. (17 July 1986) |

This caller's request to say hello to someone is not immediately put down as
the hapless Mandy's was. For one thing it is OK, as Blackburn made clear to
Mandy and everyone listening, to do 'boring dedications' in the appropriate
slot – and this is a Birthdays and Anniversaries phone-in. Moreover, rather
than barging in with an unsignalled topic-change as Mandy does, and without
waiting for permission, Simone begs her favour three times (1, 4, 6) before
proceeding to name it. In this she shows her understanding of the rules of the
game and ostensibly appears to be providing Blackburn with the cues he likes
for his line of innuendo. The asked for 'favour' is glossed by Blackburn as
sexual (3, 5) and he is momentarily disconcerted (8) when it turns out to be a
request for him to say hello to Brian. Caller's response ('because he's been acting very funny lately' (9)) is again interpreted by Blackburn as an offering to
continue his line of lewd chat, so that caller's next utterance (12) is devast-
atingly unexpected.

At first Blackburn continues with his line, and the beginning of another jokey question overlaps caller as she says 'be pregnant'. When Blackburn catches up with what she has actually said he is quite unable to assimilate it into his performance and, after a lapse into mumbled incoherence and nervous laughter, all he can do is cling to his line (15). That, however, is simply refused by the caller (16) and, when Blackburn repeats his line for a third time ('he's probably a transvestite'), caller continues with her own line by offering a gloss on Brian's strange behaviour ('he's not talking to me very nicely'). At this point all Blackburn can do is offer a feeble explanation of Brian's behaviour, a feeble hope that it will all be all right and escape to the next caller. It should be noted that Blackburn has a regular phone-in slot, Sex and Sympathy, for talking about callers' sexual problems. The point here is that Simone's mention of her possible pregnancy is situationally inappropriate and as such derails the conversation which up to this point, has developed along the usual lines of chat in the Birthdays and Anniversaries slot. Blackburn's talk collapses *not* because he cannot handle the topic, but because he cannot handle it in this particular context. His conversational collapse demonstrates the extent to which the talk in all the phone-ins is organized into routines that sustain their particular topical and relational identities.

## VI

Harold Garfinkel has argued eloquently that there is no time out from the burden of responsibility for the management and maintenance of identity. Nevertheless there are, as Erving Goffman shows us, all kinds of occasional opportunities for stepping outside of self. That is one way in which we relax or have fun:

> When an individual signals that what he is about to do is make believe and 'only' fun, this definition takes precedence; he may fail to induce the others to follow along in the fun, or even to believe that his motives are innocent, but he obliges them to accept his act as something not to be taken at face value. (Goffman 1974: 48)

Having fun involves pretending, putting temporary brackets round reality, a momentary suspension of the ordinary daily round. We have tried to bring out, in our presentation of *The Tony Blackburn Show*, not only how fun is defined, organized and projected as such, but also how it is bracketed out from ordinary reality, how it deliberately refuses to be serious.

It is clear, from the fragments of conversation considered above, that the participants in the fun – Blackburn and callers – do not stand in the same relationship to each other. Broadcasting is an institution – a power, an authority – and broadcast talk bears its institutional marks particularly in the way that it is not so much shared between participants as controlled by the broadcasters. Because the institution is, ultimately, the author of *all* the talk that goes out on air (it authorizes it) it is responsible for the talk in a way that those invited to speak are not. If an invited participant should transgress the norms (by saying 'fuck' for instance) it is the broadcasting institution rather than the transgressor who will be held accountable (cf. Lewis 1991). Thus, control and management of all talk in broadcasting must rest, first and last, with the representatives of the institutions, that is, the broadcasters.

Blackburn's control of the talk – in terms of topic management and closure – though idiosyncratic in its manner, is not in any sense particular to him. Broadcast telephone conversations, while sharing many characteristics of private phone calls, have some that mark them out as public displays produced for a listening audience. Blackburn shows this awareness routinely and it is manifest whenever he switches from talking to callers to talking to the studio or the listeners. When he pulls the plugs on a 'boring' caller this may be (subjectively) intended and heard as impolite. It may also be (objectively) intended and heard as dramatic, as 'livening things up a bit' – not so much for the caller, of course, as for other listeners for whom there may be the added frisson that – if their turn should come – they, too, might provoke, deliberately or not, the same rough treatment.

It is, from moment to moment, from one day to the next, week in week out, Blackburn's responsibility – and no one else's – to maintain the fun. For listeners and callers the fun is optional: for its presenter it is not and this is why Blackburn patrols its boundaries so carefully since he alone must manage and maintain the show's expressive idiom. To do so he has devised – formatted, we would say – an identity for the programme and himself that is routinely talked into being by himself and others. The talk is the routine, the routine is the identity. Goffman, in a particularly suggestive passage, discusses how talk routines are produced on radio. It may seem as if what he calls 'fresh talk' is constantly produced in unscripted radio talk:

> But here again it appears that each performer has a limited resource of formulaic remarks out of which to build a line of patter. A DJ's talk may be heard as unscripted, but it tends to be built up out of a relatively small number of set comments, much as it is said epic oral poetry was recomposed during each delivery. (Goffman 1981: 324)

Goffman has in mind the work of Milman Parry (1971) and Albert Lord (1960) who demonstrated how it was possible for the ancient oral tradition to produce such heroic tales as *The Iliad* and *The Odyssey*. The problem they addressed was, simply, how did the old tellers of tales know and remember such lengthy

narratives which, when transcribed, were thousands of lines long? Since each
retelling in the oral tradition must be a fresh version of the tale, what are the
techniques that enable them to be learnt, stored and reproduced afresh in each
retelling? By a study of the still-living tradition of oral epic in Southern Yugo-
slavia Parry was able to show, as Goffman puts it, how 'prose narratives, songs
and oral poetry can be improvisationally composed during presentation from
a blend of formulaic segments, set themes and traditional plots, the whole arti-
ficially tailored to suit the temper of the audience and the specificities of the
locale' (Goffman 1981: 228).

The production of the same kind of smoothly continuous talk, day in day
out, on every broadcast occasion, over a three-hour stretch poses similar problems for today's DJs. It is not difficult to show that much of Blackburn's monologue talk is a patchwork of formulaic utterances woven into set routines:

|    |    | (*Music fades*) |
|----|----|-----------------|
| 1  | TB | Paris and *I Choose You*. |
| 2  |    | It's now seven minutes before eleven o'clock. |
| 3  |    | Your main funking funketeer. |
| 4  |    | Your Boss, with all the hot sauce. |
| 5  |    | Your Leader . . . (*pause*) . . . Me. |
| 6  |    | Right. Now Dave in Greenford says 'Drive safely 'n |
| 7  |    | love you' to wife er Jill who's on her way to Radlett |
| 8  |    | at the moment. |
| 9  |    | Mark in Bermondsey sends all his love to fiancée Sally |
| 10 |    | Ann. |
| 11 |    | And also Rachel or – yes it is   Rachel in Barnet |
| 12 |    | says 'Love you' to husband Peter who's working at |
| 13 |    | Shenley Hospital hrhmm oh dear must clear my throat. |
| 14 |    | Right. Now, Em Garry's in Camden. Hello Garry. |
|    |    | (1985 undated) |

This strip of talk is embedded within a larger half-hour formatted section of
the programme called London Love in which listeners are invited to 'show you
care for the one you love' by phoning in if, for instance, they have just got
engaged or are getting married or are back from a honeymoon or want to make
up a quarrel. The phone calls are taken in pairs between suitably romantic soul
'twelve inchers'[2] and the methodological problem for the presenter is to get
from the music to the calls to the music always with an eye on the studio
clock to keep to the overall format of the show and the scheduled number of
plays within it. Here three routines are displayed: (a) continuity talk (1–5), (b)

---

[2]   As the twelve-inch vinyl discs were known, at the time, in the business. TB, as regular
listeners know, makes frequent priapic reference to his own mighty twelve-incher.

audience message (6–13) and (c) telephone chat (14). Continuity routines generally contain three elements in sequence: (i) record identification, (ii) time check, (iii) programme-presenter identification. There is more scope for variety in the third than in the first two elements. A jingle may be used or, as here, a few formulae – 'your funking funketeer', 'your Boss with all the hot sauce', 'your Leader' – from Blackburn's stock of stock phrases.

The switch from one routine to another is succinctly signalled by 'Right. Now . . .' (6) which indicates ending (Right) and beginning (Now . . . ). The next routine, audience messages, has its standard format: A in X → 'message'→ B in Y. The message may be quoted or reported. There are usually three messages, as there were three components of the preceding routine and three in the programme-presenter identification. Triads are, as Max Atkinson has shown, an extremely useful and common rhetorical device for packaging memorable and memorizable utterances (Atkinson 1984). This routine, too, is closed down and the next introduced in the same way as the preceding one: 'Right. Now . . . (14)' and into the phone-in routine.

Blackburn brings off these routines with effortless ease, including the self-monitoring utterances ('Oh dear must clear my throat') that repair momentary disruptions of the flow (cf. Goffman 1981: 290). This is the mark of his professionalism, and if lay speakers were suddenly given the DJ's talk tasks they would doubtless be dumbstruck. But this, Goffman suggests, is more for a want of tag lines than for a want of words (ibid.: 325). Regular listeners, however, know the tag lines and their appropriate usage of them and show this knowledge in conversation when they go on air in phone calls with the programme presenter.

VII

In his concluding remarks on radio talk, Goffman compares it with 'everyday face-to-face talk' without, however, commenting on or distinguishing between monologue talk (with which he has been, in fact, very largely concerned) and talk as social interaction between two or more participants. The absence of such a distinction suggests that is not significant in Goffman's terms of analysis and indeed he concludes that DJ monologue is basically the same as 'what the speaker is engaged in doing' from 'moment to moment through the course of the discourse in which he finds himself'. If face-to-face talk then is something a (male) individual 'finds himself in' he makes the best of it by selecting that footing 'which provides him with *the least threatening position* in the circumstances, or, differently phrased, *the most defensible alignment* he can muster' (ibid.; our emphases). Talk appears, in Goffman's terms, as yet another threat to face, as a kind of external imposition, to which the individual must respond self-defensively. In this curiously grim view of talk there is no perception of it as sociable interaction, as something collaboratively produced by two or more participants which, at best, is what is mutually and enjoyably achieved in Tony Blackburn's radio show:

| 14 | TB | Right. Now, Em Garry's in Camden. Hello Garry. |
|----|-----|---|
| 15 | Garry | Hello Tony. |
| 16 | TB | (*Chat up voice*) Hello. I gather you're getting |
| 17 | | married tomorrow. |
| 18 | Garry | Oh yeah 'n I'm really scared I tell you. |
| 19 | TB | After all – I'm not surprised – after all you 'nd I |
| 20 | | have meant to one another as well. |
| 21 | Garry | I know but (?) my Leader what can I do. We tried to |
| 22 | | get down 'nd see you last night as well. |
| 23 | TB | Really? |
| 24 | Garry | Yeah we couldn't. We wanted to see your twelve |
| 25 | | incher but – |
| 26 | TB | I'm – Garry! |
| 27 | Garry | Ahh. |
| 28 | TB | I'm amazed you're getting married. All those times |
| 29 | | that we spent in the sand dunes in Swanage together. |
| 30 | Garry | Ah d'you remember that time in the Bahamas? |
| 31 | TB | Yes. |
| 32 | Garry | On the beach just me 'nd you. |
| 33 | TB | When you used to whisper and nibble my ear. |
| 34 | Garry | Ahhh. |
| 35 | TB | Underneath the coconut trees. |
| 36 | Garry | And you you used to show me your twelve incher. |
| 37 | TB | And you threw it all away and you're getting married |
| 38 | | tomorrow. Don't you think you should reconsider this? |
| 39 | Garry | I think I should Tone, I think I should mate. |

In analysing this strip of talk we wish to bring out how the two participants collaborate to co-produce talk that is 'in frame', as Goffman would say, i.e. within the terms of the discursive world of *The Tony Blackburn Show*. In this respect we attend both to the content (what the talk is about) and the style (how it is talked about). We further show how both speakers, in working to produce appropriate talk, draw upon their knowledge of what Garfinkel calls 'the biography of the present situation' as sketched above, and thereby how identities are routinely reproduced and reaffirmed by talk.

Hello Garry
Hello Tony
Hello

An exchange like this is so utterly familiar that its oddity escapes us, for the fact is that neither Tony nor Garry know each other, have never met or spoken to each other before this moment. How, then, can they hail each other as familiars? We must assume, as must they, that – if not familiar with each other – they must be familiar with the programme and that this is a common knowledge and thereby a shareably relevant resource for the production of talk, both in content and manner. Thus, the embedded implicatures, as working conversational hypotheses initially made by each speaker, can be posed as follows:

> *TB*  Hello Garry (I have not spoken to you before, have never met you and don't know who you are, but I take it that you have listened to this programme before and to that extent know me, and I let you know that I make these assumptions in calling you Garry)
>
> *Garry*  Hello Tony (I have not spoken to you before, we have not met and you don't know me but I have listened to this programme before and I confirm your assumptions in calling you Tony, thereby displaying knowledge of the programme)

If TB starts with this assumption it enables him to mobilize a routine without further ado, because he can reasonably assume that caller will recognize the routine-to-be-initiated as such. One of the most economic ways of getting into a routine that Blackburn uses is voice change, which simultaneously indicates both a change of footing and the character of the new alignment. We have discussed above, in relation to several data samples, Blackburn's voice as an aspect of his chat-up routine with callers. Blackburn's repeated 'Hello', here said in a lower pitch and with a softer inflection than the first 'hello', hearably implicates intimacy. This change of voice accomplishes a number of things: first, it shifts out of the first paired greetings exchange which is a display for the general audience into particular conversation with this displayed caller. The change from DJ voice to intimate voice 'keys' the tone of the talk to be initiated, it sets the frame. Note, at this point, that an intimate tone of voice is being used with a male caller (Garry's voice, like his name, is hearably masculine).

'I gather you're getting married tomorrow' is said in the same intimate tone. Let us deal first with the technical question – how does TB know this? – before attempting to account for why he says it here in this tone of voice. Callers to this, as to other radio shows with phone-ins, get through to a switchboard in the station that handles the calls. The operators will ask callers for their names, where they come from, their telephone number and if they have anything special they want to say. These bits of information are written down on paper and handed to Blackburn in the studio who is cued, by the producer, as to who is next in the bank of callers on hold to talk to him. 'I gather' implies that Blackburn's source for the statement-query that follows is not directly Garry

− by inference, then, the station − and requests confirmation which Garry immediately produces (18).

But what is the object of this utterance at this point? Consider the predictable conversational lines that might be taken by recipients of the information that the person to whom they are speaking is to be married next day. A next turn might be to ask 'to whom?' − a question not posed until line (55) − and certainly the offer of congratulations should be forthcoming very soon, but these are not offered by Blackburn until line (96).[3] Garry's marriage − which is topically relevant *today*, in programme terms, by virtue of being tomorrow − serves as the envelope for the conversation as a whole. It is the first thing referred to after initial greetings exchange and the last thing referred to before final thank-yous and good-byes:

| 106 | *TB* | Be happily married Garry. |
|-----|------|---------------------------|
| 107 | *Garry* | Thank you very much. |
| 108 | *TB* | Thanks very much indeed for phoning. |
| 109 | | Jill's in Woodford. Hello, Jill. |
| | | (*Continues conversation with Jill*) |

The introduction of Garry's marriage at the beginning of the conversation serves not so much as a topic to be sustained in its own right, but as a foil for the routine that Blackburn wishes to establish.

What that routine is is not apparent at this point and Garry, after confirming Blackburn's statement-query, produces a response − 'n I'm really scared I tell you − that keeps up the topic of marriage-as-an-imminent-prospect. Blackburn's next turn (19–20) is, for anyone unfamiliar with the biography of the occasion, downright peculiar or 'weirdo!' as Blackburn would say (73), but in context it is routine and indeed only makes sense as a routine. It does not at first attend to Garry's response but builds on Blackburn's opening move and begins to reveal how he wants to use Garry's marriage as a conversational resource. 'After all . . . after all you'nd I have meant to each other' is said in a hearably reproachful voice that continues and makes explicit the claims to intimacy implicated in the tone of voice adopted in Blackburn's preceding turn. His interpolated reaction to Garry's response − 'I'm not surprised (you're scared)' − is a rapid change of footing, a 'normal' response in his 'normal', slightly jokey voice, a return to the real world from which the conversation is beginning to depart if Blackburn can establish his routine.

That depends on Garry's support, and that depends on Garry recognizing and keying into the fantasy routine. Garry is not in the least fazed by Blackburn's line: 'I know but . . . what can I do?' (21) acknowledges the line of reproach

---

[3]    The whole conversation is transcribed at the end of the chapter.

and plays along with it. The playfulness is underlined by the smoothly interpolated 'my Leader', said in a tone of mock deference, which claims membership of 'the gang' and displays knowledge both of the content of the discourse
of *The Tony Blackburn Show* and of its jokey, 'send-up' style. Garry has now
shown to Blackburn his understanding of the rules of his conversational game
and a general disposition to play it. But it is not yet clear, to Garry, that
Blackburn wishes to sustain his line, so Garry continues with a bit of real-
world chat – 'We tried to get down 'nd see you last night as well'.

A notable feature of the way *The Tony Blackburn Show* reaches out to its
audience, attempts to create a listening community, is the Soul Night Out that
Blackburn regularly announces on the show.[4] This is a disco, presented by
Blackburn often with a guest soul artist, in a venue somewhere in London, to
which fans of soul music and Tony Blackburn are invited. It is this that Garry
tried to attend, presumably with his bride-to-be, and which he offers here as
a topic (it is one that often crops up in phone-in talk on the programme).
In referencing it Garry further displays his membership of the programme's
listening community, but his object in introducing it here is not yet clear.
Blackburn's response token – 'Really?' (23) – is a pass that allows Garry to continue, and to make explicit what was implicit in 'We *tried* to get down' – 'we
couldn't' (24). A reason is produced for wanting to get to the show, namely the
desire to see Blackburn's twelve-incher. As heroes in the old sagas have their
trusty weapons – Achilles his spear and shield, Beowulf and Arthur their
swords – so Blackburn has his tool of heroic proportions which he may offer to
show to callers on the programme. Garry's use of the formulaic phrase – like
'my Leader' – shows his familiarity with the programme's word-hoard. More
particularly, it switches from real-world talk back to fantasy-world talk, keying
in to Blackburn's general line though not yet his particular tune.

Blackburn now, taking up the talk after a slight pause after 'but', tries to
replay that tune, having momentarily given way to Garry, 'I'm – Garry! –
( . . . ) I'm amazed you're getting married. All those times that we spent ( . . . )
together' (26–9) repeats the pattern of the first effort: 'After all – I'm not
surprised – after all you 'nd I have meant to one another' (19–20). The interpolated 'Garry!' (26), however, is in a tone of mock reproof (for mentioning
Blackburn's unmentionable) that is consonant with the rest of the utterance,
whereas the interpolated 'I'm not surprised' (19) required a momentary change
of footing back to the real world. Garry's production of Blackburn's twelve-
incher helps to retrieve the tone of the talk which the introduction of the Soul
Night Out seemed temporarily to have abandoned. But why the sand dunes in
Swanage (29) of all places? Well, the young Tony Blackburn grew up in that

---

[4]    For a vivid account of a Blackburn Soul Night Out and its audience, see Brand (1987: 70–3).

part of the world, his father being a doctor with a practice in Poole (Blackburn 1985: 4–13).

Garry's response (30) tunes in to Blackburn's line and now the conversation has clicked. Both will collaborate in the game of Let's Pretend to produce an imaginary relationship with an imaginary past, places and memories. The account we have offered of the talk thus far has attempted to show how it gets to this point where both participants have sought and found an agreed conversational framework and a shared attitude towards it. That they *can* get to this point depends, from moment to moment, as we have tried to show, on mutual knowledge and understanding of the programme's content and manner. Such knowledge is incremental. It accumulates in time as it is reproduced through time. The past of the programme is not the dead past. It is a pervasively relevant resource for renewing its identity in the particularities of the present. That identity is not wholly constructed and mediated by Tony Blackburn. Listeners, like Garry from Camden, playfully interact with the show to keep up the fun.


## VIII


It remains to link the biography of the occasion to the 'geography of the situation' (Meyrowitz 1985: 6). A broadcast programme has two spaces: that from which it speaks and that within which it is heard. Evidently programmes may be more or less oriented towards one or other of these two spaces depending on the overall communicative intentions and strategies of the programme. In hosted game shows and quizzes, as we have seen in chapter two, the fun is visibly and audibly organized in the studio before a participating studio audience. Listeners and viewers are invited to participate, *in absentia*, in the staged events taking place in the public space of the studio.

Martin Montgomery has shown how DJ talk is pervasively audience oriented: that is, its talk is directed outwards from the studio into the imagined spaces within which it is heard (Montgomery 1986). The modes of address routinely deployed by the DJ speak to an audience 'out there' which may be 'hailed' in many different ways. At the same time the talk of the DJ intermittently acknowledges the gap between speaker and listeners by references to the studio itself and what is going on in it. Montgomery restricts himself to DJ monologue and its attempts to simulate co-present conversation with the imagined audience. We have included, in our account, direct interaction between the DJ and those self-elected audience members who call in during the regular phone-in slots that are a feature of every programme.

This two-way talk underlines the ways in which the identity of the programme and its presenter are in part interactively sustained by a dialogue between institution and audience. Programme identity can thus be thought of as a relationship that lies across the public institutional space from which Blackburn speaks and the private, domestic or work spaces from which callers speak. And if that identity is perishable, the threat is likely to come less from faulty DJ talk than from caller talk that is out of frame. This can readily enough be understood in terms of the differences between the diverging circumstances of the studio and its geography, on the one hand, and that of the household or workplace, on the other.

The radio or television studio is a public place into which people come to take part in a wide variety of political, cultural, educative or entertaining programmes. In all events to enter the studio is to cross a threshold, to enter a social environment that creates its own occasions with their particular situational proprieties, discursive and performative rules and conventions. To enter this place is to assume, for the duration, a role and identity appropriate to the particular communicative event that is being staged: thus, interviewers and interviewees in political news interviews display an orientation to the character of the event by sustaining the part they are called upon to play. To be physically present in the studio, whether as programme host, participant or audience member, is to be inescapably aware of the broadcast character of the event for the technology and personnel of broadcasting – cameras, microphones, lights, production staff – are pervasively evident. The design of the setting – whether for a political interview, a chat show or a game show – structures the communicative character of the event and orients all participants (including studio audiences) to the roles and performances they are expected to produce for absent viewers and listeners. In short, those in the studio are committed to the communicative situation and their part in it.

Audience members who elect to take part in phone-ins enter the discursive space of the programme but not its physical place. They remain in their own place while dialling into a public discourse. That discourse may be defined in the first instance either by the studio or the caller. In phone discussion programmes, it is the callers who are normally expected to define the topic of their call (cf. Hutchby 1991). In *The Tony Blackburn Show*, however, callers elect to enter a conversation in which the tone and topic of the talk will be defined by Blackburn not themselves. They must enter a predefined discursive space with tightly defined boundaries. Those boundaries are liable to be transgressed, as we have seen, by callers introducing into the fantasy discourse coming from the studio their own immediate everyday problems or worries – the difficulties of obtaining a babysitter or an unexpected pregnancy, for instance. Fun is easier to sustain in a place (momentarily) dedicated to it, than one in which it is circumscribed by mundane realities.

There is, then, an inescapable lack of fit between the institutional places from which broadcasting speaks and the domestic and working places within which it is heard. If in the first place broadcasting has had to learn to adjust its discourses to fit its audiences it simultaneously requires those audiences to adjust to its discourses. Broadcasting does not, as Joshua Meyrowitz suggests, enter into the spaces of everyday life 'like a thief in the night' (Meyrowitz 1985: 117). The flaw at the heart of his critique of television as having 'no sense of place' is that he nowhere recognizes that television has its own institutional locales – above all the studio – which contribute to defining the character of broadcasting's communicative interactions. There is nothing furtive or hidden about this. The locales of radio and television manifest themselves as public and as oriented towards particular kinds of public events. Access to the public culture of the studio is open to all and voluntary. But once that domain is entered audience members must measure up to institutional expectations. In the case of *The Tony Blackburn Show* it is to maintain the fun. And if you don't like it, you can go elsewhere. As Tony Blackburn says:

> If you're offended by sex I advise you to turn to another station. There's plenty of children's programmes around. We have an adult programme going on here. (25 July 1986)

## *Appendix*

| 15 | *Garry* | Hello Tony. |
|----|---------|-------------|
| 16 | *TB* | (*Chat up voice*) Hello. I gather you're getting |
| 17 | | married tomorrow. |
| 18 | *Garry* | Oh yeah 'n I'm really scared I tell you. |
| 19 | *TB* | After all – I'm not surprised – after all you 'nd I |
| 20 | | have meant to one another as well. |
| 21 | *Garry* | I know but (?) my Leader what can I do? We tried to |
| 22 | | get down 'nd see you last night as well. |
| 23 | *TB* | Really? |
| 24 | *Garry* | Yeah we couldn't. We wanted to see your twelve |
| 25 | | incher but – |
| 26 | *TB* | I'm – Garry! |
| 27 | *Garry* | Ahh. |
| 28 | *TB* | I'm amazed you're getting married. All those times |
| 29 | | that we spent in the sand dunes in Swanage together. |
| 30 | *Garry* | Ah d'you remember that time in the Bahamas? |
| 31 | *TB* | Yes. |
| 32 | *Garry* | On the beach just me 'an you. |
| 33 | *TB* | When you used to whisper and nibble my ear. |
| 34 | *Garry* | Ahhh. |
| 35 | *TB* | Underneath the coconut trees. |
| 36 | *Garry* | And you used to show me your twelve incher. |

| 37 | *TB* | And you threw it all away and you're getting married |
| 38 | | tomorrow. Don't you think you should reconsider this? |
| 39 | *Garry* | I think I should Tone, I think I should mate. |
| 40 | *TB* | You'd have made me such a lovely wife as well. |
| 41 | *Garry* | Huh huh |
| 42 | *TB* | The way you swing that little hand-bag Garry. |
| 43 | *Garry* | Heehh |
| 44 | *TB* | And you look so nice in a cocktail dress as well |
| 45 | | in the evening. |
| 46 | *Garry* | You remember when we met in the bar? |
| 47 | *TB* | Ahh |
| 48 | *Garry* | Ahhh |
| 49 | *TB* | Those were the days, weren't they? |
| 50 | *Garry* | Oh, you're telling me Tone. |
| 51 | *TB* | D'you remember when I bought you a cocktail? |
| 52 | *Garry* | Yes yes. |
| 53 | *TB* | And the remark afterwards? Well, it's unrepeatable heh |
| 54 | *Garry* | Hehheh |
| 55 | *TB* | Hehheheh, Heheh who'y're getting married to Garry? |
| 56 | *Garry* | Ah Kerry Robertson. |
| 57 | *TB* | Kerry. |
| 58 | *Garry* | Yeah. |
| 59 | *TB* | (*Miffed*) Huh. How did you meet *her*? |
| 60 | *Garry* | Ohh |
| 61 | *TB* | I s'ppose it was on that holiday together wasn't it? |
| 62 | *Garry* | Oh well |
| 63 | *TB* | When you went off by yourself wandering along the |
| 64 | | seafront. I know Garry. I always had my suspicions |
| 65 | | about you. |
| 66 | *Garry* | Oh well (?) you give the cocktails didn't you |
| 67 | *TB* | Well that's what it was |
| 68 | *Garry* | 'n that's it 'nd I went to the toilet to have |
| 69 | | relief 'nd I went in the gels toilets. |
| 70 | *TB* | Absolutely you well you were always a bit strange and |
| 71 | | now ehheh you're getting married. |
| 72 | *Garry* | Ah |
| 73 | *TB* | You weirdo! |
| 74 | *Garry* | Ah |
| 75 | *TB* | You real weirdo you heheh |
| 76 | *Garry* | Actually now she's done she's going to two-time me |
| 77 | | for you Tone. |
| 78 | *TB* | Absolutely. |
| 79 | *Garry* | Ohh I dunno. |
| 80 | *TB* | Well, it doesn't matter Garry cos when you're married |
| 81 | | I can be your little bit on the side. |
| 82 | *Garry* | All right. |

| 83  | *TB*    | You can call me up in times of need. |
| 84  | *Garry* | Ahh thank you Tone. |
| 85  | *TB*    | Hehh |
| 86  | *Garry* | We're coming up to see you next weekend is it, next |
| 87  |         | Thursday is it the day? Well we're gonna try. |
| 88  | *TB*    | You're coming up – but you're getting married |
| 89  |         | tomorrow. |
| 90  | *Garry* | I know, doesn't matter does it? |
| 91  | *TB*    | Hehhh hehh |
| 92  | *Garry* | Well we're going out tonight. I'm goin' to get my |
| 93  |         | last fling tonight. |
| 94  | *TB*    | You're the last of the romantics you are aren't you? |
| 95  |         | Heheh so you're getting married tomorrow |
| 96  |         | congratulations |
| 97  | *Garry* | Thank you Tone |
| 98  | *TB*    | Hope you'll be very happily married 'n you're going |
| 99  |         | on honeymoon anywhere? |
| 100 | *Garry* | Er well we're going to stay over here a little while |
| 101 |         | 'nd we're waiting till next year see we're going to |
| 102 |         | see Mum in Jamaica. |
| 103 | *TB*    | Great. Well I hope that you er come and see us at the |
| 104 |         | Soul Night next Thursday. |
| 105 | *Garry* | Will do Tone. |
| 106 | *TB*    | Be happily married Garry. |
| 107 | *Garry* | Thank you very much. |
| 108 | *TB*    | Thanks very much indeed for phoning. |
| 109 |         | Jill's in Woodford. Hello Jill. |

(*Continues conversation with Jill*) (Polytechnic of Central London Collection)

# 7

---

# *Dailiness*

The question of what time is has pointed our inquiry in the direction of
Dasein, if by Dasein we mean that entity in its Being which we know as
human life; this entity in the *specificity* of its Being, the entity that we each
ourselves are, which each of us finds in the fundamental assertion: I am.
(Heidegger 1992: 6E)

I

In Division One of *Being and Time* Martin Heidegger undertakes an ontological analysis of the nature of everyday existence as being-in-the-world. His
investigation culminates in the discovery of care as the specific mark of all
possible and all actual ways of human being in the world. This astonishing
and beautiful discovery is not to be understood as a burden (the cares of the
world) nor as ethical concern (caring *for*), but as the mark of *what* matters and
*how*. That things matter for us (no matter what), the ways in which they matter
and the extent to which they do so, mark out the boundaries of our concerns.
Concern is all such things as noticing, remarking upon, attending to, observing, picking out, foregrounding and bringing to bear a focused attentiveness
upon phenomena (upon each other and our selves and circumstances) in
such ways as to find and make the matter to hand significant and meaningful in some way or other. Concern is being caught up in. It is engagement
*with*, involvement *in*. Such concern discovers (finds) the meaningfulness of
phenomena. Care is the meaning of meaning. It has no reason. It simply *is*.

*Dasein*[1] will light on some thing – no matter what – as the object of its focused attentiveness, its concern. It may be no more than idle curiosity, it may be for strategic self-interest, it may be simply for the sake of the thing itself (for its *own* sake). But whatever reason we attempt to find for whatever concern will always fail (though reasons can always be found) because concern is the *earliest* mark of our common nature. We cannot get behind it. Care is our state and way of being in all its aspects and at every level. It gathers in all ways (always) of human being which is understood, finally, as being-in-concern. For this, first and last, is what it is to be *in* the world, to be *with* others. In so far as the world is found to be meaningful and full of meaning it is so to the extent that it matters for us in the specific ways that it is found by us to matter. If nothing matters nothing means and care no longer is.

Our concern here has been and is with broadcasting and its concerns: the care-structures of radio and television. We began, in the *Social History*, with a historical reconstruction of production; more exactly, of how broadcasters went about the business of discovering what their business was to be. We showed there that they found that their job was to make programmes *for* audiences. This came to require (in this country and elsewhere) an immense institutional structure, the skills of thousands of people all geared towards the provision of programme services in such a way that they would appear as no more than what anyone would expect, as what anyone would regard as their due, as a natural, ordinary, unremarkable, everyday entitlement. The institutionalization of broadcasting can be interpreted as its routinization in order to produce and deliver an all-day everyday service that is ready-to-hand and available[2] always

---

[1]    *Dasein* = da-sein (there-being). It is best understood as human life in all its manifestations – past, present and future. It is also something that each and everyone of us possesses. *Dasein* is human being and 'being is in each case mine'. Note that it is this way round and not 'being human'. The emphasis falls on being (the ontological emphasis), and reminds us that there are many other ways of being in the world besides human being. What is the being of other animals, of fish, of trees, of rivers and rocks? Such questions are not central to *Being and Time*, but they are indicated and taken up in Heidegger's later writings. A key question in *Being and Time* is 'what is the *da* of *dasein*? What is its *there*?' Where is human being to be found or, rather, where does it find itself? Where else but in the world? Human being (*dasein*) is being-in-the-world, and what exactly that means is the fundamental issue addressed by Division One of *Being and Time*.

[2]    The terms here have a particular analytic significance in *Being and Time*. The meaningfulness of the background of everyday existence is discussed as manifest in the ways in which *equipment* (Heidegger's famous example is a hammer: here we understand radio and television in this way) is *ready-to-hand* and thereby meaningfully *available*. That is to say, everyday (humanly produced) things present themselves as useful and usable. We understand (we grasp) everyday things by knowing what to do with them and how to use them. Everyday objects are self-disclosing. They show themselves precisely as such things (as unremarkable, obvious, self-evidently what they are *for* for anyone and everyone) by virtue of their being made in such ways as to be found as usefully usable by anyone (cf. *Being and Time* 1(3)).

anytime at the turn of a switch or the press of a button. It means making programmes so that they 'work' every time – not now and again or mostly but always. And again this seems natural for us, no more than we expect. We have recovered the thought, effort and care on the part of the institutions of broadcasting that went into finding out how this could be done by the routinization of programme schedules and the serialization of production. Our account of the formation of British broadcasting, which began with politics and then moved to the production processes themselves, came through in the end to listeners and their situated everyday circumstances as the towards-which of all that preceded it.

This book, starting up from where the previous one left off (the situation of listeners), has attempted to advance that account by showing how the care (the concern) that goes into making programmes in the production process is there-to-be-found in the programmes themselves. Our way has been to reconstruct, in as much detail as possible, the coming-into-being of a programme from its initial conception through to its realization in transmission. Our analysis of that moment – the broadcast moment, the moment of transmission – treats it as an event, an occasion, that appears as the kind of event that it is by virtue of the specific concerns, commitments and involvements that go to producing it *as* entertaining or informative or whatever in its moment-by-moment unfolding. It is the how of concern, the way it is done, that produces any occasion as that which it is (that gives it its 'what').

We have shown that professionalism means producing a programme (any programme) in such a way that the effort, thought and care that goes into it does not obtrude but, to the contrary, is absorbed into the programme itself *as* that which it manifestly is. This is what is meant by quality. It is the defining characteristic of anything well done. A well-done thing is humanly pleasing because what it effortlessly gives off about itself (without ever drawing attention to its efforts) is precisely that care has gone into it – that it is replete with human thought and effort down to the smallest detail – and as such it honours those who made it and those for whom it is made. The care structure of, for instance, *Have a Go!* runs right the way through it from its gross structural, organizational features down to the momentary inflexion of a voice:

| 21 | *Pickles* | Do you do a job too? |
|----|-----------|----------------------|
| 22 | *Florrie* | Yes I'm a bus conductress. |
| 23 | *Pickles* | Are yer? |
| 24 | *Florrie* | Yes. |
| 25 | *Pickles* | An 'ow long 've you been doing that? |
| 26 | *Florrie* | Twelve year. |
| 27 | *Pickles* | Really? |
| 28 | *Florrie* | Yes. |

As transcribed this tiny snippet of the interaction between Pickles and Florrie is flat, banal and seemingly empty but, as always, it is voice that reveals attitude, disposition and demeanour. As we listen that is what we hear and attend to: not only what is said but how. Note the structure: question/response (21–2): repeat question/repeat response (23–4) – a pattern that is repeated in the next four lines (25–8). In each case the first paired exchange can be seen as designed to elicit information and does so: Florrie is a bus conductress, and she's been doing it for 12 years. The second paired exchange, in each case, adds nothing to the information produced by the preceding pair. Are they doing anything then? Could we not do without them?

Do you have a job too?
Yes I'm a bus conductress.
How long have you been doing that?
Twelve years.

It is not difficult to see that by removing the second pair in each case (and slightly modifying the wording of the first pair) the *mood* of the interaction is entirely changed. The interaction becomes brusque, more like a courtroom interrogation than a friendly conversation. And indeed the force of the second paired exchange is precisely mood-generating: 'Are yer?' 'Really?' It is what we hear in the saying that matters – that *is* the matter. 'Are you? Well now. There's a thing. Fancy that. Who'd 've thought? Well I never! Really!' Such-like things are hearable in the way of saying it, a way that discloses a concern, an involvement, a being-with and a being-towards and a being-for-the-sake-of[3] – what? – nothing more (or less) than being engaged, being caught up in talk-with-another in such a way as to find and show that the other is somehow someway interesting and worth talking to and worth listening to and that in so doing there is a pleasure to be found – a public, sayable, showable, shareable, communicable enjoyment of good company and good *craic* (as the Irish say).[4] And this is for no other or better reason than a concern, a care for its own sake, a way of being with-in-public as an end (a good) in itself.

This is not hidden. It needs no depth analysis, no expert interpretation, to find this. Such a care (like all care) is self-disclosing, and if it is careless that shows too and will give rise to noticings and remarkings. Whether careful or careless any event or occasion reveals itself as what it is in the manner of its

[3] In Heidegger's analysis these are structural aspects of the make-up of the availability of equipment that make manifest the 'purpose' or usefulness of the thing (what it is 'for', what kind of involvement it elicits). Here we understand them as structural aspects of any communicative occasion that combine to make manifest the involvement-whole of the occasion, thereby disclosing the kind of occasion that it is (cf. *Being and Time* 116–17).

[4] *Craic* (pronounced 'crack') is untranslatable. 'Was it good *craic*?' One might say of a party, a family get-together, a night out: i.e. was it a friendly, gossipy, sociable sort of thing?

moment-by-moment unfolding. It does not, of course, follow that things will necessarily be *accepted* for what they are. It might be found, for instance, that the ways of saying 'Are yer?' and 'Really!' are somehow fake. Hearably they are said emphatically, but the scale that runs from underemphasis to overemphasis is something that, while common to all, varies from person to person in terms of where the line is drawn. So that an emphatic utterance may be generally heard as emphatic but interpreted differently by different listeners in light of their own circumstances and the person that they are. If 'Are yer?' is heard as overemphatic it may be heard as violating the maxim of quantity (say no more than is necessary for the occasion). As such it may give rise to an interpretation along the lines that Pickles is 'just turning it on', 'playing it up'. He doesn't 'really *mean* it'. To those for whom sincerity is linked to authenticity – being the one and only genuine person that you are – performance is distasteful. To those who enjoy performances what counts is how well the performance is done and how far the occasion comes off.

Thus, meaning cannot be settled. This does not mean that it is always indeterminate or relative, but rather that it *shows* up differently for different people. Our interpretation does not aim to assign and fix meanings, but to show how they *may* be found by virtue of a communicative intentionality that organizes things meaningfully. There are, then, two interpretative levels: the personal assessments and evaluations that we make of any circumstances, and the (prior) organization of those circumstances in such ways as give rise to the possibility of such assessments. In producing the kinds of personal evaluations that we do we show that we have attended to the matter-to-hand and found how it matters (or not) for us. But the kinds of evaluations that are available for us to find are – in the general scope of their possibilities – by virtue of the nature of the occasion. Such has been the concern of the preceding chapters. I have tried to show the concerns of broadcasting as manifest in the organized, organizing particularities of any programme. I have tried to show how any programme is meaningfully available as that which it is and is found to be by me-or-anyone. These accounts are not – of course – in any way exhaustive. Indeed, they are the merest of beginnings. The sheer *range* of broadcast output is such that many important aspects of its work have been left unattended. News is perhaps the outstanding example. Nevertheless, I have tried (have been concerned) to show how this kind of analysis opens up and discloses the output of radio and television in its meaningfulness.

## II

Here it remains to ask one last question. Is there a particular meaningfulness to be found in the activities of radio and television? Is there a specific care structure that is manifest in each and every programme and in the totality of output? Is there an organizing principle that can account for the parts and the whole – that indeed produces a sense of the whole and the parts? We will try to show that *dailiness* is such a structure; that for radio and television it is *the* unifying structure of all its activities – the particular, distinctive, earliest mark of its being.

What is dailiness? We might begin with what it is to provide a daily service – of say bread or milk, newspapers, trains or whatever. In order to bring it about that an everyday service is produced *every* day (without exception) a routinization of the production of the service is required in such a way that that, precisely, is the outcome. Now it is one thing – complex enough – to produce a single good (a newspaper, a pint of milk) in such a way that it is there for anyone on their doorstep each morning. It is another thing to produce a daily service that fills each day, that runs right through the day, that appears as a continuous, uninterrupted, never-ending flow – through all the hours of the day, today, tomorrow and tomorrow and tomorrow. What does that *mean*? What is it to have such a service in such a way that it appears as no more than what I or anyone am entitled to expect as an aspect of my days?

Our sense of days is always already in part determined by the ways in which media contribute to the shaping of our sense of days. Would time feel different for us without radio, television and newspapers? Would it run to a different rhythm? Would it have the edge that it has today? The sense that each day is a particular day? For the effect of the temporal arrangements of radio and television is such as to pick out each day as *this* day, this day in particular, this day as its *own* day, caught up in its own immediacy, with its own involvements and concerns. The huge investment of labour (care) that goes to produce the output of broadcasting delivers a service whose most generalizable effect is to re-temporize time; to mark it out in particular ways, so that the time of day (at any time) is a particular time, a time differentiated from past time-in-the-day or time that is yet-to-come. The time of day in broadcasting is always marked as the time that it is. Its *now* is endlessly thematized in a narrative of days and their dailiness.

It would be a study in itself to show how this is so. Here we can note some of the gross ways in which the dynamics of the time-of-day and time-through-the-day encounter each other in any now-point. Breakfast radio and television thematizes itself as such in all its ways of attending to the present moment and producing it as the moment it is: breakfast time, time-to-get-up, to wash, shave, dress, clean teeth, snatch a bite to eat and off to school, factory, shop, office or wherever. Different kinds of person are implicated in this: adults, children, women and men. Each is attended to in some way in particular services. I usually get up with *Today* (BBC Radio 4), whose very name defines its function of orienting me-or-anyone to the day today. So *Today*, with its formatted time-structure, has regular time-checks, updates and reports on the weather and traffic conditions. All such matter chimes in with my concerns, the tasks that face me now, of gearing up for another day today. *Today* brings me 'news': what's happened since I went to bed, what's happening 'now', what's coming up later in the day. And this begins to give me my sense of the fullness of days – of this or any day; that today is *this* day in particular because *this* is happening. Today is not empty. It is full of matter and concerns. *What* matter, what concerns show up for me-or-anyone in *Today* or whatever I listen to, watch or read as part of the beginning of my day. Today may be a fun-day on *The Big Breakfast* (TV, Channel 4) or in the *Sun* newspaper. Different significances are picked out in different morning media services, each with their own involvement-structures, but all combining to produce the sense of the meaningfulness of days as that which we start with each and every day.

If this is our start-point, the narrative of days is the story of the movement of time through the day: the way in which any moment, in its own now-point, is caught in a double movement away from and towards. This movement shows up (grossly) in the ways that time-through-the-day is zoned from breakfast time to bed time. These zones are part of the fundamental way in which broadcast services are arranged to be appropriate to the time of day – which means appropriate to who in particular is available to watch or listen at what time and in what circumstances. So zoning adjusts services to be grossly appropriate to what people are doing and when.

In the early years of television competition between the BBC and ITV both sides observed the so-called 'toddler's truce' – the period between six and seven in the evening when there were no television services partly, it was said, to make it easier for parents to get young children to bed. In 1957 the BBC decided to fill this gap with a programme that chimed in with what viewers were thought likely to be doing at that time. Inquiries were made:

> They would be coming and going: women getting meals for teenagers who were going out and preparing supper for men who were coming in; men in the North would be having their tea; commuters in the South would be arriving home. There was no likelihood of an audience which would be ready to view steadily for half-an-hour at a time. What seemed necessary was a continuous programme held together by a permanent staff of comperes, reporters and interviewers, but consisting of separate items so that any viewer who happened to be around could dip into it knowing that something different would soon follow and that he had not lost anything by not being able to watch from the beginning. (Wyndham-Goldie 1978: 210)

The result was *Tonight*, the first major topical news magazine on television to be presented five nights a week in this country. The form and content of the programme was plainly designed in relation to expectations about what viewers

might be doing at that time and how such matters might affect their dispositions towards 'what's on'. Such institutional arrangements correspond with the
attitudes of viewers. Here is Jane, a regular viewer of *Crossroads* (a popular
early evening soap opera that ran for 12 years on ITV at the same time of day
as *Tonight*), talking to Dorothy Hobson about watching it:

J:      It's sort of tea-time viewing but not in the sense that you would
usually use tea-time viewing, do you know what I mean?

DH:    What do you mean when you say, 'Not in the sense you would normally use tea-time viewing'? How would you normally use it?

J:      Well people have got to stop and watch Crossroads 'cos it's on at tea-
time but with other things you are like rushing around getting the
tea and talking and it's sort of in the background. (Hobson 1982: 111)

A notion of 'tea-time' viewing is shared by both broadcasters and viewers and
points again to the ways in which what broadcasters do is designed to chime
in with my-time, always understood as the matter to hand, what concerns *me*
now – such as the rush and bustle of getting the family tea on the table.

Children may have gone to bed after tea 40 years ago, but not today. 'Family
viewing time', by common agreement between the broadcasters, runs until 9.00
in the evening, after which we enter a new time-zone: 'adult time' which
means adult themes (sex and bad language). Thus, the situational proprieties
of broadcasting always attend to time and place. Adult talk is appropriate late
in the day, but not earlier. Jonathan Ross established a reputation for himself
in the eighties as a master of entertaining late-night 'adult' talk on Channel 4.
Whatever tacky topic formed the substance of the talk Ross dealt with it in
such a way that the sleaze did not stick to himself or his show. It was found
that Ross was very popular with younger listeners (who should have been in
bed!), so it was decided to give him an early evening slot, setting him directly
against the master of early-evening chat, Terry Wogan and his show on BBC
1, *Wogan*. In this context Ross was not a success. 'Adult' themes were ruled
out as inappropriate to that time-of-day, but Ross's style was particular and
appropriate for that kind of talk. Without it he was ill-at-ease and it showed.
Thus, time marks the kind of thing that can be talked about and the way it can
be talked about at different times-of-day.

## III

Rigorous critics, who have 'seen through' the media, accuse the press and
broadcasting of reproducing the status quo, of creating a frozen immediacy
caught in an eternal present that obliterates the past and denies the future.

Nothing could be further from the truth, for time runs to many rhythms in the structures of broadcasting, while always converging on the now. The business (the busyness) of broadcasting is towards the production of a daily service day by day and every day. As such, although for us as viewers or listeners the services of radio and television appear *on* the day each day, broadcasting is always already ahead of itself.[5] It is always already projected beyond the day that we and it are in, and indeed it must be so in order to produce for us the day that we are in. In always being-ahead-of-itself the futuricity of broadcasting shows up: that is, the future *is* always already someway somehow structured in advance, is always anticipated (prepared for, cared for) in such structures. And this is inseparable from the pastness of radio and television which is always brought forward and projected into the future, for the future can only be anticipated in light of the past so that, in a sense, the past is ahead of us as that which (even now) is projected into the future. Thus that-which-was and that-which-is-to-be are both intrinsic to the now of broadcasting's dailiness. They encounter each other in the phenomenal now – the presencing present, the that-which-*is*, the *da* of *dasein*. The care structures of dailiness cannot be understood if broadcasting's now is thought of as blocking out the past or the future. Both are produced as what they are in our kind of society in large part by the way that the dailiness of days is constituted. Broadcasting, whose medium is time, articulates our sense of time.

Time may be understood in various ways: as natural time (day and night), abstract time (clock time) or experiential (phenomenological) time. Experiential time is *my time*: time as experienced by me-or-anyone, my own here-and-now, my situated being-in-the-world, me as a real someone someplace sometime now.[6] The time to which broadcasting directs its efforts is my-time. My-time measures all things (all concerns) from where it is, and as such its concerns are always proximal, always measured from where-I-am, how near or far, how close or distant. And such proximities are both spatial and temporal: how far or close behind from now, how close or far ahead. Phenomenological time is human time, the time of *dasein* (of being-there). It is this time to which broadcasting tunes its services. Human time is *life*time. Broadcasting is and is not in lifetime. It articulates its time-structures to human lifetime, but its time is outside human lifetime.

---

[5]   *Dasein* as being-ahead-of-itself is discussed in *Being and Time* (1(6): 236ff.).

[6]   'I am my time' is the motif running through the lecture to the Marburg theologians which Heidegger gave in 1924, entitled 'The Concept of Time' (Heidegger 1992). The lecture is generally regarded as the 'ur-form' of *Being and Time* (Gadamer 1994; Kisiel 1995), in which most of the key-concepts of the later masterpiece are introduced in programmatic form. My-world and my-time are not to be thought of as originating in a subject (a 'me') and therefore as indicating a subjective (purely personal) world and time. To the contrary, both are public structures that permit the formation of subjects and subjective worlds and times.

Time is at once reversible and irreversible, linear and cyclical. Linear time is one-way and irreversible, 'the arrow of time'. Stories and days are linear: they have a beginning, a middle, an end; morning, noon and night. Yet each day is succeeded by another day in an endless cycle of repetition. Cyclical time is reversible time. Each day is a fresh start, a new beginning, as the ebb and flow of tides washes away all manmarks on the shoreline and restores its pristine freshness at every tideturn. Human time is caught up in the to and fro of time (for time goes backwards as well as forwards). Lifetime is essentially linear, a one-way street from birth to death. Yet our day-to-day life is essentially cyclical. We live in the routine repetitive cycle of days, weeks, months and years. Do we escape the arrow of time, our being-towards-death[7] in these ways?

Hours, days, months may be the rags of time for lovers.[8] For the rest of us they are ways of marking out time into different spans whose meaningfulness is linked to projected future possibilities. What is it to live for the weekend? Or to live from year to year for that one day of carnival when the world comes alive in its fullness? Or to long for Christmas Day or one's birthday as children do? The succession of days on radio and television is not just the turn and return of the eversame. In being-ahead-of-itself broadcasting is towards a future that is not radically indeterminate but known-in-advance in significant ways, in ways that make the future significant, that bring it towards us and into our present as it moves to meet it.

Our historical study showed how this came about; how broadcasting gathered together a quite new kind of public life – a world of public persons, events and happenings – and gave this world an ordered, orderly, familiar, knowable appearance by virtue of an unobtrusively unfolding temporal sequence of events that gave substance and structure to everyday life.[9] In the course of the 1920s and 1930s a new annual calendar of events came into being, as BBC engineers arranged thousands upon thousands of outside broadcasts (OBs) from a wide variety of sources for the growing listening public. All these broadcasts were live: they existed in real time, the time of transmission being at the same time as and corresponding with the time of reception. Thus, real-world, real-time

---

[7]    Being-towards-death: the existential theme of Division 2 of *Being and Time*, the way in which the temporality of *dasein* is revealed.

[8]    'Love all alike no season knows nor clime, Nor hours, days, months which are the rags of time.' Thus lovers live (or hope they do) in a timeless now that cannot fade. Children do so really and truly. 'In the story of a human life', Doris Lessing notes, 'if it is being told true to time as actually experienced, then I'd say seventy per cent of the book would take you to age ten. At eighty per cent you would have reached fifteen. At ninety-five per cent you get to about thirty. The rest is a rush – towards eternity' (Lessing 1995: 109). The ecstatic now of childhood fades as part of growing up. The loss of its enchanted now has been a rich poetic theme since Wordsworth.

[9]    The next page or so first appeared in Scannell (1988). Cf. Scannell and Cardiff (1991: 277–89).

events – which hitherto had been accessible only to their self-selecting and particular publics – now became available for anyone. Millions of people now had access to events-in-the-world that had previously been outside their realm of possibility. These events included religious services and sacred music from churches; opera and plays from theatres and entertainment from the variety halls; dance music from cafés and hotels and concert music from the concert halls; all kinds of sporting events (racing, cricket, golf, football, to take only the most obvious instances); public speeches by public persons from all sorts of public places; and ceremonies and events that ranged from royal occasions to the song of the nightingale . . . an annual occasion on radio for a few years in the 1920s, which was to the BBC what the first cuckoo was to the letter columns of *The Times*.[10]

The cornerstone of this calendar was the religious year: the weekly observance of the Sabbath through church services and a programme schedule markedly more austere than on other days of the week; the great landmarks of Christmas, Easter and Pentecost; the feastdays of the patron saints of England, Scotland, Wales and Ireland which occasioned special programmes from the appropriate 'region', though what to do with St Patrick's Day was an annually recurring nightmare for programme-makers in Belfast. National civil holidays were celebrated in festive mood (New Year's Eve, August Bank Holiday, Whit Monday), while the solemn days of national remembrance were marked by special services and feature programmes. Sport, of course, developed its own calendar very rapidly. The winter season had its weekly observances of football, rugby and steeple-chasing, climaxing in the great feasts of the Boat Race, the Grand National and the Cup Final. Summer brought in cricket and flat racing, the test matches, Derby Day, Royal Ascot and Wimbledon.

The broadcast year – in the northern hemisphere – falls naturally into two divisions: the indoor months of autumn and winter and the outdoor months of spring and summer. One of the first things the radio manufacturers discovered was the seasonal nature of the sale of radio sets which increased sharply as winter came on. Hence, the annual trade exhibition, Radiolympia, was held in the autumn as heralding the start of 'the wireless season' (Hill 1978: 67). By the late twenties output was being planned on a quarterly basis, and the autumn season was always carefully designed to woo the 'fireside listener' with a varied menu of new plays, concerts and variety programmes. The fireside months were generally more well stocked with 'serious' listening matter, but from Whitsun onwards the lighter elements in the programmes were expected to

---

[10]  Microphones were set up in a known haunt of nightingales (a wood in Surrey) on an early summer's evening. In order to encourage the birds to pour forth their song for the ears of listeners a (lady) cellist was also set up in the wood. Thus, even if the birds remained silent there was at least something musical to be heard.

have an increasingly wider appeal. At the same time the broadcasters claimed to have redressed the balance between the seasons of the year, making it possible now to hear good plays and music through the summer months when the theatres and concert halls were normally closed (*Radio Times* 11 May 1934). Thus, programme planners tried to find broadly appropriate seasonal matter to suit the climate of the time of year and the mood and leisure activities of the audience. The highpoint of their activities were the arrangements for Christmas Day.

From the very beginning of broadcasting in Britain Christmas was always the most important date in its annual calendar. It was the supreme family festival, an invocation of the spirit of Charles Dickens, a celebration of 'Home Hearth and Happiness' (*Radio Times* 20 December 1924). It was no coincidence that John Reith, first Director General of the BBC, worked hard and long to persuade the King to speak, from his home and as head of his family, on this particular day. The royal Christmas Day broadcast (the first was in 1932) quickly became an integral part of the ritual of the British Christmas and remains so to this day – even to the point of parody. It is a classic illustration of that historical process whereby tradition is invented afresh. It seemed to set a seal on the role of broadcasting in giving expression to a sense of Britishness, of a shared way of life, in which the nation was understood through the cosy, domestic image of the family: the family audience, the royal family, the nation (the Empire) as family.

Much has changed in substance since the twenties and thirties, but the fundamental temporal structures of broadcasting remain the same. New events have been discovered, old ones discarded: less emphasis now on royal ceremony perhaps, more on sport. But now, as then, there is a stable temporal framework to the output of radio and television working through the days of the week, the months and the years. The broadcasting calendar creates a horizon of expectations, a mood of anticipation, a directedness towards that which is to come, thereby giving substance and structure (a 'texture of relevances') to everyday life. This patterned temporal regularity remains through all the years, and if it is disturbed it gives rise to noticings and remarkings. In the early 1980s the BBC decided to reschedule one of its most popular and long-running drama series, *Dr Who* – a decision which prompted the following response in the leader columns of The *Guardian*:

> All those who have grown up or grown old with *Doctor Who* (for some who watched it in the early days, tremblingly, from around the safe cover of a friendly armchair are now men of destiny and captains of what industry this country has left) know it to be as essential a part of a winter Saturday as coming in cold from heath, forest or football, warm crumpets (or pikelets, if preferred) before the fire, the signature tune of *Sports Report*, and that sense

of liberation and escapist surrender which can only come about when tomorrow is a day off too. These conditions cannot be created on Mondays and Tuesdays. Saturday will be smitten by the destruction of an essential ingredient, and *Doctor Who* will be destroyed by this violent wrenching from its natural context. (The *Guardian*, 4 January 1982: 10. Quoted in Tulloch and Alvarado 1983: 14)

For programme planners the organization of the schedules is a complex business in which decisions to move or remove particular items is part of a long-term, competitive game-plan. For listeners and viewers, schedules are part of their lives, part of their my-time, which is disturbed when things get moved about. Tea-times were disrupted in households that regularly watched *Crossroads* when the programme was moved forward by half an hour:

Well I must admit when the programme altered I altered my tea-time . . . we brought our dinner forward about ten minutes so that we are either eating it or occasionally depending on what we've had, we have something just about finished and we dive in here to watch all of it in colour. (Hobson 1982: 105)

In the case of *Doctor Who* – as the leader half-seriously suggests – the pleasures of winter weekends were in some small way caught up in the programme as an enjoyment that was there-in-advance and known to be, thereby giving structure and substance, an attitude of expectancy, to the Saturdays that were to come. Such effects are incremental. They accumulate in time as they are reproduced through time. In the course of many years broadcast output becomes sedimented in memory as traces of a common past and of the biography of individuals. Ask anyone alive at the time what they remember of wartime radio and the answer is Churchill's speeches, Tommy Handley and *ITMA*; from the fifties, the Coronation and Tony Hancock; from the sixties the assassination and funeral of Kennedy . . . a serial world punctuated by singular events. Such memories – at once individual and social in their availability for me or anyone – are not restricted to real-world persons and events. The temporal structures of radio and television – the ways in which they are articulated to my-time, to life-time – show up most clearly in that fictional narrative form which is particular to broadcasting, namely never-ending serials, or soap operas.

## IV

Soap operas are among the most remarkable things that broadcasting does.[11] How can we grasp a narrative that has been told five days a week, continuously

---

[11]    This section is largely taken from Scannell (1988).

for nearly 50 years? Such, for instance, is the length of time that *The Archers* has been running on Radio 4: over 13,000 episodes, more than 3,000 hours of transmission time (excluding omnibus repeats). What kinds of story are these, that in a perpetual 'now' are always projecting their past into a future that has no perceptible ending? Nor any originary point of departure, as Christine Geraghty points out in her excellent analysis of the narrative structure of soaps. The first episodes of *Coronation Street* or *EastEnders* already suppose that in each case the life-world of the narrative is fully given and in being and motion. The first episode simply 'cuts in' on this world as the last episode 'cuts out' of it. We are pitched into, or 'thrown' into the story, to pick it up, to figure it out and so on, just as – Heidegger argues – we are pitched or thrown into life and the world itself.[12] It is rare for these stories to die but Geraghty notes that when *Waggoner's Walk* (Radio 2) was brought to an untimely end in 1980 by BBC economies, there was no attempt to tie up all the loose ends in the last episode. 'One is left', she remarks, 'with a sense that the serial has not stopped but is still taking place' (Geraghty 1981: 11). This effect of a fictional world that exists in parallel with the actual world is the most powerful and distinctive feature of this kind of story and is the basis of the cumulative pleasures it offers to its listeners or viewers.

A sense of 'unchronicled growth' – of the objective, continuing existence outside the narrative of Ambridge (the setting of *The Archers*) or Albert Square (the setting of *EastEnders*) – is largely an effect of the way in which time passes between one episode and another. Between times the characters pursue an 'unrecorded existence' that is resumed in the next instalment. In other words, we are aware, as Geraghty suggests, that day-to-day life has continued in our absence, an awareness that is powerfully enhanced by the ways in which time in the fictional world runs in parallel with time in the actual world. Serials (in Britain) vary in the scrupulousness with which they observe real time. *The Archers* is the most punctilious in paralleling real time, so that if it is Tuesday in the narrative it is usually Tuesday in the real world. *Coronation Street* also gives the impression of marking time in its fictional life-world as running to the time of the world of its viewers, so that significant days in 'our' world (public holidays, Christmas) are marked and celebrated on the day in Coronation Street. Real-world events cross over into the story-world of the programmes, most notably in the wedding in Coronation Street planned as a double celebration to coincide with the wedding of Prince Charles and Lady

---

[12] 'Thrownness' is a key concept in *Being and Time*. 'This characteristic of Dasein's being – this "that it is" – is veiled in its "whence" and "whither", yet disclosed in itself all the more unveiledly; we call it the *thrownness* of this entity into its "there". . . . The expression "thrownness" is meant to suggest the *facticity of its being delivered over*' (*Being and Time*: 174). 'Thrownness' thus indicates the *da* of *dasein*, that its being-in-the-world is not an option for it (not a choice), but is ineluctably that which it is and has to be.

Diana Spencer. In *The Archers* real-world people occasionally appear as themselves: Princess Margaret, for instance, or (even more bizarre) Dame Edna
Everidge.[13]

It is a strange experience to watch the first-ever episode of *Coronation Street*,
recorded in grainy black and white on 9 December 1960, and to follow this with
an episode in colour from today. There, 35 years ago, is Ken Barlow (aged 21),
played by William Roache (aged 28), an anxious grammar-school boy in his
first year at college. Now, here is the self-same Ken, three-and-a-half decades
later and with a chequered career and personal life behind him – the only
member of today's cast who has been in the programme since the very first
episode. The abrupt time-leap from the first episode to the present immediately makes visible the ways in which actor and character (the two are inseparable) have aged, at exactly the same rate, over 35 years. And this confirms
the movement of time in the tale as corresponding with the movement of lifetime and its passing away.

To maintain the densely textured social world of such programmes calls
for unremitting backstage teamwork by the actors and production team. The
actors portray the characters they play as 'real people', as persons in all their
particularity. It requires considerable art to bring off this artless effect, and the
care with which the actors attend to the fine details of the management and
maintenance of the self-same identity of the characters they play shows up
clearly in, for instance, Dorothy Hobson's discussions with the cast of *Crossroads* (Hobson 1982: 87–105). The longest running programmes include a
historian or archivist in the production team to ensure that no discrepancies
appear between past and present, that characters retain consistent biographies,
and that birthdays and anniversaries are remembered on the right day from one
year to the next. For it is certain that if mistakes creep in they will be spotted
by regular listeners or viewers.

From such considerations we can begin to understand how it is that people
in these fictional worlds are knowable *in the same way* as people in the real
world are known and knowable. This is surely the remarkable, unique feature
of such stories and it enables us to account for their well-known effect as real
and life-like for their many followers – for that, indeed, is what they are. The

---

[13]    Dame Edna is a fictional character (or is she?) created by Barry Humphries. A wonderful, monstrous, blue-rinse creation, she hails from Moonee Ponds – a fearsome parody of
suburban housewives in Melbourne and everywhere. Dame Edna has long been a resident of
Britain where she is an established superstar with her own television show. It was in this
context that she appeared in *The Archers*, or rather that one of the cast of *The Archers*
appeared (or appeared to appear) in her show. For addicts of the programme it was a
delicious in-joke that it was Lynda Snell of all people (the programme's own comic parody
of a suburban housewife 'gone rural') who met Dame Edna 'in the flesh'. A truly awesome
encounter!

key is the correspondence between the movement of time in the fictional world and the real world: for, since these move in parallel and at the same pace, it follows that the lifetime of viewers and listeners unfolds at the same rate as the lives of the characters in the story. Thus, one stands in the same temporal relation to them as one does to one's own family, relatives, friends and everyday acquaintances. Moreover, access to these fictional worlds corresponds closely to the forms of access one has to the people in one's own everyday world: in both, people are encountered in similar settings and circumstances, and in the same way. And just as, in our own lives, we acquire through the years our own accumulating biography as well as an accumulating knowledge of the lives of those around us, so too, in the same way, we come to know the people in the stories. We can recall past incidents in their lives with the same facility as we can remember events in our own lives and in the lives of those we know and have known for years. We can 'drop out' of the narrative for a while and then return and pick up the threads in the same way as we drop out of and resume real life situations and relationships.

It is in such ways that these stories resonate in memory in a double sense: they are both a common cultural resource shared by millions and yet are particular to the lives of individuals. Talk about them is a staple currency of the tabloid press and of daily life everywhere that they exist. Irene Pennachioni (1984) tells of a friend on a long bus journey in the north-east of Brazil. After a while she finds herself listening to the conversation going on in front of her. Two men are avidly discussing someone they know who, it seems, has ruined and then killed his brother-in-law in order to marry his sister. Later on two more men get on the bus and loudly discuss the same man. Women join in the conversation and eventually just about everyone in the bus is talking about him in a discussion that lasts the whole journey. Pennachioni's friend is amazed at the fame of this man who is, apparently, known throughout the region – until she finally realizes that what everyone has been talking about is the villain (or hero) of the current daily *telenovela*. Such stories are good to talk about. They are talkable-about as everyday matters and in the same way. They provide a common sociable topical resource that is readily available to anyone who is a regular viewer or listener. The gossip-function of soap operas is central to their enjoyment. Such pleasure grows in time. The more you know about the characters and their past lives, the more subtle and informed will be your assessment of their behaviour in any present 'what next?' circumstances. Memory is crucial to the pleasure of soaps, but it is forward-looking rather than backward-looking. It is what is presently carried forward (what is not forgotten) by the narrative and its viewers or listeners as relevant to what is to come. Thus, memory is linked to a mood not of nostalgia but expectancy: what is to come can be anticipated in the light of a remembered past that reverberates in the future-facing present.

V

But the present cannot bring forward the past in its fullness. Geraghty (1981: 18) puts her finger on much wider issues when she observes that 'although the accumulated past is important to a serial, one could say that the ability to "forget" what has happened in the serial's past is also crucial. If the serial had to carry the heavy weight of its own past it would not be able to carry on'. This work of filtering and discarding the past, while orienting the present towards emerging events and processes, is accomplished daily and routinely by broadcast news. Philip Schlesinger, who has written most illuminatingly of the 'time culture' of news production, speaks of the way in which the whole process 'is so organised that its basic dynamic emphasises the *perishability of stories*' (Schlesinger 1978: 105, my emphasis). Soap operas and their stories may live for ever and continuously bring their past into the present, but yesterday's news is – literally – dead news. The whole emphasis in the newsroom is on 'pace' and 'immediacy', on being 'up to the minute'. When a story carries over from one day to the next, it is assumed that the audience will, after one day's exposure, be familiar enough with the subject matter to permit the 'background' to be largely taken for granted. 'It is always *today's* developments which occupy the foreground' (ibid.).

The care structures of news, all geared to today, contribute to our sense of the eventfulness of days. Our earlier analysis attended to events as occasional things whose occasionality was the mark of an eventfulness which showed up against a background of uneventful everyday existence. The care structures of news are designed to routinize eventfulness, to produce it as an everyday phenomenon every day and thereby historicizing dailiness. This, again, was something learnt. In the very early days of news broadcasting on radio, it was thought of as occasional. There was the famous moment when, on Good Friday 1930, the BBC newsreader announced, 'There is no news tonight' and that was that. This caused much amazement (and some mirth) in the press, who pointed out that there was all sorts of news that day: the death of Lady Glaney, the fire at Lord Haddo's mansion, the mountaineering accident to Professor Julian Huxley and the motor collision involving Lady Diana Cooper were just some of the things that the *Sunday Chronicle* thought might have been mentioned.[14]

Since then broadcasters have learnt how to do news gathering and telling for *The Day Today* – the title of a recent spoof series (BBC 2) that brilliantly parodied the portentous style of current television news formats. News is part of the fabric of days for us. In the course of the day it is constantly, routinely

---

[14]   That the BBC did not regard such stuff as 'news' is, of course, the point. On early BBC news-values see Scannell and Cardiff (1991: 105–33).

updated: news on the hour, and on the half-hour, breakfast news, lunch-time news, tea-time news, evening news and late-night news. News marks the structure of days, bringing it to an eventful climax with the *main* news nightly: seven o'clock news (Channel 4), nine o'clock news (BBC 1), ten o'clock news (ITV) and, for news-junkies, *Newsnight* (BBC 2) which reviews and discusses the news of the day that has gone and ends with a look ahead to next day's news.

What is all this busyness for, all this concern, this huge investment of economic, technological and human resources? What is news *about*? It is about *in* the world. It is about the world. That is its business. News for us is world-disclosing. In its busyness and concern it reveals the ways of the world, the worldliness of world. Perhaps the simplest, most fundamental thing in Heidegger's radical phenomenology was the rediscovery of *world*: the world in its immense and overwhelming facticity; the world as that which *dasein* is *in*, pitched into, *thrown* into; the world in which I have my being; the world in all its fullness and immediacy; in which I am and have to be. 'It *worlds*', 'It is worlding', Heidegger was saying in his lectures in the early twenties[15] at the very moment that people were beginning to realize what radio might do for them:

> I live in a dull, drab colliery village as far removed from real country as from real city life, a bus ride from third rate entertainments and a considerable journey from any educational, musical or social advantages of a first class sort. In such an atmosphere life becomes rusty and apathetic. Into this monotony comes a good radio set and my little world is transformed.

It worlds for *me*. Radio *worlds* for this and countless other listeners. It discloses – for the first time and routinely – the public world in its eventfulness. This world enters into countless my-worlds, so that my world is transformed: it is doubled. It is me and my immediate concerns, but now – and at the same time – such concerns extend to and include the great world beyond the immediate horizon of my time, my life. Two worlds then: my world and my being in it – the environing world of my everyday existence in which I am with others, the world of my immediate concerns – and the great world beyond the horizon of my-world, an eventful public world of public persons, doings and happenings.

These two worlds had been imaginatively thematized long before broadcasting in the European historical novel: that narrative line (picked out by Lukács) that runs from *Waverley* through *The Charterhouse of Parma* to its culminating fulfilment in *War and Peace*. In these great novels there is firstly the world of 'actual' history – of politics, war and the decisive actions of 'great men' (Napoleon, in

---

[15]    As early as 1919 in fact. 'The meaningful is the primary, (for) it gives itself immediately to me, without any detour of thought across the apprehension of a thing. Everywhere and always it signifies for me, living in an environing world; it is wholly worldlike; "*it worlds*"' (1919 lecture, quoted in Kisiel 1995: 329).

the case of Stendhal and Tolstoy). Set against this is the life-world of the novel in which (fictional) ordinary people live their ordinary lives that are, in some ways, touched by and caught up in the historical events of their time. What is fascinating about these novels is the attitudes they display to the fictional and actual worlds that are interwoven in their narratives. In all three, 'real life' is located in the uneventful daily life which makes up the fictional world of the novel, and actual history (the doings of kings, statesmen and generals) appears, in comparison, as finally unreal and remote from the fictional concerns of ordinary men and women.

By the end of the century this had changed, and the relationship between the two worlds of everyday life and public affairs had turned around. In the European drama of the late 19th century (Ibsen and Chekhov), as Raymond Williams notes, the focus of dramatic interest is ordinary life and its setting is the family home; 'but men and women stared from its windows, or waited anxiously for messages, to learn about forces "out there", which would determine the condition of their lives' (Williams 1974: 27). The gap between these two worlds – 'the immediate living areas and the directed places of work and government' – created both the need and the form of new kinds of communication, of 'news' from elsewhere, from otherwise inaccessible sources (ibid.: 26, 27). The development of mass-circulation daily newspapers was a response to such pressures:

> The development of the press . . . was at once a response to the development of an extended social, economic and political system and a response to crisis within that system. The centralisation of political power led to a need for messages from that centre along other than official lines. . . . (F)or the transmission of news and background – the whole orienting, predictive and updating process which the fully developed press represented – there was an evident need which the largely traditional institutions of church and school could not meet. . . . As the struggle for a share in decision and control became sharper, in campaigns for the vote and then in competition for them, the press became not only a new communications system but, centrally, a new social institution. (Ibid.: 21–2)

As forces beyond the immediate horizon of my-world increasingly impinged upon it and affected it – threatened to colonize it, as Habermas would say – anxiety (that defining *mood* of the late 19th and early 20th century) seeped into daily life more and more. That confidence in the normative validity of the everyday that showed so marvellously in *War and Peace* – that sense of the meaningfulness of existence as securely grounded in the being and everyday concerns of people proximally present and sufficient unto each other – began to crumble.

Even as the forces of history were apparently rebuffed by the narrative concerns of the European novel, they began to threaten the very possibility of poetry as the disenchantment of the world grew apace. This was a central motif in the poetry of Wordsworth, Keats and Baudelaire: the charm, the spell of language was broken and only with great difficulty could poetry find words for a world that was dead to its charms. As lyric poetry fell silent that sense of the domination of alien, external, uncontrollable powers gathered momentum in the late 19th century: it fused into a complex logic of domination (economic, political and cultural) – 'the steel hard cage' of modernity from which there was no escape. Meaning drained out of everyday existence and was testified to in various ways in European literature and the emerging social sciences: 'ennui' (Baudelaire), 'alienation' (Marx), 'anomie' (Durkheim), 'disenchantment' (Weber). Is not this the threnody of loss that runs from Marx, through Weber and Lukács to Adorno, Horkheimer and Marcuse and which echoes in Heidegger's writings? And this was not something 'invented' by artists and intellectuals (a mere projection of subjective mood), but was no more than *their* response to the actual experience and texture of life – the mood of the world as it showed itself in those times. That sense of the catastrophic collapse of the possibilities of ordinary, everyday existence appeared 'even' in the concerns of mass culture: 'machine civilization' (modernity *in extremis*) was portrayed apocalyptically in Fritz Lang's *Metropolis* and comically in Chaplin's *Modern Times*. It showed most terribly in totalitarian politics where life was finally rendered down to the death camps and the gulags. The nightmare of modernity was not finally dispelled until the cold war and its (literally) mad politics of Mutually Assured Destruction suddenly collapsed at the end of the eighties.

Yet all this time the life-denying forces of impersonal economic and political domination were silently mined away from within by all those forces that asserted the everyday and its concerns, that retrieved and proclaimed the social, sociable character of human life. Modern media mediated between what were thought of as 'the centre' and 'the margins': the centres of economic, political and cultural power (where the 'real' action lay) and the spaces of everyday existence in which silent masses eked out their marginal existence. Such ways of thinking were part of the very logic of domination itself, and it was against this that intellectuals, in the aftermath of the Second World War, began to turn. The writings of Lefebvre, Williams, Habermas and Goffman (to take notable instances) mark the salvaging (the redemption) of everyday life, and a recognition of it as that in which we live and have our being, which we must understand if we are to have a sense of how we live and who we are. It is part of our argument that the historical task of media in the 20th century has been to take up that task begun by literature (especially the novel) in the 19th century; namely, to mediate between a historical public world and an unhistorical my-world. A daily press begins the process that radio and television bring to fulfilment: the radical historicization and normalization of everyday life by virtue of the dailiness of news and other matter that fill the schedules through each day.


## VI

How, then, does the world in its worldliness show up for us daily in broadcast output? It is surely, in Anthony Giddens's phrase, 'a *peopled* world' – that is, a world in which people have the attributes of persons. This means that they are treated as having face, and therefore face-needs which must be attended to. Those who appear (however) on radio and television are picked out as particular individuals, not faceless, anonymous members of a mass society in which all are all alike.

It is this that has been attended to – that has been my most intimate concern – in the preceding chapters: the redemption of people, by radio and television, as particular persons in their own right. It shows in many ways, but for me most intimately and personally in voice. For what, after all, have I been studying all these years, in studying radio? *The Listener*.[16] Listening. I *listen* to radio. It speaks to me and I hear it. What do I hear if not voices in the air, and what do I hear in voices? I hear in voices the thereness of their speakers. Where they are coming from. Where they are. What they're at. A place. A person. Miss Lydia Lomas from Cressbrook, talking about her long life. Someone who speaks herself. And in this speaking is their being. Their being is manifest and manifold. It is not some fixed and singular thing. It is Tony Blackburn playing at being Tony Blackburn, talking himself (his projected self) into being. Whoever or whatever they are, they are themselves in what they say, in the *way* they say it, in the grain of the voice, the body in the voice as it speaks or sings. Vera Lynn's clear, young voice. Wilfred Pickles and Florrie, who works on the buses. Themselves uttering themselves. Their being themselves in the way that they are in the saying of it:

> Each mortal thing does one thing and the same:
> Deals out that being indoors each one dwells;
> Selves – goes itself; *myself* it speaks and spells;
> Crying *Whát I dó is me: for that I came.*

Speaking is selving. To grasp this you must hear it. Listening *before* speaking. The ontological moment in language is listening.[17] It is a primary act of attending

---

[16]    The title of the BBC's weekly magazine – first for radio and, later, television too – which began in 1930 and finally folded in the 1980s.

[17]    'Listening to . . . is Dasein's existential way of Being-open as Being-with for Others. Indeed, hearing constitutes the primary and authentic way in which Dasein is open for its

to, of noticing (of picking out significance) and as such it precedes any utterance. It is how we get into language in the first place. To hear what is in the voice is to hear the -ness of language, languageness. Its being itself in its embodied utterance. The self that is spoken is the self of the speaker *and* the self of language. Language itself. I am language. Language is me. And you. It is ours. It is what is between us. It is what we share. It is our gift from one generation to the next. I have tried to listen to what is there to be heard in the voices on air. I have tried to hear their hearable being themselves in speaking. The *dasein* of radio and television – its liveness – speaks in living voices.

In such and other ways broadcasting in its liveness rekindles the life and fire of the world in all its live and living being. 'It is most assuredly incorrect', Niklas Luhmann remarks, 'to characterize modern society as an impersonal mass society' (Luhmann 1986: 12). If by this is meant late 20th century society, this is undoubtedly so. It is part of our argument that radio and television, as they developed in the course of this century, have powerfully contributed to repersonalizing the world. It is a truism to say that television has personalized politics, for instance. But what does that mean? Let us consider, again, the transformations of publicness to which radio and television have contributed. Publicness is the irreducible mark of the intrinsically social character of life. It shows as a constitutive feature of language in its communicative and therefore necessarily public character. It is a key characteristic of world in Heidegger's analysis. How is publicness to be understood as it is displayed on radio and television?

## VII

Publicness is that which is not concealed, not hidden, not covered up, not covered over . . . in short, not secret.[18] Such apophatic definitions point up its fundamental characteristic as being available, accessible and open. But how

ownmost potentiality-for-Being . . . Dasein hears because it understands' (*Being and Time* 1(5): 206).

[18]    Heidegger's accounts of publicness are confused and confusing. It is interpreted mostly as manifest in a decayed (reified) form of something like 'public opinion' which is dominated by the 'they' (*Being and Time* 1(4): 149–68). *They* set the norms of everyday existence, resulting in an averageness, a levelling down, a standardization of ordinary experience (pp. 164–5). Publicness is inauthentic (a mark of 'fallenness'), yet it is claimed as ontologically foundational for *dasein*. How can it be both? (see Dreyfus 1994: 141–62 for an excellent discussion of the problems with 'The "who" of everyday dasein' – the theme of *Being and Time* 1(4)). Our interpretation of publicness attempts to retrieve a 'best reading' of it by linking it to the final concern of Part One, namely being-in-truth.

are things open and for whom? We have shown the everyday accessibility and availability of radio and television. Our original interpretation was in terms of the ordinary intelligibility and meaningfulness of broadcasting in all its parts and as a whole. And this intelligibility was shown to be non-exclusive. Radio and television were found to be available for me-or-anyone. If broadcasting is open in this way it can only be so for a being whose being is openness. But what does that mean?

What kind of being is it that has care as its way of being? What are the ontological conditions of being-in-concern? Being-open, Heidegger argues, is a basic structural characteristic of being-in. It is the mark of *affectedness*, of a being whose being is not closed-off but is self-disclosing. This disclosedness is what *dasein* gives off about itself and what it finds (in its concern) in all that makes up its world.[19] To be involved is not possible without a disposition to being open to involvement, involvement *with* and *in*; with others, in the world. For there to be a phenomenon such as world it *must* be a common world – a shareable, accessible, available public world. This world is not something that 'grows' out of subjects acting intersubjectively. It is not some aggregated thing as if, by simple addition, one got to some gross critical mass of something that might be called, say, 'public opinion'. Rather, that opinions are there to be had by me or anyone is by virtue of the world-in-its-publicness, and the kinds of opinion that we can find to have are indicative of the kind of world that there is.

Publicness is always already indicated as that which is familiar, for that is the mark of the availability of things *as* common, public things. Such availability rests upon their being-open for use (their being useful) in any way that matters by beings who are themselves open to their useful availability. To say that humanly made things are open to and for those for whom they are made points up the openness of human being as an *a priori*. To say that *dasein*'s being is open is tantamount to saying that it lets its own being 'show' as being open to itself, to others and the world. Only beings that are open can encounter each other.[20] Only such beings can have involvements. Only such beings can have concerns as the mark of their way of being. In the possibility of encountering, publicness is revealed as involvement with.

Before broadcasting public life was not 'for me'. It was, definitionally, beyond the reach of me-or-anyone. As such it showed up then, of necessity, as anonymous, impersonal and distant: beyond the range of my concerns. Our

[19]    On 'disclosedness' cf. Haugeland (1993).
[20]    We can of course encounter the being of other beings (dogs, cats, horses, for instance) and they us. Openness as specific to *dasein* has a triple structure of affectedness, understanding and telling (language) which other beings do not have. See *Being and Time* 1(5) for a full discussion.

stylized thematization of the 19th century in the preceding section was intended to bring this out, to show that the world as a totality – in its parts and as a whole – was 'in practice and in principle' always beyond 'my' grasp.[21] Lukács drew the correct conclusion from this – that the meaningfulness of the world *could* not be comprehended. The fracturing of the wholeness of the world – a real historical phenomenon, not a subjective projection *onto* the real – contributed to that seemingly unstanchable haemorrhage of meaning from modern life which Lukács interpreted as the phenomenon of reification. *Being and Time* can be understood, historically, in the same way – as a critique of reification and a truly heroic recovery of the meaningfulness of existence in a world whose meaning was, at the time of writing, almost completely covered over. From their very beginnings radio and, later, television have unobtrusively contributed to the recovery of the world in its meaningfulness that had become covered over in the course of societal modernization.

Heidegger glimpses this possibility in radio, in a passing reference to what was then a very new thing, in his discussion of the phenomenon of spatiality. *Dasein* encounters its world concernfully and with familiarity. The world in its availability is within the range of 'my' concerns. Thus, it is a basic spatial characteristic of *dasein* that it brings things within its grasp, within reach. 'Availability' must be understood spatially:

> *In Dasein there lies an essential tendency towards closeness.* . . . With the 'radio', for example, Dasein has so expanded its everyday environment that it has accomplished a de-severance of the 'world' – a de-severance which, in its meaning for dasein, cannot yet be visualized. (*Being and Time* 1(3): 140)

'De-severance' attempts to capture the sense of what Heidegger calls *entfernung* (*Being and Time*: 138, n. 2), which means something like to abolish distance or farness, i.e. to bring close, to bring within range. Thus, Heidegger interprets the possibility of radio as transforming spatiality; as bringing things close and hence within the reach of concern; as making the world (the great world beyond my reach) accessible and available for me or anyone. Broadcasting

[21]    This is Lukács's central perception in his analysis of the reification of consciousness, namely that 'Science' (i.e. modern knowledge) has destroyed the wholeness of the world, and (consequently) any possibility of the wholeness of being in it: 'The specialisation of skills leads to the destruction of every image of the whole. . . . The more highly developed it [knowledge] becomes and the more scientific, the more it will become a formally closed system of partial laws. It [knowledge] will then find that the world lying beyond its confines, and in particular the material base which it is its task to understand, *its own concrete underlying reality* lies, methodologically and in principle, *beyond its grasp*' (Lukács 1970: 103–4, original emphases).

has always understood this. In the portentous motto of the BBC (Nation shall speak Peace unto Nation); in the subtitle of *Panorama* (A Window on the World); in Radio 4's daily mid-day news and comment programme, *The World at One*, which signs off, each day, with the catch-phrase, 'And that's the world at 1.40!', the world-disclosing function of radio and television is unobtrusively assumed and acknowledged. But what is it that broadcasting discloses about the world, and how?

In our analysis, following Heidegger, it discloses the truth of the world, *our* world. Heidegger interprets the Greek word for truth – *aletheia* – as meaning uncoveredness, what is not concealed (cf. *Being and Time*: 262–9). In other words, truth is that which is open and manifest – that which is in plain view for all to see, that which shows up 'in the light of day' and allows itself to be seen in its own *lumen naturale*, that which is – in short – public. Truth reveals itself in its openness, in its being public. The publicness of broadcasting, then, is truth-disclosing. But how? How do things become disclosed, how do they reveal themselves as that which they are, through radio and television?

What is making-public, bringing to publicness? We have tried to show this, in the previous chapters, in our accounts and analyses of the production processes of radio and television. Making-public, in our accounts, appears as an effort to create and to allow ways of *being*-in-public for absent listeners and viewers. It seeks to do so in such a way that between the broadcast occasion and any viewer or listener there is the possibility of an *encountering*. If this is what broadcasting does then it overcomes reification, by restoring the meaningfulness of everyday existence. But how, exactly? By 'freeing' phenomena (people, events, occasions) so that they may be themselves, so that they may be that which they are *in public*.

Freeing allows being to open up, to be open, to be in the open; free *and* open. Freeing then is, precisely, liberating. It 'lets being be' (Heidegger 1993). Many of the devices of broadcasting are of this kind. Consider the structure of the interaction between, say, Harry Hopeful and Miss Lomas, discussed in chapter two. The management of the occasion is designed to free the participant (the 'ordinary person' who has never been 'on' radio before), to allow her to be herself in public and to be at ease with herself, with Hopeful, the studio audience and with us in so being. Radio 'frees' Miss Lomas in manifold ways: it enables her to be herself, to présent and présent herself, to open up and disclose her self in ways that make her self available to me or anyone. It does so enjoyably for her and us. It manages and minimizes the risks involved for her and does so on her behalf and ours as listeners. It creates a way of being in public that frees up the particular human being of someone so that it can be encountered as that which it is by me or anyone. The pleasure of such an encountering is a *real* pleasure, truly communicated, existingly so for me or anyone. That it is so is because, in part, it appears as something freely (unconditionally) given. It is a gift. A present. A making present. We saw how wartime entertainment was perceived with suspicion precisely because it seemed to be something *not* freely and unconditionally given. It came gift-wrapped with instructions: work harder, increase productivity.

This 'letting things be seen and heard as that which they are' is the way that broadcasting frees things to disclose the truth of what they are. We saw this in the ways that the microphone 'freed' the possibility of intimacy as a mode of being in public so that sincerity entered into public life. Our analysis of broadcasting's coverage of royal occasions showed its care to free the events from their own time and place so that they could, really and truly, become available as what they were for me or anyone. The desire to let things be seen as what they are has long been a principled concern of documentary practices. In *A Complaint of Rape* the formal presentational devices of 'observational' television worked to let the nature of the occasion show for me-or-anyone as that which it was. In particular, the way that the camera functioned as a recording device revealed its affectedness, its being open to what was happening, its responsiveness to and care for the matter at hand. The camera's focused and sustained attentiveness disclosed a concernfulness that opened up the possibility of being-in-concern for any viewer who cared to watch. The truth of that event is not to be thought of as residing in any judgement of it, or any consensus of opinion about it. But that opinions could be had or judgements made was a consequence of the way that the event was freed into publicness by television.

Truth, of course, may be covered over. Things may present themselves as what they are not. Or they may not be seen for what they are, in which case they remain undiscovered and unfreed. The covering over of truth is a possibility only for a being whose being is truth. That truth can be lost, or systematically and wilfully distorted or finally even denied – all this is known to us who have lived through the transformations of societal modernization in which truth has been down-sized to the sum of knowledge and power, in which it has shrunk to the force of the best information and the best argument. The dictators were rationalists: 'They were rational enough to build (tanks). Others should be rational enough to yield to them' (Horkheimer 1978: 26). Phenomenology recovers the order of truth as residing *in* things. It is not hidden, it does not lie under or behind or beneath things, and hence does not require Depth Theory to winkle it out. It is what is manifest (what shows) in things and how. If this is very obvious (as it *must* be) it yet requires a particular way of seeing and understanding in order to grasp it, for it can simply be not-seen at all.

If phenomenology sees the world differently, that difference is not particular to philosophy or its concerns.[22] Indeed, phenomenology's way of seeing is returning to the world in manifold ways today. In the last century it began to be systematically covered over. This covering over (and all its consequences) was most clearly pointed up by Dickens in the celebrated opening schoolroom scene of *Hard Times*:

> 'Girl number twenty,' said Mr Gradgrind, squarely pointing with his square forefinger . . . , 'Give me your definition of a horse.
> (Sissy Jupe thrown into the greatest alarm by this demand)
> 'Girl number twenty unable to define a horse!' said Mr Gradgrind, for the general behoof of all the little pitchers. 'Girl number twenty possessed of no facts, in reference to one of the commonest of animals! Some boy's definition of a horse. Bitzer, yours.' . . .
> 'Quadruped. Graminivorous. Forty teeth, namely twenty-four grinders, four eye-teeth, and twelve incisors. Sheds coat in the spring; in marshy countries, sheds hoofs, too. Hoofs hard, but requiring to be shod with iron. Age known by marks in mouth'. Thus (and much more) Bitzer.
> 'Now girl number twenty,' said Mr Gradgrind. 'You know what a horse is.'

Bitzer 'knows' everything about horses but knows nothing; Sissy Jupe 'knows' nothing but knows everything (her father belongs to the 'horse-riding' – a circus – and she lives and works with horses). The order of knowing that pertains to Bitzer epitomizes the reification of truth into knowledge-as-facts. The order of knowing that pertains to Sissy Jupe preserves truth as understanding of being – the being of horses. For Bitzer to get to the kind of knowledge he has depends upon treating things as Things; mere stuff, inert, dead, object-matter that can be weighed and measured and counted and taken to bits and known in this way. Modernity's world is dead. It was not God that was killed in the course of modernization but the world.[23] Is not that the greatest treason and the greatest anguish of modernity? Against what Bitzer stands for, Sissy Jupe (who knows the truth of animals existingly) is a marginal figure in a triumphant world of Facts. The order of truth that shows in her (what she *knows*) is being-in-concern. In being-amidst and being-with animals – and in

---

[22]   Phenomenology is here understood as the way of thinking which is explicated by Heidegger in *Being and Time* (cf. 49–62 for a lucid and detailed discussion of the meaning of the word's two components – 'phenomenon' and 'logos'). The philosophical 'school' of phenomenology founded by Edmund Husserl (Heidegger's teacher and supervisor) has a fundamentally different agenda to that pursued by Heidegger (cf. entries under 'Husserl', 'Heidegger' and 'phenomenology' in Honderich 1995).

[23]   And time. Time is killed by the denial of the past. This shows most clearly in all those efforts to destroy the past completely and, like the French revolutionaries, start again from 'year zero'. Killing the past always means killing people. The cold war threatened to kill the future.

so being caringly – Sissy *knows* them through and through. What she knows (what Bitzer *cannot* ever know) is their live and living being. The order of truth that shows through Sissy Jupe is the world in its liveness which is open to her through her own being-open to it, and which is closed forever to Bitzer and his world.

The truth that is recovered through what is here called phenomenology is nothing more (or less) than the truth of the world in its live and living being. It sees the same world that modernity sees – the same things in the same spaces at the same time – but it sees the world existingly. To see the world in such a way is what art has always expressed and what it tried to hang on to, even *in extremis*, throughout the historical epoch of the reification of the world from which we are beginning to emerge at the end of the 20th century. This reemergence 'frees' the world from the frozen grip of instrumental reason as exercised by 'worldless' subjects. Broadcasting has contributed to this process of freeing the world so that it can be found again as that which it truly, existingly is. It is not just this or that but all manner of things that make up the peopled busyness of the world disclosed by radio and television. What is there to be talked about is not just weighty matters as they appear in news, current affairs and social concern documentaries. There are all sorts of other things; the goings-on in soaps especially, but also fun things and odd things, and sporting 'moments' and last night's movie and a great deal else besides. The world-in-common of radio and television is by virtue of the ways in which it brings together into a common public domain what had hitherto been discrete and separate. This in part restores our sense of the wholeness of the world as disclosed routinely by broadcasting. If broadcasting were a single-issue thing it would speak only to particular interest publics. But it speaks to a *general interest public*, which it indeed created, in which each member is acknowledged as a someone with the attributes of a person, not an anonymous cipher that gets aggregated into a mass.

We have shown this as mediated through the for-anyone-as-someone structure of the communicative processes of radio and television. This structure repersonalizes public life. It overcomes depersonalized structures of indifferent being-alongside others and recovers personalized structures of solicitous being-with others.[24] The norms of sociability, sincerity and authenticity are excluded

---

[24]  Heidegger distinguishes two modes of being-with. *Indifferent* being-with is merely a kind of being present alongside others; being in the same place as others, but not affected by them, so that their presence does not matter to me nor mine to them (though there may be a care even here, as Goffman's perceptive discussion of 'civil inattention' indicates. Goffman 1963: 84–8). *Solicitous* being-with is such as to encounter the *dasein* of others. In such concern one's own *dasein* is open to others too. Such shared being-available constitutes the common ground of a shared world, a world-in-common that affects us and is affected by us. Cf. *Being and Time*: 157–9.

from depersonalized public structures as simply irrelevant to their operational effectivity. But we have shown how they are recreated and found again by radio and television so that they become taken-for-granted touchstones for assessing what we see and hear. Such criteria have nothing to do with the norms of technical efficiency (oriented to success) and everything to do with the ordinary morality of everyday existence in which people matter to each other *as* people. Broadcasting transposes the norms of everyday interpersonal existence into public life. It does so because it exists in two worlds of concern: the great world and everyone's my-world. If, as an institution, it stands in the former, it speaks (as it well knows) to listeners and viewers who live in the latter and who judge what they see and hear by the norms of social, sociable daily life.

## VIII

Our analysis of the care structures of broadcasting suggests that through them the world returns for us in its wholeness; that they help to redeem the live and living reality of everyday existence that was covered over by modernity's degradation of everydayness. The liveness of the world returns through the liveness of radio and television – their most fundamental common characteristic. This liveness is here understood as the specific temporality, the phenomenal now of broadcasting: and this now is magical. We have shown this in various ways in the preceding accounts, but particularly in that unobtrusive doubling of time and space which realizes a hitherto impossible possibility of being in two places, two times, at once.

The doubling of place has been examined in some detail in relation to events and their eventfulness. The doubling of time was found and shown by Stephanie Marriott (1996) in a brilliant analysis of instant replays in live broadcast coverage of sporting events. Marriott's linguistic analysis focuses on the interchangeability of tense in the ways that commentators, from the now in which they speak, talk through the temporal sequence of the moment that has just gone. But the crucial phenomenon which her analysis foregrounds is that although what we see is the replayed moment that has just passed (and it is this moment to which the broadcasters, in present time, attend), the background ambient sound is that of the present moment. There are then, really and truly, two different times at one and the same time: the 'then' has entered into the 'now' creating a now-and-then. These two times can – and sometimes do – collide with each other as when, for instance, a replay of say a goal-mouth incident in football is displayed on screen (and is being attended to by the sports commentator) while the background sound of the real-and-present moment indicates further eventful happenings . . . a roar from the crowd, a possible goal. Time then is, in such moments, really and truly, reversible. It goes to and fro, forwards and backwards in the phenomenal now of live transmission on radio and television. This is one aspect of the seen but unnoticed magic of the world as routinely disclosed by broadcasting; the magical liveness of a here-and-there, now-and-then. But it shows in many other ways in the edged character of the living momentum of broadcast events and occasions: the inflexion of a voice, the expression on a face, the cumulative mood-generating excitement of events in their now becoming, time and time again. Radio and television 'double' reality and in so doing create new communicative entitlements, new structures of expectancy, new ways of being in the world.

We began with that familiar everyday exchange: 'anything on telly?' 'No, nothing.' Is not that the commonplace common-sense attitude and does it not go against the grain of our interpretation? Yes and no. Yes, in that television and radio are everywhere and rightly regarded as no big deal. But then to live in the magical world has always been to live in it matter-of-factly. It is not so much the manifest ordinariness of broadcasting that is the problem, but rather that in radio and television we encounter the irreducible enigma of dailiness from which none of us escapes (cf. Haar 1993). Is it not a truth and a truism that watching television is 'a waste of time', an activity (if such it is) fit only for couch potatoes? Do we not all feel this at times, and do we not mean that we could be doing something better with our time? Adorno would interpret this in terms of the colonization of marginal 'free time' by the work ethic of capitalism (Adorno 1992). But if we interpret it in terms of Heideggerian anxiety[25] it shows up as a mild form of dread; not merely a sense of lost time, or of empty time, but of a squandering of something precious – my-time, my time on earth precious because it is finite, because I only have one life (but many lives) which must be lived before I die (so that I can *face* my death and accept my being gone with good grace). Heidegger is right to reiterate that being is 'in each case mine' by virtue of the radically indeterminate certainty of death which is mine and mine alone, which I own and must own to and which *is* my own and thus my ownmost being. Is then being absorbed in everydayness a way of avoiding any facing and dealing with that ineluctable fact of *my* existence? Does the chatter and noise of the everyday world shut out and avoid that inescapable reality?

Let us think again about the temporality of the everyday and how it connects with my being on earth, my-time, the time of my life. Let us go back again to the structures of the self: oneself, myself, ownself. The oneself (the They

---

[25] Heidegger makes much of anxiety (*angst*) as a defining mood of *dasein*. In this he is heavily indebted to Søren Kierkegaard, a major influence on the 'existential' stance to being-in-the-world that Heidegger takes up in Division 2 of *Being and Time*.

– what anyone thinks and feels) in Heidegger's terms is subsumed into the anonymous, public, worldly noise and chatter of the world. The myself is the publicly allowed possibilities of my particular tastes, interests and concerns – which constitute my particularized publicly available and displayed self – how I appear to others. The ownself is the ineffable, incommunicable self: my life, my unfolding story line, my experiences, *my* joys and sorrows, *my* cherished memories of things that happened to me, people I love (or hate) and care for (or not) and so on.

Let us set aside that third self for the moment. I have argued that radio and television have a for-anyone-as-someone structure that mediates between the for-anyone structures of publicly available anonymous (mass-produced) usable things and the for-someone structures of purely personal things (letters, 'family' snapshots and videos, etc.). The intermediary character of for-anyone-as-someone structures makes possible the use of 'we', for it is that which is mediated by the structure. Let me now interpret these distinctions temporally. Standard time (clock time) has a for-anyone structure and is clearly linked to mass-production. My-time (the time of my life) has a for-someone structure. These two incommensurate orders of temporality which correspond with two incommensurate orders of being are mediated by radio and television which have a for-anyone-as-someone temporal structure. Broadcasting takes its norm from standard clock time but its being is towards my-time. Broadcast time *faces* my-time, and in so far as it is *for* my-time it is in harmony with it. The manifold temporal arrangements of broadcasting converge into a concern to produce 'an appropriate now' for me or anyone.

What would that be? It would be something like *our* time – generational time – the time of *our* being with one another in the world. This generational time mediates between the anonymous structures of being and temporality and their personal structures. It is the temporal mediation of 'we'-ness, human social, sociable existence. Generational time displays what's going on in the world – in different parts of the world – so that what's happening enters into my concerns and my life. No matter who or where 'I' am, 'I' get caught up in such everywhere commonplace things as politics, war, murder, disaster (human and natural), sport and 'human interest' stories. I do not see and hear all this indifferently, passively. In whatever way and no matter what, I am caught up in it: what concerns *them* now concerns me. Not just a commonplace worldliness (the noise and chatter of the everyday) but a world in common, a world we share, that we inhabit (for good or ill) with others everywhere. It is this world with which I am in touch quite unremarkably everyday. It *gets* to me. It *touches* me. I *encounter* it – this worldly everyday world of concern. Its concerns are *my* concerns. Broadcasting radicalizes worldly care. Compassion fatigue, as *they* say, is one way in which this shows, but there are many others including laughter.

However, if I ask myself to whom am I answerable, to whom am I account-able – the answer that comes back is 'me'. Not the world but that third person, my *own* self, the self I own and own up to, the self that is properly mine and mine alone. It is anxiety on behalf of this self that shows in the feeling that watching telly is a waste of time, for my time is not the time of the world. The time of the world is motionless time, time at a standstill. The great French historian, Fernand Braudel, calls this time the *longue durée* and contrasts it with *histoire événementielle* – the history of events whose time-span is measured in days:

> An event is explosive, a 'nouvelle sonnante' (a matter of moment) as they said in the sixteenth century. Its delusive smoke fills the minds of its con-temporaries, but it does not last, and its flame can scarcely ever be discerned . . . . Let us say that instead of a history of events, we should speak of a short time-span, proportionate to individuals, to daily life, to our illusions, to our hasty awareness – above all the time of the chronicle and the journalist. Now it is worth noticing that side by side with the great and, so to speak, historic events, the chronicle or daily newspaper offers us all the mediocre accidents of ordinary life: a fire, a railway crash, the price of wheat, a crime, a theatrical production, a flood. It is clear, then, that there is a short time span which plays a part in all forms of life, economic, social, literary, institutional, religious, even geographical (a gust of wind, a storm) just as much as polit-ical. (Braudel 1980: 27–8)

The temporality of radio and television is evidently this eventful time, but it is rooted in motionless time. The *longue durée* shows up as a basic, structural constraint upon both the routines of daily broadcasting and the cyclical char-acter of output across the months and years. It shows up as the boundary of *available* (usable) time. How people use their time has always been a major consideration for broadcasters, and something that BBC audience research has investigated now for 60 years, since it first began in 1936. Two of the more recent surveys – *The People's Activities and Use of Time* (BBC 1979) and *Daily Life in the 1980s* (BBC 1984) – amount to major social surveys of the time-budgets of the whole British population aged five and over. What they reveal is what people *do* with their time, linearly through the day and cyclically from one day to the next.

Within the cycle of day-to-day life three major bundles of time-use are easily discerned. First, necessary or reproductive time for sleep and bodily self-maintenance. Second, coercive or work time at office, factory, school or home. Third, discretionary or free time for personal activities, leisure and relaxation. The amount of time available in the last category is determined by the prior claims of the first two, which are therefore of great interest to broadcasters who need 'first and foremost to know how many – and what kinds of – people are available to listen or view' (BBC 1979: 9). What emerges from these studies of time usage is the interlocking of life-time with the time structures and routines of the day. For what is mapped synchronically in the BBC surveys, are the different disposals of time-in-the-day by individuals at different stages in their life-times. It is above all *life-position* (that cluster of such factors as age, sex, occupation and marital status) that shapes the overall 'time-geography' – the when and where – of people's daily routines, including their routine usage of radio and television.

After surveying changes in the daily activity patterns of the British people since the late thirties, the 1979 report concludes:

> In 1975 fewer people got up earlier on weekdays than in 1939, but the changes over the last forty years have not been great. The proportions out of work have also varied a little and the working day may well have become a little shorter. Considerably less time is spent on domestic activities and meals in the evenings, and bed-times have become later by an average of rather more than half an hour for adults and one hour for children. (BBC 1979: 644)

The things that are available for people to do have spatial and temporal constraints. There are only so many hours in the day. So much time is needed for work, so much for sleep, so much for other things. The contents of radio and television, like the content of daily life, change from day to day; but their structures remain unchanging and unchanged. That is where the *longue durée*, the unheard music of slow time, shows up in radio and television. It unobtrusively structures their existential role in supporting the routine structures of our daily lives through the course of the lifetime of each and every one of us.

The time of the world goes back into an immeasurable past and forward into an immeasurable future. Compared with this, my-time is but the twinkling of an eye. It is here that we encounter the heart of darkness in everyday existence – that sure and certain knowledge that the time of the world is not my time. These two incommensurate orders of being and time show up unobtrusively everywhere on radio and television. There are many programmes 'of venerable age' (as one might say) on British radio and television today. *Desert Island Discs*, for instance, began in 1942 on the wartime Home Service – the year before I was born. It is still going strong on Radio 4 today, more than 50 years later. There is no sign of the programme ever ending, since its popularity has remained undimmed down the years. Its inventor, copyright holder and original presenter – Roy Plomley – is dead and gone. So, too, are many of those who appeared in the programme since it first began. But the programme has not aged in all that time, because it cannot. Its time is outside human time, life-time. Even if it were 'killed off' in some reorganization of the channel's schedules it does not mean that the programme is dead and gone forever as all those ever involved in it are or will be. To the contrary, it could be taken out and 'revived' at any time. And this is true of almost any programme format. In a pared-down 'bare' state any programme is a set of notations (an embryo involvement structure) that can be activated at and for any time now.

This structural characteristic, while pointing up the difference between the time of the world and my time, does not aggravate that difference. Rather it seems to mediate it *generationally*. Anyone can enter into any programme at anytime now. And this suggests that the design of programmes is not simply or only for the present generation in any particular now point, but is as much a device for handing on and handing over from one generation to the next. This shows up very clearly in long-running drama series and serials. *Dr Who* was watched as much by adults as by children (Tulloch and Alvarado 1983: 56). I myself remember watching it at home in the early sixties and 20 years later I sat with my two young sons who watched it cushion in hand. Watching it with my children was a small act of sharing something with them – something which no longer had (for me) the spell it had for them (for whom the 'Daleks' et al. were real and scary). But watching it and talking about it was a shared experience across their generation and mine. In such ways programme structures are devices for regeneration, for bringing tomorrow's generation into today's generation and, in due course, handing over and handing on to them. Thus, again, broadcasting's phenomenal now is always a past-becoming-future.

The programme structures of radio and television will produce and reproduce – as they are meant to do – the everyday human social sociable world every day endlessly. In so doing they help to constitute the meaningful background of everyday existence which they themselves foreground. Meaningfulness shows up always in small ways and little things. It is not one big thing (the delusion of intellectuals throughout the ages). If newspapers, radio and television show up as 'no big deal' – if we think of them by and large as trivial, unimportant things – that is the mark of their everydayness. What shows up for us, in the contents of newspapers and in radio and television schedules, are everyday matters. Everyday things matter for us in the ways that they show up every day on radio and television and in newspapers. It is this *every*day worldliness that is the common feature of all three: this ceaseless engagement with, this being caught up in, this being involved with, this attending to, this noticing, remarking, observing, commenting, blaming, ridiculing, laughing, worrying – it is all such and other concerns that mark out the everyday concernfulness of what we read and hear and see every day in newspapers and on radio and television. It is this that justifies the usage of *the media* as a common term for the press and broadcasting. For what is common to them is the same care structure of dailiness as it shows up in all its aspects day by day. Each day is caught up in its own concerns, its own here-and-now; that is its proper and ownmost care structure. But daily media are always already ahead of themselves in anticipation of the days to come as each day moves away from and towards: from yesterday, towards tomorrow. Radio and television face the future openly and give it a recognizable face from one generation to the next. Dailiness is caught up in time's various rhythms and ways of being. Historical studies of the press and broadcasting – whose dailiness *is* their care structure – can show us how. How we ourselves assess that care and those concerns is, of course, another matter.

# References

Adorno, T. (1992) 'Free Time', *The Culture Industry* (J. M. Bernstein, ed.). London: Routledge.

Adorno, T. and Horkheimer, M. (1985) 'Enlightenment as mass deception', *Dialectic of Enlightenment*. London: Verso.

Althusser, L. (1971) 'Ideology and ideological state apparatuses', *Lenin and Philosophy and Other Essays*. London; New Left Books

Atkinson, M. (1984) *Our Masters' Voices*. London: Methuen.

Barthes, R. (1977) 'The grain of the voice', *Image-Music-Text*. London: Fontana.

Barthes, R. (1984) *Camera Lucida*. London: Fontana

Bausinger, H. (1984) 'Media, technology and daily life', *Media Culture & Society* 6(4): 343–52.

BBC (1979) *The People's Activities and Use of Time*. London: BBC Publications.

BBC (1984) *Daily Life in the 1980s* London: BBC Publications.

Benjamin, W. (1973) 'The work of art in the age of mechanical reproduction', *Illuminations*. London: Fontana.

Blackburn, T. (1985) *Tony Blackburn, 'The Living Legend': An Autobiography*. London: W. H. Allen.

Bourdieu, P. (1984) *Distinction: A Sociological Critique of the Judgment of Taste*. London: Routledge.

Brand, G. (1987) 'Tony Blackburn: The construction and maintenance of a broadcast identity and a broadcast universe'. Media Studies dissertation, University of Westminster.

Brand, G. and Scannell, P. (1991) 'Talk, identity and performance: *The Tony Blackburn Show*', *Broadcast Talk* (P. Scannell, ed.). London: Sage.

Braudel, F. (1980) *On History*. London: Weidenfeld and Nicolson.

Bridson, G. (1971) *Prospero and Ariel*. London: Victor Gollancz.

Briggs, A. (1970) *The War of Words: The History of Broadcasting in the United Kingdom*, Volume III. Oxford: Oxford University Press.

Briggs, A. (1979) *Sound and Vision: The History of Broadcasting in the United Kingdom*, Volume IV. Oxford: Oxford University Press.

Brown, P. and Levinson, S. (1987) *Politeness*. Cambridge: Cambridge University Press.

Burke, P. (1993) *The Art of Conversation*. Cambridge: Polity Press.

Button, G. (ed.) (1991) *Ethnomethodology and the Human Sciences*. Cambridge: Cambridge University Press.

Calder, A. (1971) *The People's War*. London: Panther Books.

Calhoun, C. (ed.) (1992) *Habermas and the Public Sphere*. London: MIT Press.

Camporesi, V. (1994) 'American broadcasting and the BBC, 1930–1955', *Media Culture & Society* 17(4).

Cannadine, D. (1983) 'The context, performance and meaning of ritual: the British monarchy and the "invention of tradition"', *The Invention of Tradition* (E. Hobsbawm and T. Ranger, eds). Cambridge: Cambridge University Press.

Cardiff, D. and Scannell, P. (1986) '"Good luck war workers!" Class, politics and entertainment in wartime broadcasting', *Popular Culture and Social Relations* (T. Bennett, C. Mercer and J. Woollacott, eds). Milton Keynes: Open University Press.

Carrithers, M., Collins, S. and Lukes, S. (1987) *The Category of the Person*. Cambridge: Cambridge University Press.

Chaney, D. (1986) '"A symbolic mirror of ourselves": Civic ritual in mass society', *Media Culture & Society: A Critical Reader* (R. Collins et al., eds). London: Sage.

Davidoff, L. and Hall, C. (1987) *Family Fortunes: Men and Women of the English Middle Class, 1780–1850*. London: Routledge.

Dayan, D. and Katz, E. (1992) *Media Events: The Live Broadcasting of History*. Cambridge, Mass.: Harvard University Press.

Dimbleby, J. (1975) *Richard Dimbleby*. London: Hodder & Stoughton.

Dreyfus, H. L. (1994) *Being-in-the-World*. Cambridge, Mass.: MIT Press.

Elster. J, (1991) *Sour Grapes: Studies in the Subversion of Rationality*. Cambridge: Cambridge University Press.

Foster, M. (1983) 'Having a Go.' Media Studies dissertation, University of Westminster.

Foucault, M. (1977) *Discipline and Punish*. Harmondsworth: Penguin Books.

Frith, S. (1986) 'Art versus technology: the strange case of popular music', *Media Culture & Society* 8(3): 263–80.

Frith, S. (1988) *Music For Pleasure*. Cambridge: Polity Press.

Gadamer, H.-G. (1994) *Heidegger's Ways*. Albany: State University of New York Press.

Garfinkel, H. (1984) *Studies in Ethnomethodology*. Cambridge: Polity Press.

Geraghty, C. (1981) 'The continuous serial: a definition', *Coronation Street* (R. Dyer et al., eds). London: BFI TV Monograph, 13.

Giddens, A. (1984) *The Constitution of Society*. Cambridge: Polity Press.

Giddens, A. (1992) *The Transformation of Intimacy: Sexuality, Love and Eroticism in Modern Societies*. Cambridge: Polity Press.

Goffman, E. (1956) *The Presentation of Self in Everyday Life*. Harmondsworth: Penguin Books.

Goffman, E. (1963) *Behaviour in Public Places*. New York: Free Press of Glencoe.

Goffman, E. (1968) *Stigma: Notes on the Management of Spoiled Identity*. Harmondsworth: Penguin Books.

Goffman, E. (1972) *Interaction Ritual*. Harmondsworth: Penguin Books.

Goffman, E. (1974) *Asylums*. Harmondsworth: Penguin Books.

Goffman, E. (1975) *Frame Analysis*. Harmondsworth: Penguin Books.

Goffman, E. (1981) *Forms of Talk*. Oxford: Basil Blackwell.

Haar, M. (1993) 'The enigma of everydayness', *Reading Heidegger* (J. Sallis, ed.). Bloomington & Indianapolis: Indiana University Press.

Habermas, J. (1989) *The Structural Transformation of the Public Sphere*. Cambridge: Polity Press.

Habermas, J. (1991) *The Theory of Communicative Action* (Volumes 1 and 2). Cambridge: Polity Press.

Hall, E. T. (1959) *The Silent Language*. Garden City, NY: Doubleday.

Haugeland, J. (1993) 'Dasein's disclosedness', *Heidegger: A Critical Reader* (H. L. Dreyfus and H. Hall, eds). Oxford: Blackwell.

Heidegger, M. (1962) *Being and Time*. Oxford: Blackwell.

Heidegger, M. (1992) *The Concept of Time*. Oxford: Blackwell.

Heidegger, M. (1993) 'On the essence of truth', *Basic Writings* (D. Krell, ed.). London: Routledge.

Heritage, J. (1984) *Garfinkel and Ethnomethodology*. Cambridge: Polity Press.

Heritage, J. (1985) 'Analyzing news interviews: aspects of the production of talk for an overhearing audience', *Handbook of Discourse Analysis, Volume 3: Discourse and Dialogue* (T. A. van Dijk, ed.). London: Academic Press.

Heritage, J. and Greatbatch, D. (1992) 'On the institutional character of institutional talk: the case of news interviews', *Talk and Social Structure* (D. Boden and D. Zimmerman, eds). Cambridge: Polity Press.

Hill, J. (1978) *The Cat's Whisker: Fifty Years of Wireless Design*. London: Oresko Books.

Hobson, D. (1982) *'Crossroads': The Drama of a Soap Opera*. London: Methuen.

Hoggart, R. (1962) *The Uses of Literacy*. Harmondsworth: Penguin Books.

Honderich, T. (1995) *The Oxford Companion to Philosophy*. Oxford: Oxford University Press.

Horkheimer, M. (1978) 'The end of reason', *The Essential Frankfurt School Reader* (E. Arato and P. Piccone, eds). Oxford: Blackwell.

Hutchby, I. (1991) 'The organisation of talk on talk radio', *Broadcast Talk* (P. Scannell, ed.). London: Sage.

Jefferson, D. (1984) 'On the organisation of laughter in talk about troubles', *Structures of Social Action* (J. Maxwell Atkinson and J. Heritage, eds). Cambridge: Cambridge University Press.

Jennings, H. and Madge, C. (eds) (1987) *May the Twelfth: Mass Observation Day Survey, 1937*. London: Faber and Faber.

Johnson, L. (1988) *The Unseen Voice: A Cultural Study of Early Australian Radio*, London: Routledge.

Kisiel, T. (1995) *The Genesis of Heidegger's 'Being and Time'*. Berkeley and Los Angeles: University of California Press.

Kuhn, A. (1978) 'The Camera I: Observations on documentary', *Screen* 19(2): 71–84.

Langer, J. (1981) 'Television's "personality system"', *Media Culture & Society* 3(4): 351–65.

Leech, G. (1983) *Principles of Pragmatics*. London: Longman.

Lessing, D. (1995) *Under My Skin*. London: Flamingo.

Levinson, S. (1983) *Pragmatics*. Cambridge: Cambridge University Press.

Lewis, C. A. (1924) *Broadcasting From Within*. London: George Newnes.

Lewis, P. (1991) 'Referable words in radio drama', *Broadcast Talk* (P. Scannell, ed.). London: Sage.

Lewis, V. (1975) *Vocal Refrain*. London: W. H. Allen.

Livingstone, S. and Lunt, P. (1994) *Talk on Television*. London: Routledge.

Lord, A. (1960) *The Singer of Tales*. New York: Atheneum.

Luhmann, N. (1986) *Love as Passion*. Cambridge: Polity Press.

Lukács, G. (1970) *History and Class Consciousness*. London: Merlin Press.

Marriott, S. (1996) 'Time and time again: "live" television commentary and the construction of replay talk', *Media Culture & Society* 18(1).

Matheson, H. (1933) *Broadcasting*. London: Thornton Butterworth.

Meyrowitz, J. (1985) *No Sense of Place*. New York: Oxford University Press.

Montgomery, M. (1986) 'DJ talk', *Media Culture & Society* 8(4).

Montgomery, M. (1991) '*Our Tune*: a study of a discourse genre', *Broadcast Talk* (P. Scannell, ed.). London: Sage.

Morley, D. (1986) *Family Television*, London: Comedia.

Moules, J. (1983) *Our Gracie: The Life of Dame Gracie Fields*. London: Robert Hale.

*New Grove Dictionary of Music and Musicians* (1980). London: Macmillan.

Parry, A. (ed.) (1971) *The Making of Homeric Verse: The Collected Papers of Milman Parry*. Oxford: Oxford University Press.

Pegg, M. (1983) *Broadcasting and Society, 1918–1939*. London: Croom Helm.

Pennachioni, I. (1984) 'The reception of popular television in North-East Brazil', *Media Culture & Society* 6(4).

Peters, J. Durham (1993) 'Distrust of representation: Habermas on the public sphere', *Media Culture & Society* 15(4).

Peyre, H. (1965) *Literature and Sincerity*. New Haven, Conn.: Yale University Press.

Pickles, W. (1949) *Between You and Me*. London: Werner Laurie.

Pickles, W. (1978) *Have Another Go*. London: David and Charles.

Randell, D. M. (ed.) (1986) *New Harvard Dictionary of Music*. Cambridge, Mass.: Harvard University Press.

Roache, W. (1993) *Ken and Me*. London: Simon and Schuster.

Sacks, H. (1992) *Lectures on Conversation*, 2 volumes. Oxford: Blackwell.

Scannell, P. (1979) 'The social eye of television, 1946–1955', *Media Culture & Society* 1(1).

Scannell, P. (1988) '*Radio Times*: the temporal arrangements of broadcasting in the modern world', *Television and Its Audience* (P. Drummond and R. Paterson, eds). London: British Film Institute.

Scannell, P. (1989) 'Public service broadcasting and modern life', *Media Culture & Society* 11(2).

Scannell, P. (ed.) (1991a) *Broadcast Talk*. London: Sage.

Scannell, P. (1991b) 'The relevance of talk', *Broadcast Talk* (P. Scannell, ed.). London: Sage.

Scannell, P. (1993) 'Time, space and place in broadcasting', *Kringkasting og Kino* (K. Skretting, ed.). Oslo: Norges forskningsråd avd. NAVF.

Scannell, P. and Cardiff, D. (1991) *A Social History of British Broadcasting: Serving the Nation, 1923–1939*. Oxford: Basil Blackwell.

Schegloff, E. (1979) 'Identification and recognition in telephone conversation openings', *Everyday Language: Studies in Ethnomethodology* (G. Psathas, ed.). New York: Irvington.

Schegloff, E. A., Jefferson, G. and Sacks, H. (1977) 'The preference for self-correction in the organization of repair in conversation', *Language* 53.

Schlesinger, P. (1978) *'Putting Reality Together': BBC News*. London: Constable. See also 2nd edn (1986), London: Methuen, for a useful new introduction.

Sennett, R. (1985) *The Fall of Public Man*. London: Faber.

Sieveking, L. (1934) *The Stuff of Radio*. London: Cassell.

Silverstone, R. (1994) *Television and Everyday Life*. London: Routledge.

Silvey, R. (1977) *Who's Listening? The Story of BBC Audience Research*. London: Allen and Unwin.

Simmel, G. (1950) 'Sociability', *The Sociology of Georg Simmel*. Glencoe, Il.: Free Press of Glencoe.

Smulyan, S. (1994) *Selling Radio: The Commercialization of American Broadcasting, 1920–1934*. Washington: Smithsonian Institution Press.

Stone, L. (1979) *The Family, Sex and Marriage in England, 1500–1800*. Harmondsworth: Penguin Books.

Stone, L. (1987) *The Past and Present Revisited*. London: Routledge and Kegan Paul.

Taylor, C. (1989) *Sources of the Self: The Making of the Modern Identity*. Cambridge: Cambridge University Press.

Taylor, C. (1995) *Philosophical Arguments*. Cambridge, Mass.: Harvard University Press.

Thomas, H. (1977) *With an Independent Air*. London: Weidenfeld and Nicolson.

Thompson, J. B. (1994) 'Social theory and the media', *Communication Theory Today* (D. Crowley and D. Mitchell, eds). Cambridge: Polity Press.

Tolson, A. (1991) 'Televised chat and the synthetic personality', *Broadcast Talk* (P. Scannell, ed.). London: Sage

Trilling, L. (1971) *Sincerity and Authenticity*. London: Oxford University Press.

Tulloch, J. and Alvarado, M. (1983) *'Dr Who': The Unfolding Text*. London: Macmillan.

Weber, M. (1947) *The Theory of Social and Economic Organization*. New York: Oxford University Press.

Weber, M. (1971) *The Protestant Ethic and the Spirit of Capitalism*. London: Unwin University Books.

Whitehead, K. (1989) *The Third Programme: A Literary History.* Oxford: Clarendon Press.

Williams, R. (1974) *Television: Technology and Cultural Form.* London: Fontana.

Williamson, J. (1984) '"Police": Victims of verité?' Media Studies dissertation, University of Westminster.

Wolfe, K. (1984) *The Churches and the British Broadcasting Corporation, 1922–1956.* London: SCM Press.

Wood, R. (1979) *A World in Your Ear.* London: Macmillan.

Wyndham-Goldie, G. (1978) *Facing the Nation: Television and Politics, 1936–1976.* London: The Bodley Head.

# Index

absent audiences   29–30, 42, 56, 79
    and live broadcasting   84
    and sacred events   77, 79
abstract time   152
Adorno, T.   21, 163, 173
aesthetic judgement   73–4, 116
Althusser, L.   13
*Archers, The*   157, 158
Atkinson, Max   134
Auden, W. H.
    *Musée des Beaux Arts*   97
audience–broadcaster relationships
    11 14, 19
    as unforced relationship   23–4, 76
audiences
    in *Billy Welcome* (listening)   41
    as citizens   88
    common ground with programme-
        makers   16
    and DJ talk   139–40
    as nation   88
    studio   25, 28–9, 30, 33–5, 42
    in *The Tony Blackburn Show*
        127–31, 132, 138
    *see also* absent audiences; listeners;
        viewers

authenticity   93–116, 171–2
    of experiences in general and
        particular   99–102
    and the modern media   90
    of ordinary experiences   93–5
    and sincerity   148
    and story-telling on television   108
    of witnesses   95 102
auto-cues   14–15
autumn broadcasting season   154

Barber, Jack   42
Barnes, George   11
Barthes, R.   14, 36, 68
BBC (British Broadcasting
    Corporation)
    audiences   11–12
    and the coronation of 1953   80–6
    and crooning   64–5, 71
    early evening television   150–1
    and the Great British Public   43
    Light Programme   48
    Listener Research unit   10, 56
    newsreaders   14, 41
    and programme planning   9–10
    Radio 1   119, 120, 121

Radio 4   149–50, 157
  and the State Opening of Parliament
    (1958)   87–8
  surveys of time-budgets   175–6
  Talks Department   12–13
  *The Tony Blackburn Show*
    120–43
  Third Programme   11–12
  and wartime propaganda   37, 39–48
*Being and Time* (Heidegger)   5, 89,
    144–5, 147, 153, 157, 167–8
being-in-concern   166
being-open   166
Benjamin, Walter   90
Bennett, Eric   71, 72
*Billy Welcome*   25, 37–48
Black, Peter   82
Blackburn, Tony   117–43, 164
  airing of personal views   120, 122–3
  changes of voice   125–7, 129
  conversational collapse   130–1
  corny gags   118–19, 124–5
  empathy games   126
  and fun radio   123–4
  personal life   119–20, 121
  personalized jingle   119
  send-up of himself   124–5
  and soul music   123
  *see also Tony Blackburn Show, The*
Bloody Sunday
  witnesses to events of   99–102
Bowlby, Al   64
Braudel, Fernand   175
breakfast radio and television   149–50
Bridson, Geoffrey   26, 37–8, 39
Briggs, A.   72, 80
Brown, P.   20

cameras *see* television cameras
Cannadine, D.   83, 89
Cardiff, D.   12, 25, 37, 64
care structures   144–77
  of dailiness   152, 177–8
  *Have a Go!*   146–8
  of news   160
Carrithers, M.   7

*Cathy Come Home*   116
Christmas Day broadcasting   155
Churchill, Winston   81
*Classic Soil, The*   35
coming-into-being
  of programmes   8, 146
commercial broadcasting   11
  and the 1953 coronation   86
  and the State Opening of Parliament
    (1958)   87–8
common ground
  and intentionality   16–17
communicative ethos
  of broadcasting   20–1, 23
  of politeness   19–20
  of *The Tony Blackburn Show*   118
communicative intentionality   148
  of documentaries   110–14
  theory of   3, 15, 17–18, 21
*Complaint of Rape, A*   102–17, 169
conflicting rationalities of broadcasting
    21
conversation analysis   17, 19
  *see also* talk
coronation
  of Elizabeth II (1953)   80–6
  of King George VI   77–9
  of Queen Victoria   83
*Coronation Street*   74, 157–8
critical tradition
  and public ceremony   75–6
crooning   62–5
Crosby, Bing   63
*Crossroads*   151, 156, 158
cyclical time   153

dailiness   149–56, 173, 175–8
  broadcasting's temporality as   5
  historicizing   160
  of news   164
*Dasein*   144
  and availability   167
  being-open   166
  and dailiness   152
  defining   145
  of events   92

and phenomenological time 152
of radio and television 165
and thrownness 157
and the world 161
Day, Robin 87–8
*Day Today, The* 160
Dayan, D. 6
*Desert Island Discs* 176–7
Dickens, Charles
*Hard Times* 170–1
Dickson, Dorothy 71
Dimbleby, Jonathan 80–5
Dimbleby, Richard 83–4, 85–6,
87–8
disasters
witnesses to 95–8
disk jockeys 117–43
documentaries
*A Complaint of Rape* 102–17, 169
communicative intentionality of
110–14
Donaghue, Phil 25
*Dr Who* 155–6, 177
drama
late 19th century European 162
Du Cane, Jean Merrill 71
Durkheim, E. 163

editing process
and communicative intentionality
18
Eliot, George
*Middlemarch* 94
Elizabeth II, Queen
coronation 80–6
State Opening of Parliament (1958)
87–8
events
attitude of broadcasting to 80–6
aura of presence 90–1
as broadcast 79–80
*Dasein* of 92
outside broadcasting of 153–4
real-world in soap operas 157–8
royal ceremonies 76–88, 89, 169
Everidge, Dame Edna 158

everyday life 163–4
experiences
in general and particular 99–102
ordinary 93–5
self- and other-related 114

face-needs 20, 24, 164
fictional worlds
in historical novels 162
in soap operas 158–9
Fields, Gracie 72
Fisher, Geoffrey, Archbishop of
Canterbury 80, 81, 82
for-anyone-as-someone structures
174
Foucault, M. 76
Fred Hartley Sextet 66
Frith, Simon 62
FTAs (face threatening actions) 20
'fundamental vocabulary' 4
futuricity of broadcasting 152

Gadamer, Hans-Georg 93
Garfinkel, Harold 131, 135
Garnsey, Cheryl 127
generational time 174
George VI, King
coronation of 77–9
Geraghty, Christine 157, 160
Giddens, Anthony 164
Gilliam, Lawrence 37, 43
Goffman, Erving 17, 20, 36, 131,
132–3, 134–5
golf tournaments
Masters from Augusta 91–2
Graves, Cecil 64
Greatbatch, D. 13
Grenfell, Joyce 66
Grice, Paul H. 17, 20

Habermas, Jürgen 21, 75–6, 162
Hall, Edward 64
*Hard Times* (Dickens) 170–1
Harding, Archie 25–6
*Harry Hopeful* 24–37, 38, 41, 42, 46,
47, 48, 168

*Have a Go!*   25, 48–57
    care structure of   146–8
hearable audiences   28–9
Heidegger, Martin   5
    *Being and Time*   5, 89, 144–5, 147,
        153, 157, 167–8
    on the oneself   13–14, 173–4
    and the rediscovery of world   161
    *see also* Dasein
Heritage, J.   13
historical novels   161–2
Hobson, D.   156, 158
Horkheimer, M.   21, 163

identity
    and disk jockeys   117–43
    regional and local   30–1
    of serial productions   10
ideological interpellation   13
individual personality
    and voice   36–7
Industrial Revolution
    radio programmes on   35–6
institutional occasions   18–19
institutionalization of broadcasting   9,
    145–6
intentionality
    and common ground   16–17
    *see also* communicative intentionality

Joyce, William ('Lord Haw Haw')   38

Kaltenbourn, W. V.   86
Kant, I.   73
Katz, E.   6
Kennedy, John F.
    assassination of   91, 97, 156
Kuhn, A.   111

Lang, Fritz   163
language
    and listening   164–5
'language games'   4
laughter
    of studio audiences   28–9, 30, 33–5
Levinson, S.   20

*lieder* singing   61, 62
lifetime   153
Lind, Jenny   61
linear time   153
listeners
    assessment of programmes   7
    and the myself   13
    *see also* audiences; viewers
listening   164–5
live broadcasting   153–4
    and absent audiences   84
    of sacred events   77–86
    of sporting events   172–3
    State Opening of Parliament   87–8
Lord, Albert   132
Luhmann, Niklas   58, 165
Lukács, G.   21, 161, 163, 167
Lyle, Sandy   91–2
Lynn, Vera   62–3, 65–74, 164
    as butt of satire   71–2
    press reports on   62–3, 66, 70–2

Marriott, Stephanie   172
Marx, Karl   163
meaning
    loss of with modernity   163
    and utterance   17–18
meaningfulness
    of broadcasting   21, 148–9
    of everyday existence   177
    of programmes   7–8, 15, 16
    of the world   167
media
    and authenticity   90
    and dailiness   178
    and everyday life   163
    and public ceremony   75, 76
    and witnesses to disasters   95–8
media studies   4
memory
    and soap operas   159
    social   91
Meyrowitz, Joshua   141
*Middlemarch* (Eliot)   94
Miller, Gavin   113
modernity   163, 170

Montgomery, M. 13, 139
mood
    and broadcasting commentaries on
        public events 88–9
    of interactions 147
moral assessments of stories 116
motives for programmes 8–9
Murrow, Ed 86
myself, the 13, 173–4

narratives
    in *A Complaint of Rape* 115
    oral traditions 132–3
    and sincerity 74
narrator-as-witness 102
natural time 152
*News of 100 Years Ago* 35
news reports 160–4
    meaningfulness of 148
    and witnesses to disasters 95–8
newscasters
    look-to-camera 14 15
newspapers
    development of mass circulation
        162
    *see also* press reports
newsworthiness of events 95 8
Nicholls, Frank 26

oneself 13, 173–4
opera singing 61
oral traditions 132–3
ordinariness of broadcasting 6, 173
'ordinary effect' 15
ordinary experiences
    authenticity of 93–5
outside broadcasts (OBs) 153–4
ownmost self 14, 173–4, 175

Parry, Milman 132
particularity of programmes 8
Peel, John 117
Pennachioni, Irene 159
'people' programmes 25
pep talks
    and wartime propaganda 45–6

performance
    expected ways of performing
        102–6
    relation between performers and 57
    and sincerity 58, 73
'personality system' of broadcasting
    118
Peters, John Durham 75, 76
phenomenological time 152
phenomenology 169–71
Phillips, Frank 41
Pickles, Wilfred 25, 164
    in *Billy Welcome* 38–43
    in *Have a Go!* 49–56, 57, 147, 148
poetry
    and modernity 163
politeness
    communicative ethos of 19–20
political reality
    and media studies 4
press reports
    on *A Complaint of Rape* 116
    on the coronation of 1953 82–3
    on Vera Lynn 62 3, 66, 70–2
private life
    and broadcasting 21
professionalism in broadcasting 84–5,
    146
professionals
    and sincerity 59–60
programme planning (scheduling)
    9–10
programmes
    coming-into-being 8, 146
    meaningfulness of 7–8
    motives for 8–9
    organizing schedules 156
    serial production 10–11, 146
    speciality of 11
    *see also* radio programmes; television
        programmes
propaganda
    Second World War 23, 37, 39–48,
        50, 70
public ceremonies 75–92
public life

and broadcasting   21, 153
refeudalization of   75
public mood
  and broadcasting commentaries on
    public events   88–9
public opinion   166
public–private relationship
  and radio   69, 89
publicness   165–72

radio
  breakfast   149–50
  disk jockeys   117–43
  impact of on ordinary people
    89–90
  soap operas   157, 158
  as transforming speciality   167–8
Radio Caroline   118–19
Radio London   119
  *The Tony Blackburn Show*   118,
    120–43
radio programmes
  *Billy Welcome*   25, 37–48
  coronation of King George VI   77
  crooning   63–5
  *Desert Island Discs*   176–7
  *Harry Hopeful*   24–37, 38, 41, 42,
    46, 47, 48, 168
  *Have a Go!*   25, 48–57
  *News of 100 Years Ago*   35
  *Sincerely Yours, Vera Lynn*   65–74
  talk routines on   132–9
  *The Archers*   157, 158
  *The Classic Soil*   35
  *The Tony Blackburn Show*   118,
    120–43
  *Waggoner's Walk*   157
  *We Speak for Ourselves*   37–9, 50
  *Workers Playtime*   45–6
*Radio Times*   10
Radiolympia   154
reification   167
Reith, John   155
religious broadcasting   154
religious singing   60–1
Roache, William   74

Rorty, Richard   4
Ross, Jonathan   151
royal ceremonies   76–88, 89, 169
royal Christmas Day broadcast   155
Ryan, A. P.   71

Sacks, Harvey   93–4, 94–5, 96, 98
sacred events
  live coverage of   77–86, 90
Scannell, P.   12, 20, 25, 37, 64
Schegloff, E.   17
Schlesinger, Philip   160
Schubert, Franz   61
Schumann, Robert   61
seasonal broadcasting   154–5
Second World War
  *Billy Welcome*   25, 37–48
  factory feature programmes   25,
    37–48
  propaganda   23, 37, 39–48, 50, 70
  radio programmes   156
  *Sincerely Yours, Vera Lynn*   65–74
self
  particularized   13–14
serial productions   10–11, 146
Shapley, Olive   35
Shelton, Anne   71
Siepmann, Charles   29, 31
Simmel, G.   22–3, 35, 56
*Sincerely Yours, Vera Lynn*   65–74
sincerity   58–74, 171–2
  and aesthetic judgement   73–4
  and authenticity   148
  and intimate relationships   59
  and performance   58
  and professionals   59–60
  and singing   60–5, 67–74
  trivialization of   70
singing   60–5
  and depersonalized voices   69
  *lieder*   61, 62
  at the microphone (crooning)
    62–5, 68–9
  opera   61, 62
  religious   60–1
soap operas   156–9

sociability 4, 22–57, 171–2
 and talk 23
*Social History of British Broadcasting*
 1–2
social occasions 18
soul music 123, 138
space
 situated experiential character of
 89
speech *see* talk
sporting events
 live broadcasting of 172–3
Stone, Lew 64
studio audiences 25, 28–9, 30, 33–5,
 42
studios
 radio and television 140

talk
 and broadcasting's communicative
 style 24
 conversation analysis 17, 19
 everyday face-to-face 134
 institutional 19
 laughter-seeking 34
 routines on *The Tony Blackburn
 Show* 132–9
 and sociability 23
 style of in broadcasting 12–13
talk-in-public 35
'tea-time' viewing 151, 156
technical innovations
 and documentaries 111
 singing at the microphone 62–5
tele-prompters 14–15
telephone conversations
 in *The Tony Blackburn Show*
 128–31, 132
 Tony Blackburn's voice in 125–7
television
 'adult time' 151
 breakfast 149, 150
 and the coronation of 1953 80–6
 documentaries 102–17, 110–14, 169
 experiences of victims and witnesses
 101–2

'family viewing time' 151
newscasters 14–15
soap operas 156–9
studios 106
'tea-time' viewing 151, 156
'toddler's truce' time 150
television cameras
 in *A Complaint of Rape* 107–8,
 111–14, 115, 169
 and the coronation of 1953 80–1,
 84
television programmes
 *A Complaint of Rape* 102–17, 169
 *Coronation Street* 157–8
 *Crossroads* 151, 156, 158
 *Dr Who* 155–6, 177
 *EastEnders* 157
 *The Day Today* 160
 *Tonight* 150–1
Thatcher, Margaret 125
Thomas, Howard 65–6, 71
Thompson, John 76
thrownness 157
time
 abstract 152
 cyclical 153
 and dailiness 149–56, 175–8
 doubling of 172–3
 generational 174, 177
 lifetime 153
 linear 153
 my-time 176
 natural 152
 phenomenological time 152
 and programme production 9–11
 seasonal broadcasting 154–5
 situated experiential character of 89
 in soap operas 157
 social surveys of time-budgets
 175–6
 'time culture' of news production
 160
*Today* (BBC Radio 4) 149–50
*Tonight* (BBC television) 150–1
*Tony Blackburn Show, The* 118,
 120–43

audience 127–31
  London Love 133–4
  phone-in features 120–1
  Soul Night Out 138
totalitarian politics 163
Trilling, Lionel 70
truth 168–71

United States
  crooning 63
  network television coverage of the
    1953 coronation 86
  'people' programmes 25
utterance
  and meaning 17–18

Victoria, Queen 83
viewers
  and *A Complaint of Rape* 107–8, 114
  assessment of programmes 7
  and the myself 13
  as witnesses 101
  *see also* audiences; listeners
voices
  changes of voice by Tony
    Blackburn 125–7, 129
  communicable qualities 28

and personal identity 36–7, 68–9
professional 125
singing 68–9
Vera Lynn 67–8

*Waggoner's Walk* 157
*War and Peace* (Tolstoy) 161, 162
wartime broadcasting *see* Second
    World War
*We Speak for Ourselves* 37–9, 50
Weber, M. 21, 163
'We'll Meet Again' 66, 73
Westminster Abbey 80–1
Wiggins, Maurice 82, 91
Williams, Raymond 23
Winfrey, Oprah 25
witnesses
  to disasters 95–8
  to events of Bloody Sunday
    99–102
Wogan, Terry 117, 151
Wolfe, Kenneth 81
Wood, R. 80
*Workers Playtime* 45–6
worlds
  fictional 158–9, 162
  public and everyday 161–4, 172